ADVANCE PRAISE FOR
America's New War on Poverty

"I've never seen a book quite like this. These searing first-hand portraits take you into people's life stories in many ways: through memoirs, newspaper articles, fiction. And when the stories make you angry, there's no excuse not to get involved, because the short profiles of public and private programs interspersed throughout the book even give you the phone number to call—and the hope, in this otherwise cynical time, that we *can* do something about poverty."

ADAM HOCHSCHILD
Author

"This remarkable and timely book packs three decades of experience between two covers, combining hard facts with powerful personal stories and solutions that work."

PETER EDELMAN
Professor, Georgetown University
Law Center (on leave)

"Everyone who wants to combat the politics of cynicism and fear should have this user-friendly compendium, chock full of writings by today's best thinkers and activists. It's inspiring!"

MARGARET BRODKIN
Executive Director of Coleman Advocates for Children and Youth,
and author of *Every Kid Counts*

"The biggest wrong thing that most Americans believe is that the War on Poverty created most of the poverty we have today. Blackside has boldly and persuasively corrected the historical record, and so has led us to begin thinking again about what we need to do about our most severe domestic problem."

NICHOLAS LEMANN
Author, *The Promised Land*

"These compelling stories put a human face on the staggering problem of poverty in America today."

SENATOR BARBARA BOXER

"This collection of essays and reportage powerfully captures what Mother Teresa called America's poverty of loneliness, but it also reminds us that we are not without hope. As this anthology points out, there are programs, both private and public, that make a difference. This book serves as a call for action."

ALEX KOTLOWITZ
Author, *There Are No Children Here*

AMERICA'S NEW WAR ON POVERTY

COMPILED AND EDITED BY
ROBERT LAVELLE
AND THE STAFF OF BLACKSIDE, INC.

Foreword by Daniel Schorr

Introduction by Henry Hampton

COMPANION TO THE PUBLIC TELEVISION SERIES
America's War on Poverty

AMERICA'S NEW
War on Poverty

A READER FOR ACTION

KQED
BOOKS

SAN FRANCISCO

KQED Books & Tapes
2601 Mariposa St.
San Francisco, CA 94110

PUBLISHER:	Pamela Byers
BOOK DESIGN:	Janis Owens
PRINTING SERVICES:	Penn&Ink

For KQED:
President & CEO: Mary G.F. Bitterman
Vice President for
Publishing & New
Ventures: Mark K. Powelson

For America's New War on Poverty:
Editor: Robert Lavelle
Research coordinator: Ann Bennett
Researchers: Patricia Garcia-Rios, and Lalitha Rajan
Writers: Hannah Benoit, Roger House, Robert Lavelle, and Susan Pittman
Advisors: Arthur Blaustein, Pablo Eisenberg, Chester Hartman, Rob Hollister, and James Jennings
Intern: Marc Mandel

Library of Congress Cataloging-in-Publication Data
Lavelle, Robert, 1954–
  America's new war on poverty : a reader for action / compiled and edited by Robert Lavelle and the staff of Blackside, Inc.
    p. cm.
  "Companion to the Public television series: America's war on poverty."
  Includes bibliographical references.
  ISBN 0-912333-37-5 (pbk.) : 12.95
  1. Economic assistance, Domestic—United States. 2. Poverty—United States. 3. Poor—United States. I. Blackside, Inc. II. Title.
HC110.P63L36 1995
362.5'8'0973–dc20   94-40666
                                                         CIP

Educational, community, and non-profit groups wishing to order this book at attractive quantity discounts may contact:

KQED Books & Tapes
2601 Mariposa St.
San Francisco, CA 94110

ISBN 0-912333-37-5

Manufactured in the United States of America
10 9 8 7 6 5 4 3 2 1

Acknowledgments for permission to reprint copyrighted material appear on pages (246-247).

Distributed to the trade by Publishers Group West

If there is no struggle,
there is no progress.

FREDERICK DOUGLASS
1876

CONTENTS

List of Program Profiles / viii
About this Book / ix

Foreword by Daniel Schorr / xi
Introduction by Henry Hampton / xiii

PROLOGUE: Everything Has Changed,
Except the Way We Think

Secession of the Successful / *xvi*
by Robert B. Reich

Poverty and Power / *xxv*
by James Jennings

Are We a Humane Nation? / *xxix*
by Arthur I. Blaustein

Part 1: When Children Are Poor / 2

SAWDUST / 4
by Chris Offutt

WHAT IS POVERTY? / 14
by Carolyn Shaw Bell

SO HOW DID I GET HERE? / 18
by Rosemary Bray

SHARERS / 31
by Connie Porter

EXCERPT FROM
BASTARD OUT OF CAROLINA / 41
by Dorothy Allison

THE CIRCUIT / 45
by Francisco Jiménez

THE MANFUL LIFE OF
NICHOLAS, 10 / 53
by Isabel Wilkerson

THE LESSON / 65
by Toni Cade Bambara

LESSONS FOR A NEW WAR ON
POVERTY / 76
An interview with Marian Wright Edelman

**Part 2: Poverty, Families, and
Friends / 78**

GETTING NOWHERE / 80
by Tony Horwitz

GETTING THE FACTS OF LIFE / 88
by Paulette Childress White

ON AND THEN OFF WELFARE / 99
An interview with Jacqueline Pope

DOUGLAS, WYOMING:
An oral history / 101
by Connie Arthur

CONFRONTING SLAUGHTER IN THE
STREETS / 110
by Brent Staples

ON THE MEANING OF PLUMBING
AND POVERTY / 118
by Melanie Scheller

THE DEATH OF A FARM / 124
by Amy Jo Keifer

CIRCLING RAVEN / 127
by Janet Campbell Hale

DANIEL / 136
by Lars Eighner

EXCERPT FROM
RACHEL AND HER CHILDREN / 142
by Jonathan Kozol

Part 3: Communities in Poverty / 150
EXCERPT FROM
THE MILAGRO BEANFIELD WAR / 152
by John Nichols

ERNESTO J. CORTES, JR.: Organizer / 163
An interview by Bill Moyers

TRAVELS / 176
by Alice Walker

INSIDE TREY-NINE / 182
by reporters at Newsweek

THE TRIPLE WHAMMY / 193
An interview with Sylvester Monroe

LIKE A PRISON / 196
by David Gonzalez

IN THE FIELDS OF KING COAL / 207
by Fenton Johnson

WORKING WITH VOLUNTEERS / 217
An interview with Sue Ella Kobak

CONCLUSION: Ideas, Strategies, and
Resources
"Them" or "Us"? / 220
by Michael Katz
Responsibility for Reducing Poverty / 223
by Peter B. Edelman
Communitarian vs. Individualistic
Capitalism / 227
by Lester Thurow

*Appendix A: Giving Service: Resources for
Action as Citizen, Neighbor, Community
Member and Employee / 233*

*Appendix B: Policy, History and Poverty: An
Annotated Bibliography,
by James Jennings / 235*

*Appendix C: Stories and Voices:
35 Novels to Continue the Dialogue,
by Arthur I. Blaustein / 239*

About the contributors / 243

Notes / 244

Sources / 246

Acknowledgments / 248

LIST OF PROGRAM PROFILES

A Better Chance / 194

AFDC / 30

AIDS Action Council / 141

The Algebra Project / 74

AmeriCorps / 219

Appalshop / 16

Avance / 161

BOCES / 52

Children's Defense Fund / 77

City Year / 205

Coalition for the Homeless / 148

Community Building in Partnership / 117

Cooperative Home Care Associates / 181

COPS / 175

Delta Service Corps / 180

Dineh / 134

Dudley Street Neighborhood Initiative / 162

Families First / 108

Farmworker Justice Fund, Inc. / 51

Food Stamp Program (USDA) / 100

Gautreaux / 113

Head Start / 44

"I Have a Dream" Foundation / 75

Job Corps / 87

Linking Lifetimes / 63

Literacy Volunteers of America / 206

National Family Farm Coalition / 126

New Settlement Apartments / 116

Operation Exodus Inner City / 114

Options for Recovery / 107

Parents Anonymous / 109

Parents as Teachers / 40

PrairieFire Rural Action / 123

Service for Shelter / 149

STAR / 62

Teach for America / 135

Teens on Target / 195

Three Chicago Strategies / 115

Youth Volunteer Corps of America / 204

VISTA / 17

World SHARE / 39

YouthBuild / 64

The title of this book is meant to be both descriptive and prescriptive. It describes programs across the country that are fighting poverty. And, because these efforts aren't nearly enough, it prescribes that we all take responsibility, whatever our political backgrounds, for engaging in a fight against economic inequality. In putting this project together we were not so naive as to think it feasible for the federal government to launch a bold effort to eradicate poverty. With the middle class itself struggling to hold its ground, there is no will for massive governmental action to help fight poverty. In this climate, the government is seen by many as the enemy, the creator of problems. Unfortunately, by extension (some would argue by design), many voters also see poor people themselves as problems. Nevertheless, in assembling this book we have come to believe that the American people and the institutions with which we are affiliated *can* launch a war on poverty. We also believe that, in concert with local, state, and federal governments, we can do a great deal to combat this pernicious injustice.

The goal of this book is to contribute in some small way to a meaningful and reasonable discussion about poverty in America. It is difficult to say when poverty dropped off the list of things we Americans could discuss in public with civility and a sense of shared purpose — but it is clear that the topic cannot be broached today without setting off a noisy, bitter, and usually unproductive debate.

The short stories, fiction excerpts, and personal essays presented here are at the heart of this book. Because a number of analytic books on poverty are already available (and because this book has been compiled for the general reader), we have tried to limit the policy-oriented discussion to the prologue and conclusion. The stories and essays were chosen to show the many manifestations of poverty today, to offer a glimpse of the human faces that usually are hidden behind the statistics and policies — and to do so in a way that neither romanticizes "the poor" nor separates them from the nonpoor as helpless victims. Most of the contributors have written from firsthand experience.

The selected writings are framed by graphs, facts, and statistics that we have included in an attempt to place personal stories into a larger context. The risk here, of course, is that these data might distractingly intrude upon the narrative — and this is of particular concern in the case of the fiction selections. We have therefore designed the book so that the reader may choose to read the supplemental material or ignore it.

The programs that are profiled in this book were selected on the basis of a variety of criteria. We chose innovative programs from which we could learn a great deal; successful and effective programs; and/or programs that counterbalanced the problems presented in the excerpts. We want to leave the reader with a sense of hope and resolvability, not only because hope makes these problems easier to grapple with, but because there is in fact an enormous amount of creative, successful, and innovative work being done today by private, public, and informal organizations. The programs profiled here offer just a glimpse of the wide array of work being done today. In future editions of the book we hope to profile additional organizations and programs.

One of the assumptions we have made in pulling this material together is that we cannot effectively redress income inequality, economic and racial segregation, and other issues of poverty without talking about them directly and openly. The discussion has gone underground. We speak in code — "welfare," "race," "jobs," "entitlement," "empowerment" — or we don't speak at all. It is not enough that numerous programs are already fighting against the inequalities in our society. If we are unable to talk about these issues, then the successful programs will only be isolated victories. Without the goodwill of the general public, it would be politically, economically, and socially difficult to build lasting improvements. It is our hope that the stories and programs in this book will prompt readers to reconsider their assumptions about poverty in America and to resolve to take action on their beliefs.

Please send your comments and suggestions for future editions to: America's New War on Poverty/Blackside, Inc., 486 Shawmut Avenue, Boston, MA 02118.

Robert Lavelle
Editor

BY DANIEL SCHORR

In 1966, when I hung up my foreign correspondent's trench coat and was brought home by CBS to be "re-Americanized," poverty became part of my beat. Having lived long in Europe, where the sharper edges of deprivation are generally softened by a long-accepted welfare safety net, I was struck by the Johnsonian rhetoric of "war on poverty." It seemed to denote some newly discovered foe requiring an emergency mobilization of resources and manpower.

My early education in poverty came in visits to inner city ventures in "community action" under the aegis of Economic Opportunity, contacts with the militants of welfare rights movement, and coverage of Senate committees exploring hunger — another name for poverty — in the South. The trip that made the deepest impression on me was with Senator Robert Kennedy through the Mississippi Delta, seeing a depth of poverty that I — and he —had not imagined. He kept shaking his head, as we went from hovel to hovel, saying, "This is unacceptable...unacceptable."

But to most of America it was acceptable. I soon found that a wall of voluntary ignorance and ingrained prejudice ran through America — and right through the CBS newsroom. When I offered stories on abject conditions, news executives came back with demands for stories on welfare cheating and misappropriation of poverty funds — the kind of thing middle-class people talked about, reading the *Wall Street Journal* on their commuter trains.

Controversy is the stuff of journalism, and controversy based on race and class distinction is the stuff of middle-class journalism. So, I found that the easiest way to get on air with the innovative Head Start experiment in preschool education was to cover the struggle of the Head Start project, Child Development Group of Mississippi, to survive the assault of the Mississippi white establishment. The "Burn, baby, burn!" rhetoric of Stokely Carmichael and H. Rap Brown made more acceptable fodder for the Evening News than black moderate appeals for inner city investment.

The clashes of OEO Director Sargent Shriver with congressional opponents were more newsworthy than what Shriver was trying to accomplish — and, in some measure, succeeding. The effort of Governor Ronald Reagan to hamstring Legal Services in California and Senator George Murphy to abolish it nationwide made a "better story" than the bold effort, supported by the conscience-stricken American Bar Association, to provide legal representation to the poor. A welfare rights sit-in at the office of the Secretary of Health, Education and Welfare attracted attention to the movement, as planned, but not to what the movement was about.

Looking back, with more regret than anger, I am aware that the full story of the "war on poverty" was never really told. The many ailments that would have gone untreated that were treated in Neighborhood Health Centers. They are now called Community Health Centers and they are a familiar part of the American landscape. The many children who got their feet on the education ladder through Head Start, now so deeply embedded in American life that it resists constant efforts to cut its funding.

The conventional wisdom, which is not wise at all, is the Reaganite slogan that "we fought a war against poverty, and poverty won." It has become commonplace to cite the antipoverty campaign of the sixties in a cliché about "throwing money at problems." It is the kind of rhetoric that underpins efforts to cut back on welfare, or in the most extreme Charles Murray version, to scrap it altogether.

A generation ago the War on Poverty ended not in defeat, but in surrender. Despite several important, but unheralded, victories in that skirmish, a generation later, poverty is more widespread and runs deeper. The current political lexicon about poverty, suggesting welfare children having welfare children in some inexorable cycle, is meant to convey futility. One looks for a Kennedy or a Johnson to sound the trumpet call that abandoning an underclass is "unacceptable."

Coping with the blight of poverty today will be more difficult than a generation ago. But it is important to try and, to the extent that neglect today seeks its justification in a misreading of the past, it is also important to revisit the campaign against poverty in the sixties.

I am delighted about Blackside's television series, which re-examines the War on Poverty, and about this companion volume, which concerns itself instead with the present. Together they should serve to focus attention anew on that continuing shame — poverty in America.

Daniel Schorr, senior news analyst,
National Public Radio, former CBS reporter.

INTRODUCTION

BY HENRY HAMPTON

I enjoyed a privileged childhood. Not the least of my privileges was working with and learning from my father. When I was fourteen, I worked in my father's medical office during the summer. It was during those days that I came in close contact with people who might now be defined as poor. It was a summer of learning that was to touch my life forever.

My father was a successful general practitioner and surgeon whose practice was largely based on the thousands of working class and recently arrived African Americans who flooded St. Louis during the forties and fifties. They worked hard in the tough jobs available to them, but they and their middle class peers jointly suffered the outrages of segregation, racism, limited opportunity, and the always present reality of bad schools, inadequate housing, and too little political power.

My father's response to the racism that confronted him was to take an aggressive stance …be smarter, be richer, be confident. As I grew to adulthood in the midst of the civil rights movement, I came to see that my father's individual response to racism was not feasible for so many others. My father's response was peculiar to his personality and his own circumstances. But his aggressiveness, his confidence in establishing goals and devoting energy to achieving them were lessons that I continue to hold as invaluable. The most important lesson I learned from him that summer of 1954, however, was something else.

My father often bartered his services for food or work. Or he would charge his patients only a dollar. He insisted on getting something. What he taught me firsthand was that when you are working with people who have less than you, people who are in so many ways poor, don't just give them what they might need. Instead, establish dignity and mutual respect by taking the transaction seriously, by conversing, by establishing a human connection. In many ways, that is what we at Blackside are trying to do with our War on Poverty project — with the historical documentary series we are trying to establish meaningful human connections to the past. And with this book, we are hoping to establish meaningful connections among people living in poverty, people living on the edge of poverty, and those who live their lives with no more awareness of poverty than they glean from the facts, figures, and sensational stories on the evening news.

To people living in poverty, struggling with the brutal reality of too many needs and too few resources, and to others who find themselves overburdened and anxious about their own foothold in the middle class, history may seem like a luxury that can await calmer times. But it cannot. A nation cannot live peaceably when the gap between affluence and poverty becomes as wide as ours is becoming. America must take on the responsibility to fight poverty not only out of fear of what might happen if we don't, but out of a true hope in the American Possibility. Equitable economic opportunity is the silent partner to democracy. One without the other is not sustainable. We must fight poverty today and a key part of that fight is in understanding our history. History is the rudder that can keep us on course in the midst of storms.

This book and the historical documentary series *America's War on Poverty* to which it is a companion have at their center one basic question: What is the responsibility of our government to its citizens, and of the citizens to their government? Few would disagree that we have entered a new era in our history. Because the cold war is over, because of a realignment of international allegiances, because of new technologies and international economic development, political and economic power is changing at the local, national, and international level. It is under such pressure that weaknesses can destroy the whole. Our greatest failure as a nation remains our inability to deal with racism and poverty.

We undertook the making of this historical documentary series because we believe it is important to deliver stories that confirm the enormous human potential and the leadership that came out of this much maligned and misinterpreted period of history. Before we can take advantage of all that we have learned during the War on Poverty and in the intervening years, we must first demythologize that war.

The campaign was not an unqualified success, but even its failures had many positive benefits. More often than not, when failure occurred, it was due to a lack of readiness and the conscious hostile objections of those who disagreed with its intent. We chose to tell this story because today we need to be reminded of a moment when a responsible activist government attempted to highlight the problems of poverty and race and move those issues to a higher priority for the good of the nation.

This book offers many telling lessons in contemporary poverty. It also profiles some of the leaders and activists who are today struggling with issues of poverty in America. We need a new war on poverty — not with a capital W and a capital P, perhaps not even constricted within the confines of a win-or-lose "war" metaphor, and not led by a federal government that over the course of three decades has lost the public's confidence as an effective agent of change. But we need to fight against poverty and we need to be visible in our caring. Effectiveness comes as much from leadership, from moral vision, as it does from good ideas.

We need leadership. There are some leaders in the contemporary political field, but few are bold enough, few have the courage. Emerson offered us one notion of courage. He wrote that "the great part of courage is having done the thing before." We have fought poverty before. We ought not walk away from all we have learned just because the war became a skirmish and because the very idea of combatting poverty became political fodder for mean-spirited people. There is much work to be done. The stories in this book demonstrate that. The profiles of the programs and leaders who have kept on with innovation and perseverance offer us numerous ideas. What is needed now is the public will to address these problems. Conventional wisdom has it that it is political poison to talk about poverty or about antipoverty programs. Our belief in the effectiveness of our public institutions has become so eroded that showing compassion or hope or a belief that we can and ought to combat poverty is seen by many as ludicrous. But that level of hopelessness and cynicism is untenable if we are to grow either as a democratic power or as an economic power.

In truth, we have learned an enormous amount about fighting poverty since 1964. That history and the years since have taught us lessons...about the importance of building coalitions, about the role that government at the municipal, state, and federal level can play, about the role of the law, about the importance of planning and anticipating obstacles, about the need for flexibility and the importance of communicating ideas to the public. We are now in a position to accomplish a great deal. To succeed we must create an environment that makes it politically feasible or acceptable for "leaders" to lead us forward. We must develop a moral atmosphere that encourages people to participate, to take action against the problems of poverty around them. Most of us understand the diagnosis of what ails our nation; the issue now is to chart a course of treatment. And we must have a vision for our future as well. The writer Roberto de Roberto said that among all human constructions, the only ones that withstand the dissolving hands of time are the castles in the air. It is our dreams that drive us forward, the dreams that give us courage to meet the challenges of a time such as ours.

Henry Hampton,
executive producer, documentary series
America's War on Poverty

Everything Has Changed Except the Way We Think

SECESSION OF THE SUCCESSFUL

ROBERT B. REICH

The idea of "community" has always held a special attraction for Americans. In a 1984 speech, President Ronald Reagan celebrated America's "bedrock" — "its communities where neighbors help one another, where families bring up kids together, where American values are born." Governor Mario M. Cuomo of New York, with a very different political leaning, has been almost as lyrical. "Community...is the reality on which our national life has been founded," he said in 1987.

There is only one problem with this picture. Most Americans no longer live in traditional communities. They live in suburban subdivisions bordered by highways and sprinkled with shopping malls, or in tony condominiums and residential clusters, or in ramshackle apartment buildings and housing projects. Most of them commute to work and socialize on some basis other than geographic proximity. And most people pick up and move to a different neighborhood every five years or so.

But Americans generally have one thing in common with their neighbors: they have similar incomes. And that simple fact lies at the heart of the new community. This means that their educational backgrounds are likely to be similar, that they pay roughly the same in taxes, and that they indulge in the same consumer impulses. "Tell me someone's ZIP code," the founder of a direct-mail company once bragged, "and I can predict what they eat, drink, drive — even think."

Americans who own their homes usually share one political cause with their neighbors: a near obsessive concern with maintaining or upgrading property values. And this common interest is responsible for much of what has brought neighbors together in recent years. Complete strangers, although they may live on the same street or in the same condominium complex, suddenly feel intense solidarity when it is rumored that low-income housing will be constructed in their midst or that a poorer school district will be consolidated with their own.

The renewed emphasis on "community" in American life has justified and legitimized these economic enclaves. If generosity and solidarity end at the border of similarly valued properties, then the most fortunate can be virtuous citizens at little cost. Since most people in one neighborhood or town are equally well off, there is no cause for a guilty conscience. If inhabitants of another area are poorer, let them look to one another. Why should *we* pay for *their* schools?

So the argument goes, without acknowledging that the critical assumption has already been made: "we" and "they" belong to fundamentally different communities. Through such reasoning, it has become possible to maintain a self-image of generosity toward, and solidarity with, one's "community" without bearing any responsibility to "them" — the other "community."

America's high earners — the fortunate top fifth — thus feel increasingly justified in paying only what is necessary to insure that everyone in their community is sufficiently well educated and has access to the public services they need to succeed.

Last year, the top fifth of working Americans took home more money than the other four-fifths put together — the highest portion in postwar history. These high earners will relinquish somewhat more of their income to the federal government this year than in 1990 as a result of last fall's tax changes, although considerably less than in the late 1970s, when the tax code was more progressive. But the continuing debate over whether the wealthy are paying their fair share of taxes obscures a larger issue, with more profound implications for America: The fortunate fifth is quietly seceding from the rest of the nation.

This is occurring gradually, without much awareness by members of the top group — or, for that matter, by anyone else. And the government is speeding this process as Washington shifts responsibility for many public services to state and local governments.

The secession is taking several forms. In many cities and towns, the wealthy have in effect withdrawn their dollars from the support of public spaces and institutions shared by all and dedicated the savings to their own private services. As public parks and playgrounds deteriorate, there is a proliferation of private health clubs, golf clubs, tennis clubs, skating clubs, and every other type of recreational association in which costs are shared among members. Condominiums and the omnipresent residential communities dun their members to undertake work that financially strapped local governments can no longer afford to do well — maintaining roads, mending sidewalks, pruning trees, repairing street lights, cleaning swimming pools, paying for lifeguards, and, notably, hiring security guards to protect life and property. (The number of private security guards in the United States now exceeds the number of public police officers.)

Of course, wealthier Americans have been withdrawing into their own neighborhoods and clubs for generations. But the new secession is more dramatic because the highest earners now inhabit a different economy from other Americans. The new elite is linked by jet, modem, fax, satellite, and fiber-optic cable to the great commercial and recreational centers of the world, but it is not particularly connected to the rest of the nation.

That is because the work this group does is becoming less tied to the activities of other Americans. Most of their jobs consist of analyzing and manipulating symbols — words, numbers, or visual images. Among the most prominent of these "symbolic analysts" are management consultants, lawyers, software and design engineers, research scientists, corporate executives, financial advisors, strategic planners, advertising executives, television and movie producers, and other workers whose job titles include terms like "strategy," "planning," "consultant," "policy," "resources," or "engineer."

These workers typically spend long hours in meetings or on the telephone and even longer hours in planes or hotels — advising, making presentations, giving briefings, and making deals. Periodically, they issue reports, plans, designs, drafts, briefs, blueprints, analyses, memorandums, layouts, renderings, scripts, or projections. In contrast with people whose jobs tend to be tedious and repetitive, symbolic analysts find their work varied and intellectually challenging. In fact, the work is often enjoyable.

These symbolic analysts are in ever greater demand in a world market that places an increasing value on identifying and solving problems. Requests for their software designs, financial advice, or engineering blueprints come from all parts of the globe. This largely explains why most (but by no means all) symbolic analysts have become wealthier, even as the ever-growing worldwide supply of unskilled labor continues to depress the wages of other Americans.

Successful Americans have not completely disengaged themselves from the lives of their less fortunate compatriots. Some devote substantial resources and energies to helping the rest of society, not through their tax payments, but through voluntary efforts. "Generosity is a reflection of what one does with his or her resources — and not what he or she advocates the government do with everyone's money," Ronald Reagan said in 1984.

The argument is fair enough. Government is not the only device for redistributing wealth. In his speech accepting the presidential nomination at the Republican National Convention in 1988, George Bush said that the real magnanimity of America was to be found in a "brilliant diversity" of private charities, "spread like stars, like a thousand points of light in a broad and peaceful sky."

No nation congratulates itself more enthusiastically on its charitable acts than America, none engages in a greater number of charity balls, bake sales, benefit auctions, and border-to-border hand holdings for good causes. Much of this is sincerely motivated and admirable.

But close examination reveals that many of these acts of benevolence do not help the needy. Particularly suspect is the private giving of those in the top income-tax bracket. Studies have revealed that their largess does not flow mainly to social services for the poor — to better schools, health clinics, or recreational centers. Instead, most voluntary contributions of wealthy Americans go to the places and institutions that entertain, inspire, cure, or educate wealthy Americans — art museums,

opera houses, theaters, orchestras, ballet companies, private hospitals, and elite universities.

And even these charitable contributions are relatively skimpy. Last year, American households with incomes of less than $10,000 gave an average of 5.5 percent of their earnings to charity or to a religious organization; those making more than $100,000 a year gave only 2.9 percent. After the 1986 tax-code overhaul reduced the benefits of charitable giving, the very rich became even stingier. According to Internal Revenue Service data, taxpayers earning $500,000 or more slashed their average donations to $16,062 in 1988 from $47,432 in 1980.

Corporate philanthropy is following the same general pattern. In recent years, the largest American corporations have been sounding the alarm about the nation's fast deteriorating primary and secondary schools. Few are more eloquent and impassioned about the need for better schools than American executives. "How well we educate all of our children will determine our competitiveness globally, and our economic health domestically, and our communities' character and vitality," said a report of The Business Roundtable, a New York–based association of top executives.

Accordingly, there are numerous "partnerships" between corporations and public schools: scholarships for poor children qualified to attend college, and programs in which businesses adopt individual schools by making conspicuous donations of computers, books, and, on occasion, even money. That such activities are loudly touted by corporate public relations staffs should not detract from the good they do. Despite the hoopla, business donations to education and charitable causes actually tapered off markedly in the 1980s, even as the economy boomed. In the 1970s, corporate giving to education jumped an average of 15 percent a year. In 1990, however, giving was only 5 percent over that in 1989; in 1989, it was 3 percent over 1988. Moreover, most of this money goes to colleges and universities — in particular, to the alma maters of symbolic analysts, who expect their children and grandchildren to follow in their footsteps. Only 1.5 percent of corporate giving in the late 1980s was to public primary and secondary schools.

Notably, these contributions have been smaller than the amounts corporations are receiving from states and communities in the form of subsidies or tax breaks. Companies are quietly procuring such deals by threatening to move their operations — and jobs — to places around the world with a more congenial tax climate. The paradoxical result has been even less corporate revenue to spend on schools and other community services than before. The executives of General Motors, for example, who have been among the loudest to proclaim the need for better schools, have also been among the most relentless in pursuing local tax abatements and in challenging their tax assessments. G.M.'s successful efforts to reduce its taxes in North Tarrytown, New York, where the company has had a factory since 1914, cut local revenues by $1 million in 1990, part of a larger shortfall that forced the town to lay off scores of teachers.

The secession of the fortunate fifth has been most apparent in how and where they have chosen to work and live. In effect, most of America's large urban centers have splintered into two separate cities. One is composed of those whose symbolic and analytic services are linked to the world economy. The other consists of local service workers — custodians, security guards, taxi drivers, clerical aides, parking attendants, sales people, restaurant employees — whose jobs are dependent on the symbolic analysts. Few blue-collar manufacturing workers remain in American cities. Between 1953 and 1984, for example, New York City lost about 600,000 factory jobs; in the same interval, it added about 700,000 jobs for symbolic analysts and service workers.

The separation of symbolic analysts from local service workers within cities has been reinforced in several ways. Most large cities now possess two school systems — a private one for the children of the top-earning group and a public one for the children of service workers, the remaining blue-collar workers, and the unemployed. Symbolic analysts spend considerable time and energy insuring that their children gain entrance to good private schools, and then small fortunes keeping them there — dollars that under a more progressive tax code might finance better public education.

People with high incomes live, shop, and work within areas of cities that, if not beautiful, are at least esthetically tolerable and reasonably safe; precincts not meeting these minimum standards of charm and security have been left to the less fortunate.

Here again, symbolic analysts have pooled their resources to the exclusive benefit of themselves. Public funds have been spent in earnest on downtown "revitalization" projects, entailing the construction of clusters of post-modern office buildings (complete with fiber-optic cables, private branch exchanges, satellite dishes, and other communications equipment linking them to the rest of the world), multilevel parking garages, hotels with glass-enclosed atriums, upscale shopping plazas and galleries, theaters, convention centers, and luxury condominiums.

Ideally, these complexes are entirely self-contained, with air-conditioned walkways linking residences, businesses, and recreational space. The lucky resident is able to shop, work, and attend the theater without risking direct contact with the outside world — that is, the other city.

Carrying the principle a step further, several cities have begun authorizing property owners in certain affluent districts to assess a surtax on local residents and businesses for amenities unavailable to other urban residents, services like extra garbage collections, street cleaning, and security. One such New York district, between 38th and 48th Streets and Second and Fifth Avenues, raised $4.7 million from its residents in 1989, of which $1 million underwrote a private force of uniformed guards and plainclothes investigators. The new community of people with like incomes and with the power to tax and enforce the law is thus becoming a separate city within the city.

When not living in urban enclaves, symbolic analysts are increasingly congregating in suburbs and exurbs where corporate headquarters have been relocated, research parks have been created, and bucolic universities have spawned entrepreneurial ventures. Among the most desirable of such locations are Princeton, New Jersey; northern Westchester and Putnam Counties in New York; Palo Alto, California; Austin, Texas; Bethesda, Maryland; and Raleigh-Durham, North Carolina.

Engineers and strategists of American auto companies, for example, do not live in Flint or Saginaw, Michigan, where the blue-collar workers reside; they cluster in their own towns of Troy, Warren, and Auburn Hills. Likewise, the vast majority of the financial specialists, lawyers, and executives working for the insurance companies of Hartford would never consider living there; after all, Hartford is the nation's fourth poorest city. Instead, they flock to Windsor, Middlebury, West Hartford, and other towns that are among the wealthiest in the country.

This trend, too, has been growing for decades. But technology has accelerated it. Today's symbolic analysts linked directly to the rest of the globe can choose to live and work in the most pastoral of settings.

The secession has been encouraged by the federal government. For the last decade, Washington has in effect shifted responsibility for many public services to local governments. At their peak, federal grants made up 25 percent of state and local spending in the late 1970s. Today, the federal share has dwindled to 17 percent. Direct aid to local governments, in the form of programs introduced in the Johnson and Nixon administrations, has been the hardest hit by budget cuts. In the 1980s, federal dollars for clean water, job training and transfers, low-income housing, sewage treatment, and garbage disposal shrank by some $50 billion a year, and Washington's share of spending on local transit declined by 50 percent. (The Bush administration has proposed that states and localities take on even more of the costs of building and maintaining roads, and wants to cut federal aid for mass transit.) In 1990, New York City received only 9.6 percent of all its revenue from the federal government, compared with 16 percent in 1981.

States have quickly transferred many of these new expenses to fiscally strapped cities and towns, with a result that by the start of the 1990s, localities were bearing more than half of the costs of water and sewage, roads, parks, welfare, and public schools. In New York State, the local communities' share has risen to about 75 percent of these costs.

Cities and towns with affluent inhabitants can bear these burdens relatively easily. Poorer ones, faced with the twin problems of lower incomes and greater demand for social services, have had far more difficulty. And as the gap between the richest and poorest communities has widened, the shift in responsibility for public services to cities and towns has functioned as another means of relieving wealthier Americans of the cost of aiding less fortunate citizens.

The result has been a growing inequality in basic social and community services. While the city tax rate in Philadelphia, for example, is about triple that of communities around it, the suburbs enjoy far better schools, hospitals, recreation, and police protection. Eighty-five percent of the richest families in the greater Philadelphia area live outside the city limits, and 80 percent of the region's poorest live inside. The quality of a city's infrastructure — roads, bridges, sewage, water treatment — is likewise related to the average income of its inhabitants.

The growing inequality in government services has been most apparent in the public schools. The federal government's share of the costs of primary and secondary education has dwindled to about 6 percent. The bulk of the cost is divided about equally between the states and local school districts. States with a higher concentration of wealthy residents can afford to spend more on their schools than other states. In 1989, the average public school teacher in Arkansas, for example, received $21,700; in Connecticut, $37,300.

Even among adjoining suburban towns in the same state the differences can be quite large. Consider three Boston-area communities located within minutes of one another. All are predominantly white, and most residents within each town earn about the same as their neighbors. But the disparity of incomes between towns is substantial.

Belmont, northwest of Boston, is inhabited mainly by symbolic analysts and their families. In 1988, the average teacher in its public schools earned $36,109. Only 3 percent of Belmont's 18-year-olds dropped out of high school, and more than 80 percent of graduating seniors chose to go on to a four-year college.

Just east of Belmont is Somerville, most of whose residents are low-wage service workers. In 1988, the average Somerville teacher earned $29,400. A third of the town's 18-year-olds did not finish high school, and fewer than a third planned to attend college.

Chelsea, across the Mystic River from Somerville, is the poorest of the three towns. Most of its inhabitants are unskilled, and many are unemployed or only employed part time. The average teacher in Chelsea, facing tougher educational challenges than his or her counterparts in Belmont, earned $26,200 in 1988, almost a third less than the average teacher in the more affluent town just a few miles away. More than half of Chelsea's 18-year-olds did not graduate from high school, and only 10 percent planned to attend college.

Similar disparities can be found all over the nation. Students at Highland Park High School in a wealthy suburb of Dallas, for example, enjoy a campus with a planetarium, indoor swimming pool, closed-circuit television studio, and state-of-the-art science laboratory. Highland Park spends about $6,000 a year to educate each student. This is almost twice that spent per pupil by the towns of Wilmer and Hutchins in southern Dallas County. According to Texas education officials, the richest school district in the state spends $19,300 a year per pupil; its poorest, $2,100 a year.

The courts have become involved in trying to repair such imbalances, but the issues are not open to easy judicial remedy.

The four-fifths of Americans left in the wake of the secession of the fortunate fifth include many poor blacks, but racial exclusion is neither the primary motive for the separation nor a necessary consequence. Lower-income whites are similarly excluded and high-income black symbolic analysts are often welcomed. The segregation is economic rather than racial, although economically motivated separation often results in *de facto* racial segregation. Where courts have found a pattern of racially motivated segregation, it usually has involved lower-income white communities bordering on lower-income black neighborhoods.

In states where courts have ordered equalized state spending in school districts, the vast differences in a town's property values — and thus local tax revenues — continue to result in substantial inequities. Where courts or state governments have tried to impose limits on what affluent communities can pay their teachers, not a few parents in upscale towns have simply removed their children from the public schools and applied the money they might otherwise have willingly paid in higher taxes to private school tuitions instead. And, of course, even if statewide expenditures were better equalized, poorer states would continue to be at a substantial disadvantage.

In all these ways, the gap between America's symbolic analysts and everyone else is widening into a chasm. Their secession from the rest of the population raises fundamental questions about the future of American society. In the new global economy — in which money, technologies, and corporations cross borders effortlessly — a citizen's standard of living depends more and more on skills and insights, and on the infrastructure needed to link these abilities to the rest of the world. But the most skilled and insightful Americans, who are already positioned to thrive in the world market, are now able to slip the bonds of national allegiance, and by so doing disengage themselves from their less favored fellows. The stark political challenge in the decades ahead will be to reaffirm that, even though America is no longer a separate and distinct economy, it is still a society whose members have abiding obligations to one another.

Adapted for the *New York Times Magazine*, January 20, 1991 from *The Work of Nations: Preparing Ourselves for 21st-Century Capitalism*, 1991.

POVERTY AND POWER

JAMES JENNINGS

For more than 20 years, urban poverty in this country has been getting worse. And as the spring 1992 rebellions in Los Angeles and several other cities underscored, social welfare policies have failed to arrest this deterioration. They have neither strengthened the social infrastructure of neighborhoods nor ensured opportunities for socioeconomic mobility for vast and growing numbers of poor Americans, especially blacks and Latinos.

Faced with these failures of politics and policy, people in a number of American cities are pursuing new strategies for fighting urban poverty. Where conventional policies treat poor people as clients who need services; the new strategies are based on ideas of community-building and enpowerment; they encourage mobilization by poor people themselves around their own self-defined interests. A few foundations are providing scattered support for such projects. But neither the media nor policy-makers have been paying much attention....

In his classic work, *The Affluent Society* (1958), John Kenneth Galbraith urged Americans not to treat poverty as an "afterthought." Galbraith was writing at a time of growing affluence, but his point retains all of its original force. Millions of Americans are "official-

ly" poor, and millions more are officially "near poverty." Since 1965, the U.S. Census Bureau has used a mechanical formula to define the official poverty line. According to this formula — which set the 1992 poverty threshold for a family of four at $13,547 — the U.S. poverty population now includes 17.7 million whites, 10.2 million blacks, and 6.3 million Latinos. The numbers have been growing for 20 years. In 1965, approximately 33.2 million persons lived in households below the official poverty level, representing 17 percent of the U.S. population. By 1973, both the absolute number of persons living in poverty (23 million), and the rate of poverty (11 percent) had declined significantly. By 1988, however, the number of persons in poverty was back up to 31.9 million, 13.1 percent of the population. In 1990, 31.9 percent of all blacks lived below the official poverty level, compared to 28.1 percent of Latinos, and 8.8 percent of the white population.

The racial gap in poverty rates has also persisted. The ratio of the black poverty rate to the white rate has changed little over the past half century, despite changes in family structure, attitude toward work, and levels of schooling — the factors that many analysts take as the principal causes of poverty. In 1939, the poverty rate for black families was at least three times the rate for white families. In 1970, and still in 1988, the black poverty rate was three times the white poverty rate! This racial gap is evident among children, the elderly, and even among female-headed families.

The pervasiveness, persistence, and growth of urban poverty suggest that poverty is neither an economic aberration nor a reflection of the morals, or lack thereof, of 34 million poor adults and children — or the millions more who are near poor. Rather, the problem of poverty reflects the declining number of jobs paying decent living wages, an increasingly inequitable distribution of wealth, continuing racial divisions, and *the absence of poor people themselves from the analysis or political resolution of the problem of poverty.*

The exclusion of poor people from official policy discussion — their political demobilization — may be an important factor in the failure of conventional policies to arrest persistent poverty. This depoliticization encourages a conception of the poor as targets for services and treatment, not as equal citizens, as civic partners in setting or acting on the public agenda. It has permitted public discourse to turn away from structural causes and to focus on the vague symbolism of "dependency," "irresponsibility," and "welfare reform."

Politicians from both parties gain political advantage by encouraging, perhaps even manipulating, this unfounded symbolism while at the same time pushing similar policy responses to persistent poverty. The Family Support Act of 1988 — highly touted, but now about to be discarded — won broad bipartisan support from Presidents Reagan and Bush, a Democratic congress, and many Democratic governors, including then Governor Bill Clin-

ton. It was hailed as the legislation that would finally bring the "welfare mess" under control. But it has been ineffective not only because of inadequate funding, but also because it reflects an a historical view of poverty and a conventional idea of poor people as mere recipients of state benefits.

The relatively quick failure of this legislation has heralded the current call by both parties to "end welfare as we know it." In many states, this means the adoption of punitive and Draconian measures aimed at forcing poor people into low-wage jobs, cutting food stamps, limiting the number of years that a person may receive AFDC [Aid to Families with Dependent Children] benefits, punishing poor and single women who decide to give birth to more than one child, fingerprinting AFDC recipients, and developing costly bureaucracies to follow, and monitor, the activities of poor people, especially in black and Latino communities.

Although they are invisible in current public discourse — or appear only as recipients — poor people have a long tradition of mobilizing against poverty. The Civil Rights Movement itself is a premier example of a political response to poverty by the poor. Martin Luther King, Jr., believed that after successfully completing the legislative battle against segregation, the Civil Rights Movement needed to develop a massive civil disobedience campaign — a national mobilization of poor people — to end poverty in the United States. As he explained in his 1967 article, "Martin Luther King Defines Black Power," *political* decisions on behalf of those with power and wealth produce poverty; it would, therefore, take counterpower to reduce or eliminate poverty.

The National Welfare Rights Organization (NWRO), founded in 1966, provides another example of how poor people attempted to use political mobilization to reduce poverty. NWRO sought to organize poor women around four principles: adequate income, dignity, justice, and democracy for all poor people. Although it was defunct by 1975, the NWRO had a significant impact on increasing and liberalizing welfare benefits for women and children, and gave rise to chapters of the grassroots organization ACORN [Action for Community Organization and Reform Now] in many American cities.

The political mobilizations of the 1960s contributed to a significant reduction in poverty over the decade. In 1960, for example, 65.5 percent of all black children (under 18 years of age) lived in poverty; by 1970, this figure declined to 41.5 percent. This figure has since increased again, in part because of the decline of a national movement for social and economic change, led by, and on behalf of, poor people. The resurgence in the rate of child poverty — particularly among black children — is more a reflection of the depoliticization of poor people, than of the pathologies attributed to them in standard academic and political discussion.

Excluded from public discussion, poor people are seeking once more to organize politically in response to the problem of poverty. *Community building* is one such response.

A second line of response is *advocacy and mobilization* of the kind pursued by the NWRO. More recently, the Coalition for Basic Human Needs and the Human Services Coalition in Massachusetts have pursued lobbying strategies and annually published a "Poor People's Budget" showing how a more equitable distribution of state dollars could reduce the level of poverty. In Detroit, an organization of welfare recipients and the homeless have mobilized the poor community under a campaign, "Up and Out of Poverty Now," which targets demonstrations against unsupportive elected officials. In Minneapolis, the Welfare Rights Committee has organized a campaign to resist such welfare reform initiatives as the Clinton administration's two-year limit and workfare proposals.

Another organization controlled by poor people and dedicated to eradicating poverty through political action is the Milwaukee-based Congress for a Working America (CFWA). As one observer put it, "the group is…strongly committed to involving welfare recipients and the working poor in changing public policy." CFWA's campaign to eliminate poverty has achieved some important successes. In 1989, CFWA won a major legislative battle when the Wisconsin legislature adopted a statewide earned-income tax credit which supplements the federal earned-income tax cred-it. Only a handful of states have earned-income tax credits and, due to CFWA's efforts, Wisconsin is the only one that ties the tax cred-it to family size.

Successes — whether of community-build-ing or of advocacy and mobilization — are rou-tinely challenged and may not survive the onslaught of interests seeking to protect wealth and power. But they remain important mod-els that could be strengthened through greater political and community mobilization. And only such mobilization — organized, led, and sustained by poor people — can guarantee antipoverty policies that reflect poor people's interests and well-being and put an end to poverty "as we know it."

FROM: *The Boston Review*, June–September, 1994.

ARE WE A HUMANE NATION?

ARTHUR I. BLAUSTEIN

In 1964, this nation undertook a course of action designed to combat "the paradox of poverty amidst plenty." In doing so, President Lyndon Johnson decided upon a broadside effort to seriously attack the root causes of poverty: inadequate health care, impaired education, lack of decent jobs, deteriorating housing, and decaying neighborhoods. When Johnson requested — and Congress passed — the Economic Opportunity Act, it also signified a moral commitment on the part of our political leadership to pursue the unfulfilled goals of equality, justice, and opportunity.

It truly was a historic moment — one worth recalling with pride — for it was a time when Americans demonstrated their commitment, openness, and generosity. A new federal agency was created to spearhead and coordinate this endeavor: the Office of Economic Opportunity (OEO), which had the responsibility for initiating several programs, including Head Start, Volunteers in Service to America (VISTA), Legal Services, Job Corps, Upward Bound, Foster Grandparents, Community Economic Development, and Community Action; all of which were direct and specific, aimed at pressing national problems.

It was a time of enthusiasm and hope. People not only thought about what was right and talked about what was wrong, but they also accepted personal responsibility for actually doing something about righting those wrongs. The nation's spirit was enlivened by the tens of thousands of young (and not-so-young) Americans who volunteered for the Peace Corps, VISTA, Legal Services, and the Teacher Corps, or who supplemented their education by providing worthwhile social services to the poor through the more than 900 Community Action Agencies (CAAs) established across the country.

I do not have to tell you that times have changed. Nowadays, people complain a lot, but they do not take personal responsibility for anything other than their own ambition, career, or security. On campus and off, rather than activism, idealism, and vitality, the mood has shifted to apathy, fatalism, passivity, and privatism: "Look out for No. 1," — those who can't are shiftless, a drag on the economy.

Times also have changed for our disadvantaged youth. In the 1960s, there was hope: Upward Bound, the Neighborhood Youth Corps, and the Job Corps held out a helping hand. Youngsters who had never before had a chance believed that the dream of achieving selfhood could become a reality. By the early 1980s, though, that hope had been dashed, and it was replaced with despair, as youngsters turned to drugs, crime, and violence.

It is important to clarify this reality, for along the way, in deliberate efforts to destroy the credibility of these programs, conservative politicians began manipulating symbols in order to stigmatize them. During the Nixon era, the president himself began to refer to them as "minority" and "welfare" programs, rather than as "opportunity" ones, thereby switching the message from a positive to a negative one. This kind of deceit and distortion was not an accident; it was designed to exploit fear and racial divisiveness.

By the time we reached the 1980s, we had entered an era that officially — at the highest levels of government — condoned and even encouraged negative attitudes, code words, and symbols directed against the poor in particular, and toward basic human and social service programs in general. Those conservative politicians, especially Ronald Reagan, who did so were adept at moralizing endlessly over the issues: the "problems" of the unemployed and underemployed, the homeless and hungry, of alcoholism, drug abuse, mental illness, infant mortality, child and spouse abuse, and disrupted families. But they have neither the heart nor the will for the rigorous thoughts and work of finding cures or even just relieving some of the suffering and symptoms.

There is a price to be paid for Reagan's reduction of human and social services. The price is that these cutbacks did not reduce crime; they increased it. They did not promote better family life; they destabilized it. They did not reduce alcoholism; they increased it. They did not increase respect for the law; they weakened it.

The four particular elements of the Reagan administration's policies that have served to undermine our social equilibrium are (1) the massive across-the-board cuts in social and human service programs; (2) the transfer of federal authority and program responsibility to states with diminished resources; (3) the abolition of delivery systems provided for in the Economic Opportunity Act; and (4) the abdication of moral leadership.

Commitment to Equality

I want to quote from a tribute to Jane Addams made in 1960 by the distinguished writer and historian Archibald MacLeish because it touches my sense of the meaning of the war on poverty. Jane Addams, he said,

> was not working for her immigrants and her poor: she was committing herself with them to the common life — that life our generation watches more and more as spectators, as though it were not common, as though it were a life for someone else. She was as explicit about that as a woman could be. She was not, she said, a reformer: she wanted to establish a place (Hull House) "in and around which a fuller life might grow for others and for herself." And having made that much clear she then reversed her words to make her declaration clearer still. "The good we secure for ourselves is precarious and uncertain until it is secured for all of us and incorporated into our common life."

No, Hull House changed Chicago and changed the United States, not because it was a successful institution but because it was an eloquent action by a woman capable of action regardless of the dark ahead. We talk as though the great question before our society was whether the things that need to be done in America to keep this last best hope of earth alive should be done by the federal government or by the states or perhaps the cities or by industries or by some other kind of organization. But that, of course, is not the question. The question before our society is simply whether or not these things *will be done*. And the answer is that they will be done if we ourselves see to it as Jane Addams and her friends saw it — if we accept, as she accepted, responsibility for our lives. That, when all is said and done, is why our time remembers her — that she accepted for herself responsibility for the "common life."

Serving the Poor

I cite this passage because it best describes for me the spirit and the intentionality of the Economic Opportunity Act, its programs and the people who worked at OEO. In 1965, the concept of Hull House was institutionalized through the Economic Opportunity Act with the establishment of over 900 CAAs, an indispensable step forward in the delivery of social services to our nation's poor. These multiservice agencies have provided basic life-support services to millions of Americans.

In reviewing the policies of the past 25 years, we have seen various strategies and theories come and go — a welfare reform strategy, a private-sector job strategy, a minority-entrepreneurship strategy, a special-revenue strategy. Yet, I believe that if we had never passed the original legislation, the Economic Opportunity Act of 1964, which created an independent federal agency supporting CAAs — and the Community Economic Development Amendment in 1966 that established Community Development Corporations (CDC) — we would have to invent it today. It created the only coherent delivery mechanisms — imperfect as they may be — that relate policies and programs to people. That is the genuine achievement of the Economic Opportunity Act.

Lost in the cliches, slogans, and double-talk of the conservative antigovernment criticism are the solid accomplishments. The value of these programs, services, and innovations has been obscured; the extraordinary contributions have been slighted. I believe that it is particularly important during a period of passivity, privatism, and rhetoric to recall a time when responsibility for the "common life," as Jane Addams put it, was the law of the land. When our government actually provided the kind of moral leadership that is consistent with the values of a just, humane, and truly democratic society.

954 Points of Light

At this point, when we should be reaping a substantial peace dividend, I believe that a rediscovery of the spirit and a re-enactment of the content of the Economic Opportunity Act would be the most healthy response possible to cope with our present social and community problems. If President Bush is serious about establishing "a thousand points of light," he need not look very far or very long. There are 954 points of light out there now: They are called community action agencies. They have been burning the midnight oil for too long and are in need of some fuel.

With the demise of the Cold War, only a tragic failure of nerve can prevent the administration from acting upon the remarkable opportunity that history is now offering: that of reordering our national priorities. Not only the 34 million poor in America, not only the 45 million near-poor (who are one accident, lay-off, illness, or divorce away from poverty); but also each and every one of us who cares about the future of our nation must ask the question, "If not now, when?"

Politics today, in a period of limited economic growth, seems to have reached a level of abstractness that removes it from the commonplace circumstances of ordinary Americans. When a sane and civilized family runs into tough financial times, two things happen. The one thing that they do do is to assure that those members of the family who are least able to fend for themselves are given the protection and minimum amenities necessary for survival. The one thing that they do not do is to allow those who have more than enough and are enjoying luxuries to continue to hoard. There

are certain natural principles of behavior, of caring and decency, that have prior claim over untested game plans of economic theorists or politicians on the make.

Our founding fathers were well aware of what was needed: They knew that a vital and healthy federal government is indispensable to the well-being of a self-governing people. They believed in the ability of government to secure and protect the liberties of all our people — the weak as well as the strong. That is, after all, what democracy is all about.

Finally, it must be said in response to the downgrading of national commitment to economic opportunity, in response to our government's avoidance of our growing social problems and its abdication of moral leadership that only those people have a future, and only those people can be called humane and historic, who have an intuitive sense of what is important and significant in both their national and public institutions, and who value them. It is this conviction, and the continuing belief in the common-sense vision of the American promise, that allows us to recall the significance of the goals and principles embodied in the Economic Opportunity Act. And to remind ourselves that the struggle for genuine equality, justice, and economic opportunity is still the most important endeavor of our time.

FROM: *San Jose Mercury News*, December 24, 1989.

AMERICA'S NEW WAR ON POVERTY

PART ONE

When Children Are Poor

Unfortunately, many Americans live on the outskirts of hope — some because of their poverty, some because of their color, and all too many because of both. Our task is to help replace their despair with opportunity.

President Lyndon B. Johnson

in his first inaugural address

January 8, 1964

When Lyndon Johnson announced his poverty initiative in 1964, he spoke to a public that enjoyed unprecedented growth and prosperity — a public for whom the realization that there was poverty amidst this plenty was shocking. In what seemed to be an economically propitious moment, poverty was discovered anew. This also happened at a time when the civil rights movement offered its greatest moral lessons to the broader American public. Television and newspaper coverage of children and adults demonstrating against segregation being met with attacking police dogs in Birmingham, Alabama, and of the peaceful and enormous gathering at the March on Washington brought the public to a moral height rarely reached in civic life. Within five months of the March on Washington, President Johnson declared a "war on poverty."

The response to this recognition of poverty was consistent with the American image of self help. What poor people needed was better training, better education, more skills, and counseling; in short, the cause of poverty was the personal characteristics of poor people. Improve the character of poor people and you can end poverty. Few people would argue the need for education, nutrition, and training. President Johnson called it opportunity, but he left it to the marketplace to actually provide the opportunities — the jobs. He set about improving the labor force. If given a chance, the talents of people will always win out — this is the American way.

Even today, despite our abundant cynicism, most nonpoor Americans still believe in the fairness of the game of success in the United States. We believe there exists a level playing field for all contestants, and that cream rises to the top. Poor boys (and perhaps someday girls) can grow up to become president. We believe in the innocence and promise of children. While we may cling intuitively to this mythology, the evidence that contradicts it grows every day.

Babies born on the same day in the same county but at different hospitals (one in the wealthy part of town, the other not) will grow up to lead radically different lives. Poverty is not now — if it ever was — a crucible that tests moral character. It is, instead, a symptom of a debilitating disease that affects both the patient and the onlooker. Winston Churchill once noted that "there is no finer investment for any community than putting milk into babies." The stories, data, and essays that follow make it clear that we are not yet investing in our future.

Sawdust

CHRIS OFFUTT

Chris Offutt, the author of this short story, grew up in the Appalachian region of eastern Kentucky. In "Sawdust" he offers a portrait of white rural poverty. As Junior says of his town, "This is a place people move away from." Mr. Offutt also gives us a sense of what it is like to try to learn in situations where learning is considered a luxury more than a necessity. In 1991, 16 percent of the U.S. adult population had not attained a high school diploma.

Not a one on this hillside finished high school. Around here a man is judged by how he acts, not how smart he's supposed to be. I don't hunt, fish, or work. Neighbors say I think too much. They say I'm like my father and Mom worries that maybe they're right.

When I was a kid we had a coonhound that got into a skunk, then had the gall to sneak under the porch. He whimpered in the dark and wouldn't come out. Dad shot him. It didn't stink less but Dad felt better. He told Mom that any dog who didn't know coon from skunk ought to be killed.

"He's still back under the porch," Mom said.

"I know it," Dad said. "I loved Tater, too. I don't reckon I could stand to bury him."

He looked at my brother and me.

"Don't you even think of putting them boys under that porch," Mom yelled. "It's your dog. You get it."

She held her nose and walked around the house. Dad looked at us again. "You boys smell anything?"

My eyes were watered up but I shook my head no.

"Dead things stink," said Warren.

"So does a wife sometimes," Dad said, handing me his rifle. "Here, Junior. Put this up and fetch my rod and reel."

Chris Offutt grew up and attended college in the Appalachian region of eastern Kentucky. He is the author of *Kentucky Straight* and *The Same River Twice: A Memoir*. His writing has also appeared in several literary magazines.

I ran into the house for his fishing pole. When I got outside, Dad was on his knees shining a flashlight under the porch. Back in the corner lay old Tater, dead as a mallet. "Blind casting," Dad said. "This might turn out fun."

He spread his legs and whipped the rod and the line went humming under the porch. He reeled in a piece of rag. Dad threw again and hooked Tater but only pulled out a hunk of fur. On the next cast, his line got hung. He jerked hard on the fishing pole. The line snapped, the rod lashed over his shoulder and hit Warren in the face. Mom came running around the house at Warren's screams.

"What'd you do now?" she said.

"Line broke," Dad said. "Eight-pound test. Lost a good split sinker, too."

"Why don't you cut a hole in the floor and fish him out like an ice pond!"

"Don't know where my saw's at."

"That's the worst of it! You'd have gone and done it."

She towed Warren up the gray board steps into the house. Dad broke the fishing pole across his knee. "Never should have had no kids," he said, and threw the ruined rod over the hill. A jaybird squalled into the sky. Dad grabbed my shoulders and leaned his face to mine.

"I wanted to be a horse doctor," he said, "but you know what?"

I shook my head. His fingers dug me deep.

"I quit sixth grade on account of not having nothing to wear. All my kin did. Every last one of us."

He turned loose of me and I watched his bowed back fade into the trees. Wide leaves of poplar rustled behind him.

A FEW YEARS LATER Dad gave his gun away and joined the church. He got Warren a pup that fell off the porch and broke its leg. Dad cried all day. I was scared, but Mom said his crying was a sign that both his oars were back in the water. She told me to be proud. That Sunday, Dad climbed on top of a church pew in the middle of service. I thought he'd felt the Lord's touch and would start talking in tongues. The preacher stopped his sermon. Dad looked around the room and swore

Summary

Between 1982 and 1992, there was a 50 percent decrease in the number of coal mining jobs.

Loss of Coal Mining Jobs

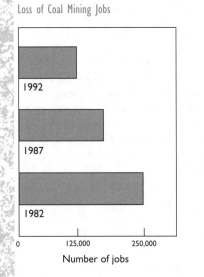

Source: U.S. Statistical Abstract, 1993.

to high heaven he would heal our pup's busted leg or die trying. Mom made him sit down and hush. I got scared again.

After church Dad carried the pup out the ridge to a hickory where he tried all day to fix its leg. He was still yelling at God when Mom sent us to bed. She found Dad in the morning. He'd taken off his belt and hanged himself. On the ground below him lay the pup, all its legs broken. It was still alive.

WARREN AND I both quit school. He got a job and saved his money. I took to the woods hunting mushrooms, ginseng, and mayapple root. I've been places a rabbit wouldn't go.

Last fall Warren pushed a trailer up a hollow and moved into it. He said the one thing I was good for was taking care of Mom. Twice a week I walked to the Clay Creek Post Office at the foot of the hill. It and the church was all we had and they sat side by side between the creek and the road. Most people went to both but Mom and I divided it up. I got more mail than her and she took enough gospel for the whole county. I subscribed to a peck of magazines and read everything twice, even letters and household hints. They stopped coming because I never paid.

Some days I went to the post office early to look at crooks the government wants. Sixty photographs were stapled together like a feed store calendar, and the faces were just regular folks. Under each one was a list of what the person did, where his scars were, and if he was black or white. It seemed odd to show a picture of a man and say what color he was. Around here, we're mostly brown. I wouldn't mind talking to somebody of another color but they don't ever come around these parts. Nobody does. This is a place people move away from.

One afternoon I saw a sign in the post office about a GED. Anyone could take the high school test from a VISTA center in town, and that set me to thinking on what Dad said about quitting school. He never read anything but the King James Bible and about a hundred maps. Dad collected maps the way some men kept dogs—big maps and little maps, favorites and no-counts. I've seen him study maps over a tree stump till way past dark. He wanted to know where the Land of Nod was at and who all lived there. The preacher told him it was lost in the Flood. Dad didn't think so.

"Everywhere has to be somewhere," he always said.

The GED fretted me for two days' worth of walking in the woods. I almost stepped on a blue racer sunning on a rock. We watched each other for a spell, him shooting a little forked tongue out and me not able to think of nothing but taking that test. Most people run from a snake without ever knowing if it was poison or just alive. The GED was the same way. Failing couldn't hurt me, and getting it would make everybody on the hill know I wasn't what they thought. Maybe then they'd think about Dad differently, too.

The next morning I hitchhiked to Rocksalt and stood on the sidewalk. People stared from cars. My hand was on the test place doorknob and sweat poured off me. I opened the door. The air was cool and the walls were white. Behind a metal desk sat a lady painting her fingernails pink. She looked at me, then at her nails.

"The barbershop is next door," she said.

"I don't want a haircut, ma'am. I might could use one but that ain't what I come to town for."

"It ain't," she said like she was mocking me. She talked fast and didn't always say her words right. I wondered what brought her to the hills. Things must be getting pretty bad if city people were coming here for work.

"I'll take that GED," I said.

"Who sent you?"

"Nobody."

She stared at me a long time. Her hand moved like she was waving away flies and when the nail polish was dry, she opened a drawer and gave me a study book. It was magazine size with a black plastic binder.

"Come back when you're ready," she said. "I'm here to help you people."

I was five hours getting home and the heat didn't bother me a bit. By the time I got to the house, somebody had seen me in town and told a neighbor, who told Mom at the prayer meet-

It is hard to be an island of excellence in a sea of indifference.

ERNEST BOYER
President, Carnegie Foundation for the Advancement of Teaching

Poverty is not just an individual affair. It is also a condition, a relationship to society, and to all the institutions which comprise society.

SARGENT SHRIVER
Head of Office of Economic Opportunity under President Lyndon Johnson

ing. That's the way it is around here. A man can sneeze and it'll beat him back to the porch.

"They say you're fixing to get learned up on us," she said. "You might read the Bible while you're at it."

"I done did. Twice."

"I ain't raised no heathen then."

After supper I hit those practice tests. My best was reading and worst was math. A man can take a mess of figures and make it equal out to something different. Maybe some people like math for that, but a pile of stove wood doesn't equal a tree. It made me wonder where the sawdust went to in a math problem. After all that ciphering, there wasn't anything to show for the work, nothing to clean up, nothing to look at. A string of numbers was like an owl pellet lying in a game path. You knew a bird had flew over, but not the direction.

Warren pulled his four-wheel-drive pickup into the yard, honking the horn. He used to work in town until they built a car plant in Lexington. Now he drives three hours a day to work and back. He's got a video dish, a microwave, and a VCR.

His boots hit the porch and the front door slammed. He walked in our old room. "What do you know, Junior? All on your ownself and afraid to tell it."

I shook my head. After Dad died, Warren went all out to make people like him. I went the other way.

"Hear you're eat up with the smart bug," he said. "And taking that school test in town."

"Thinking on it."

"You ought to let up on that and try working. Then you can wear alligator-hide boots like these."

He pulled a pants leg up.

"Where'd you get them from" I said.

"Down to Lex. They got a mall big as two pastures laid end to end. I bought these boots right out of the window. Paid the man cash, too."

"He saw you coming, Warren. They ain't made no alligator nothing in nigh ten years. Government's got them took care of."

"What makes you know so much?"

"Read it in a magazine."

Warren frowned. He doesn't put much store in anything but TV. Commercials are real people to him. I knew he was getting mad by a neck vein that popped up big as a night crawler.

"I ought to kick your butt with these boots," he said.

"That won't make them gator."

"It won't take the new out either." He scuffed my workshoes that were ordered from the Sears and Roebuck catalog. "You're still wearing them goddam Wishbook clod-hoppers."

"Warren!" Mom screeched from the kitchen.

She doesn't mind cussing too awful much but taking the Lord's name in vain is one thing she won't stand for. Dad used to do it just to spite her.

"You know what GED stands for?" Warren said. "Get Even Dumber."

He stomped outside, started his truck, and rammed it through the gears. Road dust rose thick as smoke behind him. I watched the moon haul itself above Redbird Ridge. Night crawled up the hollow. I went outside and sat on Dad's old map-stump. A long time ago I was scared of the dark until Dad told me it was the same as day, only the air was a different color.

IN A WEEK I'd taken every practice test twice and was ready for the real one. Everybody on the hill knew what I was doing. The preacher guaranteed Mom a sweet place in heaven for all her burdens on earth. He said I was too hardheaded for my own good.

I got to thinking about that in the woods and decided maybe it wasn't a bad thing to be. I'm not one to pick wildflowers and bring them inside where they'll die quicker. And I'll not cut down a summer shade tree to burn for winter firewood. Taking the GED was the first time I'd ever been stubborn over the doing of something, instead of the not doing. Right there's where Dad and me were different. He was hardheaded over things he never had a say in.

In the morning I left the hill and walked halfway to town before getting a ride that dropped me off at the test place. The lady was surprised to see me. She wrote my name on a form, and asked for fifteen dollars to take the test. I didn't say anything.

Summary

One-sixth of all rural Americans live in poverty.

Suburban/Rural/Urban Poverty

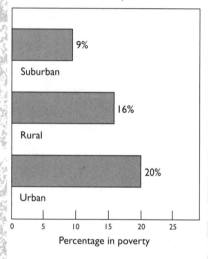

Percentage in poverty

Source: Center on Budget and Policy (1992).

"Do you have the fee?" she asked.

"No."

"Do you have a job?"

"No."

"Do you live with family?"

"Mom."

"Does she have a job?"

"No."

"Do you receive welfare assistance?"

"No, ma'am."

"Then how do you and your mother get along?"

"We don't talk much."

She tightened her mouth and shook her head. Her voice came slow and loud, like I was deaf.

"What do you and your mother do for money?"

"Never had much need for it."

"What about food?"

"We grow it."

The lady set her pencil down and leaned away from the desk. On the wall behind her hung a picture of the governor wearing a tie. I looked through the window at the hardware store across the street. Dad died owing it half on a new chain saw. We got a bill after the funeral and Mom sold a quilt her great-aunt made, to pay the debt.

I was thinking hard and not getting far. There wasn't anything I had to sell. Warren would give me the money but I could never ask him for it. I turned to leave.

"Junior," said the lady. "You can take the test anyway."

"I don't need the help."

"It's free when you're living in poverty."

"I'll owe you," I said. "Pay you before the first snow."

She led me through a door to a small room with no windows. I squeezed into a school desk and she gave me four yellow pencils and the test. When I finished, she said to come back in a month and see if I passed. She told me in a soft voice that I could take the test as many times as necessary. I nodded and headed out of town toward home. I couldn't think or feel. I was doing good to walk.

EVERY NIGHT Mom claimed a worry that I was getting above my raisings. Warren wouldn't talk to me at all. I wandered the hills, thinking of what I knew about the woods. I can name a bird by its nest and a tree by its bark. A cucumber smell means a copperhead's close. The sweetest blackberries are low to the ground and locust makes the best fence post. It struck me funny that I had to take a test to learn I was living in poverty. I'd say the knowing of it is what drove Dad off his feed for good. When he died, Mom burned his maps but I saved the one of Kentucky. Where we live wasn't on it.

I stayed in the woods three weeks straight. When I finally went to the post office, the mail hadn't run yet. It was the first of the month and a lot of people were waiting on government checks. The oldest sat inside, out of the sun, and the rest of us stood in willow shade by the creek. A Monroe boy jabbed his brother and pointed at me.

"If it ain't the doctor," he said, "taking a break off his books."

"Hey, Doctor, you aiming to get smart and rich?"

"Yeah," said his brother. "He's going to start a whorehouse and run it by hand."

Everybody laughed, even a couple of old women with hair buns like split pine cones. I decided to skip the mail and go home. Then the one boy made me mad.

"I got a sick pup at the house, Doctor. You as good on them as your daddy was?"

Way it is around here, I had to do more than just fight. Sometimes a man will lay back a year before shooting somebody's dog to get back at its owner, but with everyone watching, I couldn't just leave. I walked to their pickup and kicked out a headlight. The youngest Monroe came running but I tripped him and he rolled in the dirt. The other one jumped on my back, tearing at my ear with his teeth. His legs had a hold I couldn't break. He kept hitting the side of my face. I fell backwards on the truck hood and he let go of me then. Two old men held back the other boy. I crossed the creek and climbed the steep hill home, spitting blood all the way.

Mom never said a word after she heard what the fight was over. Warren came by the next night.

"I got one at the creek and the other at the head of Bobcat Holler," he said. "They'll not talk that way no more."

"Whip them pretty bad?"

"They knowed they was in a fight."

Warren'd taken a lick or two in the jaw, and his neck vein was puffed out again. A railroad tie won't knock him over.

"You still getting that GED?" he said.

"Friday."

"I'm getting me a TV that runs on batteries."

"What for?"

"To sit and look at."

"Same with me, Warren. Same with me."

He pushed his fingers at a swollen place below his cheekbone. His shoulders sagged. "I'll fight for you, Junior. And for Daddy, too. But I never could figure what either of you ever was up to."

He went outside and opened the truck door with his thumbs. The knuckles of both hands were split, and bending his fingers would open the scabs. One was already leaking a little. He started the truck in second gear so he wouldn't have to shift, and drove away with his palms. I watched him till the dust settled back to the road.

ON FRIDAY I walked the ridgeline above the creek all the way to town. Rocksalt lay in a wide bottom between the hills. I'd never seen it from above and it looked pretty small, nothing to be afraid of. I went down the slope, crossed the creek, and stepped onto the sidewalk. For a long time I stood in front of the test center. I could leave now and never know if I passed or flunked. Either one scared me. I opened the door and looked in.

"Congratulations," said the lady.

She handed me a state certificate saying I'd achieved a high school degree. My name was written in black ink. Below it was a gold seal and the governor's signature.

"I have a job application for you," she said. "It isn't a promise of work but you qualify now. Employment is the next step out."

"All I wanted was this."

"Not a job?"

"No, ma'am."

She sighed and looked down, rubbing her eyes. She leaned against the doorjamb. "Sometimes I don't know what I'm doing here," she said.

"None of us do," I said. "Most people around here are just waiting to die."

"That's not funny, Junior."

"No, but what's funny is, everybody gets up awful early anyhow."

"I like to sleep late," she said.

She was still smiling when I shut the door behind me. I'd come as close as a man could get to finishing school and it didn't feel half bad. At the edge of town I looked back at the row of two-story buildings. Dad used to say a smart man wouldn't bother with town, but now I knew he was wrong. Anybody can go there any time. Town's just a bunch of people living together in the only wide place between the hills.

I left the road and walked through horseweed to the creek bank. It was a good way to find pop bottles and I still owed the state fifteen dollars.

FROM: *Kentucky Straight*, 1992.

> *If a free society cannot help the many who are poor, it cannot save the few who are rich.*
>
> JOHN F. KENNEDY
> 35th U.S. President

What is poverty?

BY CAROLYN SHAW BELL

Eligibility for public housing, government loans for college, and low-cost health insurance usually refer to the poverty level. Subsidies may go to those with incomes "up to three times the poverty level," or "at or below 150 percent of the poverty threshold." The current minimum wage is said to be "below the poverty line" and everyone knows that food stamps and Medicaid go to those who are poor.

Every year the U.S. Bureau of Labor Statistics (BLS) goes through the exercise of counting the poor. It describes poor people — their age, education, location, race, family composition, and employment. Instead of defining "the poverty threshold of income," it calculates 61 different levels of poverty for elderly couples, for one person, and for families with different numbers of adults and children.

But the figures use a definition of poverty itself almost 30 years old. Policy still depends on the pioneering work of Mollie Orshansky, a brilliant economist who invented the basic method in 1965, and who received little or no credit for her research, even as it affected millions of lives. She knew that, in the mid-1960s, people spent about one-third of their income for food. She defined poverty, therefore, as three times the dollar amount needed to buy a nutritious but low-cost diet.

The U.S. Department of Agriculture had the nutritional expertise: It produced three meal plans, with menus and shopping lists, for people at various income levels. BLS field workers shopped in different stores to get prices for the foods listed. The one-third ratio between food expenditures and the total came from a U.S. Census survey of income and spending. So multiplying the cost of the economy meal plan by three yielded an income at the upper limit of poverty. These were hard, empirical data, free of any judgment of what people "ought to spend" for food or rent or clothing.

Most previous efforts at defining poverty itemized, for a "working girl" or "the typical steelworker's family" or some other household, the "necessities" or "the bare minimum" for food, clothing, shelter, and other appurtenances of living. Such lists dated back to mid-Victorian England; in the United States, they were drawn up by settlement-house workers, state boards determining minimum wages, commissions settling wage disputes, and charitable organizations raising funds to help the poor. All the lists showed that nobody could agree on what poor people really needed.

The Orshansky method precluded such dissension. It automatically yielded different poverty incomes for different-sized families, living on farms or in cities, or consisting of a retired couple. Start with the Department of Agriculture's recommended meal plan for families of different types, price the actual food required, figure out a week's food expenditure and multiply by three, which is the factor drawn from data on what real people really spent for food. If food costs amounted to one-third of the average income, then an economy food plan should amount to one-third of an economy income, that is, an income pretty much at the minimum. Anyone with less income could safely be called poor.

Although Orshanksy's work is still basic to the figures, they are far removed from the realities of empirical data and generally agreed on methods of earlier days. For one thing, people today spend about 15 percent of their income on food, not 25 to 33 percent. Orshanksy deplored the continued use of her method years after it was invented, and few experts defend it today for calculating subsidies for health insurance or a floor for minimum wages. But no alternative has yet been agreed on.

The other two significant methods for identifying poverty incomes prove fairly simple. One turns to consumers for their judgment. Asking people for the weekly or monthly sum to be used as a poverty line, for a family of three (mother, two children) or four (parents and two children) has been part of public opinion polls for years. The responses fall within a fairly close range — setting the poverty level of income well above the official figure. This means, of course, that people think poverty is more widespread than the official data show.

The other definition identifies poverty in relation to the current median income, which is higher than what half the population receives and lower than what half the population receives. For example, defining poverty as 50 percent of the median would yield, in 1992, $13,000 as the poverty level for families consisting of an elderly couple because the median income for such families was $26,000. But the official poverty figure was only $8,500, about one-third the median income.

In Sweden, the poverty-level income is about 60 percent of the median Swedish income; and in other European countries it varies between 40 and 60 percent. The relative income method of calculating poverty has several advantages. First, it is simplicity itself. Second, it reflects changes in the income of other, non-poor families. Third, it has been widely accepted in other countries and has proved workable.

Changing the current definition of poverty is long overdue. But when a new, better definition of poverty appears, the country should plan to review it regularly, instead of waiting another 30 years.

Carolyn Shaw Bell is the Katharine Coman emerita professor of economics at Wellesley College.

FROM: *The Boston Globe*, July 12, 1994.

Appalshop

Appalshop is a media-arts center in the small town of Whitesburg, Kentucky, dedicated to enabling the people of the Appalachian Mountains to tell their stories. Over the years, Appalshop artists have produced a wide range of films, plays, magazines, books, concerts, radio programs, and festivals celebrating and investigating Appalachian life.

The people in this coal mining region have historically been depicted in a stereotyped manner: either as passive victims of unemployment and illiteracy or as the hicks of Li'l Abner and The Beverly Hillbillies.

In 1969, the federal Office of Economic Opportunity established the Community Film Workshop Council of Appalachia — one of 10 film workshops set up across the nation with the goal of helping people learn job skills and show their lives and culture as they saw it.

The workshop appealed to Elizabeth Barret, a University of Kentucky student who joined in 1973. "The films were about my home region, and they were done in a different way than anything I had seen before." She went on to produce "Long Journey Home," an hour-long documentary exploring migration to and from Appalachia.

For more than two decades, Appalshop artists have created films, collected oral histories, staged community plays and concerts, and established a training program for young people.

For more information, write Appalshop, 306 Madison Street, Whitesburg, KY 41858; (606) 633-0108.

VISTA

Volunteers in Service to America

Volunteers in Service to America (VISTA) enlists full-time volunteers to work in community-based projects aimed at bettering the lives of poor people while fostering self-reliance. Created as part of the Economic Opportunity Act of 1964, VISTA is now administered by the Corporation for National Community Service.

For the duration of their full-time, one-year (minimum) assignments, VISTA volunteers live in the communities they serve. They are paid a poverty-level wage by VISTA, but they work directly for local programs — programs that address such basic needs as shelter, food, health, neighborhood revitalization, and literacy. One VISTA might find herself training food bank volunteers while another might help organize a home rehabilitation project.

While many of the first VISTA volunteers were middle-class white college students or recent graduates, today's 4,000 VISTA volunteers are much more diverse: about one-third are minorities; 15% are skilled retired persons; and 50% are recruited directly from the community that is being served.

During the Reagan administration, the program's budget was slashed nearly in half, but VISTA was revitalized by President Clinton's national service initiative, AmeriCorps. In its first 30 years, over 100,000 VISTA volunteers have served in 12,000 projects throughout America, from inner-city New York to the migrant worker camps of California.

Today's VISTA volunteers do more than provide direct services; they also participate in "institution building" and the mobilization of resources. At the Chadwick Residence in Syracuse, New York, a women's shelter, VISTAs not only helped recruit community volunteers for the program, they also trained those community members to do the recruiting in the future. Thus, the VISTA volunteers achieved their mandate of "working themselves out of a job." Said Barbara Fioramonti of Catholic Services, which oversees the residence: "They left something permanent for the community to continue as a way of helping itself move ahead."

For more information, contact VISTA, 1100 Vermont Avenue, NW, Washington, DC 20525; (800) 942-2677.

Photo: Kim Beury, September 1994

So How Did I Get Here?

ROSEMARY BRAY

Roughly one-third of welfare recipients are white and one-third are black. The ratio of white-to-black recipients has remained constant for at least the last 20 years. Nonetheless, as Rosemary Bray points out in this essay, "the 'welfare question' has become the race question...in disguise."

Growing up on welfare was a story I had planned to tell a long time from now, when I had children of my own. My childhood on Aid to Families with Dependent Children (AFDC) was going to be one of those stories I would tell my kids about the bad old days, an urban legend equivalent to Abe Lincoln studying by firelight. But I know now I cannot wait, because in spite of a wealth of evidence about the true nature of welfare and poverty in America, the debate has turned ugly, vicious, and racist. The "welfare question" has become the race question and the woman question in disguise, and so far the answers bode well for no one.

In both blunt and coded terms, comfortable Americans more and more often bemoan the waste of their tax money on lazy black women with a love of copulation, a horror of birth control, and a lack of interest in marriage. Were it not for the experiences of half my life, were I not black and female and of a certain age, perhaps I would be like so many people who blindly accept the lies and distortions, half-truths, and wrongheaded notions about welfare. But for better or for worse, I do know better. I know more than I want to know about being poor. I know that the welfare system is designed to be inadequate, to leave its constituents on the edge of survival. I know because I've been there.

And finally, I know that perhaps even more dependent on welfare than its recipients are the large number of Americans

Rosemary Bray is the author of *Martin Luther King*, a children's biography to be published in January 1995 by Green Willow Books. Her political memoir, *Unafraid of the Dark*, will be published in 1995 by Random House. From 1987 to 1992 she was an editor for *The New York Times Book Review*. Ms. Bray now lives in Detroit, Michigan.

who would rather accept this patchwork of economic horrors than fully address the real needs of real people.

M y m o t h e r c a m e t o C h i c a g o in 1947 with a fourth-grade education, cut short by working in the Mississippi fields. She pressed shirts in a laundry for a while and later waited tables in a restaurant, where she met my father. Mercurial and independent, with a sixth-grade education, my Arkansas-born father worked at whatever came to hand. He owned a lunch wagon for a time and prepared food for hours in our kitchen on the nights before he took the wagon out. Sometimes he hauled junk and sold it in the open-air markets of Maxwell Street on Sunday mornings. Eight years after they met — seven years after they married — I was born. My father made her quit her job; her work, he told her, was taking care of me. By the time I was four, I had a sister, a brother, and another brother on the way. My parents, like most other American couples of the 1950s, had their own American dream — a husband who worked, a wife who stayed home, a family of smiling children. But as was true for so many African-American couples, their American dream was an illusion.

The house on the corner of Berkeley Avenue and 45th Street is long gone. The other houses still stand, but today the neighborhood is an emptier, bleaker place. When we moved there, it was a street of old limestones with beveled-glass windows, all falling into vague disrepair. Home was a four-room apartment on the first floor, in what must have been the public rooms of a formerly grand house. The rent was $110 a month. All of us kids slept in the big front room. Because I was the oldest, I had a bed of my own, near a big plate-glass window.

My mother and father had been married for several years before she realized he was a gambler who would never stay away from the track. By the time we moved to Berkeley Avenue, Daddy was spending more time gambling, and bringing home less and less money and more and more anger. Mama's simplest requests were met with rage. They fought once for hours when she asked for money to buy a tube of lipstick. It didn't help that I always seemed to need a doctor. I had allergies and

> *To be a poor man is hard, but to be a poor race in a land of dollars is the very bottom of hardships.*
>
> W . E . B . D U B O I S
> Writer, Educator, Lecturer

Summary

As of 1986, the U. S. Department of Agriculture's estimated average monthly cost for a moderate-level family to raise a 12-year-old in the urban South was four times higher than a child's share of the median state maximum Aid to Families with Dependent Children grant for a family of three.

Living on Welfare

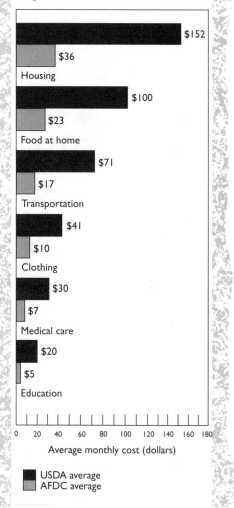

Average monthly cost (dollars)

- ■ USDA average
- ▨ AFDC average

Source: *A Children's Defense Budget* (1989).

bronchitis so severe that I nearly died one Sunday after church when I was about three.

It was around this time that my mother decided to sign up for AFDC. She explained to the caseworker that Daddy wasn't home much, and when he was he didn't have any money. Daddy was furious; Mama was adamant. "There were times when we hardly had a loaf of bread in here," she told me years later. "It was close. I wasn't going to let you all go hungry."

Going on welfare closed a door between my parents that never reopened. She joined the ranks of unskilled women who were forced to turn to the state for the security their men could not provide. In the sterile relationship between herself and the State of Illinois, Mama found an autonomy denied her by my father. It was she who could decide, at last, some part of her own fate and ours. AFDC relegated marginally productive men like my father to the ranks of failed patriarchs who no longer controlled the destiny of their families. Like so many of his peers, he could no longer afford the luxury of a woman who did as she was told because her economic life depended on it. Daddy became one of the shadow men who walked out back doors as caseworkers came in through the front. Why did he acquiesce? For all his anger, for all his frightening brutality, he loved us, so much that he swallowed his pride and periodically ceased to exist so that we might survive.

In 1960, the year my mother went on public aid, the poverty threshold for a family of five in the United States was $3,560, and the monthly payment to a family of five from the State of Illinois was $182.56, a total of $2,190.72 a year. Once the $110 rent was paid, Mama was left with $72.56 a month to take care of all the other expenses. By any standard, we were poor. All our lives were proscribed by the narrow line between not quite and just enough.

What did it take to live?

It took the kindness of friends as well as strangers, the charity of churches, low expectations, deprivation, and patience. I can't begin to count the hours spent in long lines, long waits, long walks in pursuit of basic things. A visit to a local clinic (one housing doctors, a dentist, and a pharmacy in an incredibly crowded series of rooms) invariably took the better part of a day; I never saw the same doctor twice.

It took, as well, a turning of our collective backs on the letter of a law that required reporting even a small and important miracle like a present of five dollars. All families have their secrets, but I remember the weight of an extra burden. In a world where caseworkers were empowered to probe into every nook and cranny of our lives, silence became defense. Even now, there are things I will not publicly discuss because I cannot shake the fear that we might be hounded by the state, eager to prosecute us for the crime of survival.

ALL MY MEMORIES of our years on AFDC are seasoned with unease. It's painful to remember how much every penny counted, how even a gap of 25 cents could make a difference in any given week. Few people understand how precarious life is from welfare check to welfare check, how the word "extra" has no meaning. Late mail, a bureaucratic mix-up…and a carefully planned method of survival lies in tatters.

What made our lives work as well as they did was my mother's genius at making do — worn into her by a childhood of rural poverty — along with her vivid imagination. She worked at home endlessly, shopped ruthlessly, bargained, cajoled, charmed. Her food store of choice was the one that stocked pork and beans, creamed corn, sardines, Vienna sausages, and potted meat all at 10 cents a can. Clothing was the stuff of rummage sales, trips to Goodwill, and bargain basements, where thin cotton and polyester reigned supreme. Our shoes came from a discount store that sold two pairs for five dollars.

It was an uphill climb, but there was no time for reflection; we were too busy with our everyday lives. Yet, I remember how much it pained me to know that Mama, who recruited a neighbor to help her teach me how to read when I was three, found herself left behind by her eldest daughter, then by each of us in turn. Her biggest worry was that we would grow up uneducated, so Mama enrolled us in parochial school.

When one caseworker angrily questioned how she could afford to send four children to St. Ambrose School, my mother, who emphatically declared, "My kids need an education," told

Summary

In 1991, the number of white mothers on welfare was about equal to the number of African American mothers.

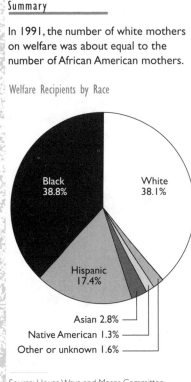

Welfare Recipients by Race

Black 38.8%
White 38.1%
Hispanic 17.4%
Asian 2.8%
Native American 1.3%
Other or unknown 1.6%

Source: House Ways and Means Committee.

FACT

The inflation-adjusted value of Aid to Families with Dependent Children (AFDC) plus food stamps declined by 26 percent between 1972 and 1992.

(Source: U.S. House of Representatives, Committee on Ways and Means, *Overview of Entitlement Programs: 1993 Green Book*.)

her it was none of her business. (In fact, the school had a volume discount of sorts; the price of tuition dropped with each child you sent. I still don't quite know how she managed it.) She organized our lives around church and school, including Mass every morning at 7:45. My brother was an altar boy, I laid out the vestments each afternoon for the next day's Mass. She volunteered as a chaperon for every class trip, sat with us as we did homework she did not understand herself. She and my father reminded us again and again and again that every book, every test, every page of homework was in fact a ticket out and away from the life we lived.

MY LIFE ON WELFARE ended on June 4, 1976 — a month after my 21st birthday, two weeks after I graduated from Yale. My father, eaten up with cancer and rage, lived just long enough to know the oldest two of us had graduated from college and were on our own. Before the decade ended, all of us had left the welfare rolls. The eldest of my brothers worked at the post office, assumed support of my mother (who also went to work, as a companion to an elderly woman), and earned his master's degree at night. My sister married and got a job at a bank. My baby brother parked cars and found a wife. Mama's biggest job was done at last; the investment made in our lives by the State of Illinois had come to fruition. Five people on welfare for 18 years had become five working, taxpaying adults. Three of us went to college, two of us finished; one of us has an advanced degree; all of us can take care of ourselves.

Ours was a best-case phenomenon, based on the synergy of church and state, the government and the private sector, and the thousand points of light that we called friends and neighbors. But there was something more: What fueled our dreams and fired our belief that our lives could change for the better was the promise of the civil rights movement and the war on poverty — for millions of African-Americans the defining events of the 1960s. Caught up in the heady atmosphere of imminent change, our world was filled not only with issues and ideas but with amazing images of black people engaged in the struggle for long-denied rights and freedoms. We knew other people lived differently than we did, we knew we didn't have much, but we didn't mind, because we knew it wouldn't be long. My mother borrowed a phrase I had read to her once from Dick Gregory's autobiography: "Not poor, just broke." She would repeat it often, as often as she sang hymns in the kitchen. She loved to sing a spiritual Mahalia Jackson had made famous: "Move On Up a Little Higher." Like so many others, Mama was singing about earth as well as heaven.

These are the things I remember every time I read another article outlining America's welfare crisis. The rage I feel about the welfare debate comes from listening to a host of lies, distortions, and exaggerations — and taking them personally.

I am no fool. I know of few women — on welfare or off — with my mother's grace and courage and stamina. I know not all women on welfare are cut from the same cloth. Some are lazy, some are ground down. Some are too young; many are without husbands. A few have made welfare fraud a lucrative career; a great many more have pushed the rules on outside income to their very limits.

I also know that none of these things justify our making welfare a test of character and worthiness, rather than an acknowledgment of need. Near-sainthood should not be a requirement for financial and medical assistance.

But all manner of sociologists and policy gurus continue to equate issues that simply aren't equivalent — welfare, race, rates of poverty, crime, marriage, and childbirth — and to reach conclusions that serve to demonize the poor. More than one social arbiter would have us believe that we have all been mistaken for the last 30 years — that the efforts to relieve the most severe effects of poverty have not only failed but have served instead to increase and expand the ranks of the poor. In keeping women, children, and men from starvation, we are told, we have also kept them from self-sufficiency. In our zeal to do good, we have undermined the work ethic, the family, and, thus, by association, the country itself.

So how did I get here?

DESPITE ATTEMPTS to misconstrue and discredit the social programs and policies that changed — even saved — my life, certain facts remain. Poverty was reduced by 39 percent

FACT

Only 3 percent of the nation's doctors and lawyers and less than 1 percent of the nation's architects are black.

(Source: Census Bureau, 1990.)

MYTH

Most Americans believe that the average family with a single mother and two children on AFDC receives $650 per month.

FACT

According to the U.S. Department of Health and Human Services, the average is $376.

(Source: A Report on Americans' Attitudes Toward Poverty — poll conducted in late 1994.)

Summary

In 1993, about half of mothers on welfare who left the rolls did so because they had increased earnings, while only 11 percent of them stopped receiving Aid to Families with Dependent Children payments because of marriage, remarriage, or reconciliation.

How Women Leave Welfare

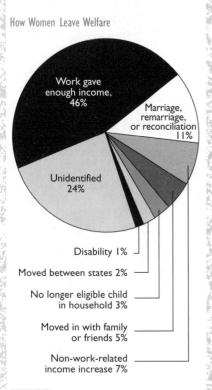

Work gave enough income, 46%

Marriage, remarriage, or reconciliation 11%

Unidentified 24%

Disability 1%

Moved between states 2%

No longer eligible child in household 3%

Moved in with family or friends 5%

Non-work-related income increase 7%

Source: LaDonna A. Pavetti, *The Dynamics of Welfare and Work: Exploring the Process by Which Young Women Work Their Way Out of Welfare* (John F. Kennedy School of Government, Harvard University: Thesis, 1993).

between 1960 and 1990, according to the Census Bureau, from 22.2 percent to 13.5 percent of the nation's population. That is far too many poor people, but the rate is considerably lower than it might have been if we had thrown up our hands and reminded ourselves that the poor will always be with us. Of black women considered "highly dependent," that is, on welfare for more than seven years, 81 percent of their daughters grow up to live productive lives off the welfare rolls, a 1992 Congressional report stated; the 19 percent who become second-generation welfare recipients can hardly be said to constitute an epidemic of welfare dependency. The vast majority of African-Americans are now working or middle class, an achievement that occurred in the past 30 years, most specifically between 1960 and 1973, the years of expansion in the very same social programs that it is so popular now to savage. Those were the same years in which I changed from girl to woman; learned to read and think; graduated from high school and college; came to be a working woman, a taxpayer, a citizen.

In spite of all the successes we know of, in spite of the reality that the typical welfare recipient is a white woman with young children, ideologues have continued to fashion from whole cloth the specter of the mythical black welfare mother, complete with a prodigious reproductive capacity and a galling laziness, accompanied by the uncaring and equally lazy black man in her life who will not work, will not marry her, and will not support his family.

Why has this myth been promoted by some of the best (and the worst) people in government, academia, journalism, and industry? One explanation may be that the constant presence of poverty frustrates even the best-intentioned among us. It may also be because the myth allows for denial about who the poor in America really are and for denial about the depth and intransigence of racism regardless of economic status. And because getting tough on welfare is for some a first-class career move; what better way to win a position in the next administration than to trash those people least able to respond? And, finally, because it serves to assure white Americans that lazy black people aren't getting away with anything.

Many of these prescriptions for saving America from the welfare plague not only reflect an insistent, if sometimes unconscious, racism but rest on the bedrock of patriarchy. They are rooted in the fantasy of a male presence as a path to social and economic salvation and in its corollary — the image of woman as passive chattel, constitutionally so afflicted by her condition that the only recourse is to transfer her care from the hands of the state to the hands of a man with a job. The largely ineffectual plans to create jobs for men in communities ravaged by disinvestment, the state-sponsored dragnets for men who cannot or will not support their children, the exhortations for women on welfare to find themselves a man and get married, all are the institutional expressions of the same worn cultural illusion — that women and children without a man are fundamentally damaged goods. Men are such a boon, the reasoning goes, because they make more money than women do.

Were we truly serious about an end to poverty among women and children, we would take the logical next step. We would figure out how to make sure women who did a dollar's worth of work got a dollar's worth of pay. We would make sure that women could go to work with their minds at ease, knowing their children were well cared for. What women on welfare need, in large measure, are the things key to the life of every adult woman: economic security and autonomy. Women need the skills and the legitimate opportunity to earn a living for ourselves as well as for people who may rely on us; we need the freedom to make choices to improve our own lives and the lives of those dear to us.

"The real problem is not welfare," says Kathryn Edin, a professor of sociology at Rutgers University and a scholar in residence at the Russell Sage Foundation. "The real problem is the nature of low-wage work and lack of support for these workers — most of whom happen to be women raising their children alone."

Completing a five-year study of single mothers — some low-wage workers, some welfare recipients — Edin is quantifying what common sense and bitter experience have told millions of women who rotate off and on the welfare rolls: Women, particularly unskilled women with children, get the worst jobs

Summary

As of 1990, the gap in salaries between men and women was smallest among white women, who earned 72 cents for every dollar white men earned. African-American women earned 65 cents for every dollar while Hispanic women earned a mere 57 cents for every dollar.

Female/Male Earnings, by Race

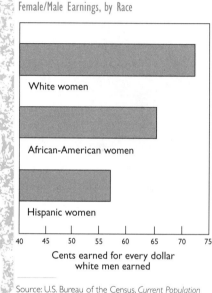

Cents earned for every dollar white men earned

Source: U.S. Bureau of the Census, *Current Population Reports* (1991).

Summary

On the average, single mothers spend about half their monthly income on rent. The rent burden (percentage of income devoted to housing) reached its peak in 1985 (60 percent) and in 1989 was estimated at 46 percent.

Paying the Rent

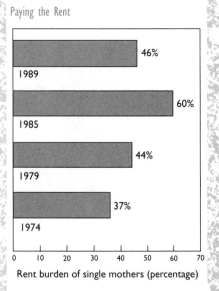

Rent burden of single mothers (percentage)

Source: American Housing Survey.

available, with the least amount of health care, and are the most frequently laid off. "The work place is not oriented toward people who have family responsibilities," she says. "Most jobs are set up assuming that someone is minding the kids and doesn't need assistance."

But the writers and scholars and politicians who wax most rhapsodic about the need to replace welfare with work make their harsh judgments from the comfortable and supportive environs of offices and libraries and think tanks. If they need to go to the bathroom midsentence, there is no one timing their absence. If they take longer than a half hour for lunch, there is no one waiting to dock their pay. If their baby-sitter gets sick, there is no risk of someone having taken their place at work by the next morning. Yet these are conditions that the low-wage women routinely face, which inevitably leads to the cyclical nature of their welfare histories. These are the realities that many of the most vocal and widely quoted critics of welfare routinely ignore. In his book, *The End of Equality*, for example, Mickey Kaus discusses social and economic inequity, referring to David Ellwood's study on long-term welfare dependency without ever mentioning that it counts anyone who uses the services for at least one month as having been on welfare for the entire year.

In the heated atmosphere of the welfare debate, the larger society is encouraged to believe that women on welfare have so violated the social contract that they have forfeited all rights common to those of us lucky enough not to be poor. In no area is this attitude more clearly demonstrated than in issues of sexuality and childbearing. Consider the following: A *Philadelphia Inquirer* editorial of December 12, 1990, urges the use of Norplant contraceptive inserts for welfare recipients — in spite of repeated warnings from women's health groups of its dangerous side effects — in the belief that the drug "could be invaluable in breaking the cycle of inner-city poverty." (The newspaper apologized for the editorial after it met widespread criticism, both within and outside the paper.) A California judge orders a woman on welfare, convicted of abusing two of her four children, to use Norplant; the judge's decision was appealed. The Washington state legislature considers approving cash payments of up to $10,000 for women on welfare who agree to be sterilized. These and other proposals, all centering on women's reproductive capacities, were advanced in spite of evidence that welfare recipients have fewer children than those not on welfare.

The punitive energy behind these and so many other Draconian actions and proposals goes beyond the desire to decrease welfare costs; it cuts to the heart of the nation's racial and sexual hysteria. Generated neither by law nor by fully informed public debate, these actions amount to social control over "those people on welfare" — a control many Americans feel they have bought and paid for every April 15. The question is obvious: If citizens were really aware of who receives welfare in America, however inadequate it is, if they acknowledged that white women and children were welfare's primary beneficiaries, would most of these things be happening?

WELFARE HAS BECOME a code word now. One that enables white Americans to mask their sometimes malignant, sometimes benign racism behind false concerns about the suffering ghetto poor and their negative impact on the rest of us. It has become the vehicle many so-called tough thinkers use to undermine compassionate policy and engineer the reduction of social programs.

So how *did* I get here?

I kept my drawers up and my dress down, to quote my mother. I didn't end up pregnant because I had better things to do. I knew I did because my uneducated, Southern-born parents told me so. Their faith, their focus on our futures are a far cry from the thesis of Nicholas Lemann, whose widely acclaimed book *The Promised Land* perpetuates the myth of black Southern sharecropping society as a primary source of black urban malaise. Most important, my family and I had every reason to believe that I had better things to do and that when I got older I would be able to do them. I had a mission, a calling, work to do that only I could do. And that is knowledge transmitted not just by parents, or school, or churches. It is a palpable thing, available by osmosis from the culture of the neighborhood and the world at large.

> *Welfare is hated by those who administer it, mistrusted by those who pay for it, and held in contempt by those who receive it.*
>
> PETER C. GOLDMARK
> Former Budget Director, NY State
> President, Rockefeller Foundation

FACT

More American children lived in poverty in 1992 than in any year since 1965, although our Gross National Product grew 53.2 percent during the same period.

(Source: Children's Defense Fund, 1994.)

Summary

Nearly one child in eight (12.9 percent) is being raised on government welfare through Aid to Families with Dependent Children (AFDC).

Children on Welfare

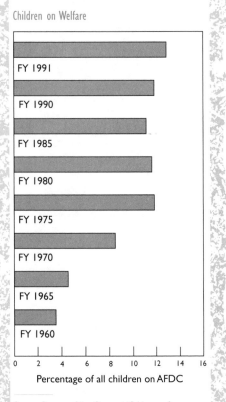

Source: Bureau of the Census; U.S. House of Representatives.

Add to this formula a whopping dose of dumb luck. It was my sixth-grade teacher, Sister Maria Sarto, who identified in me the first signs of a stifling boredom and told my mother that I needed a tougher, more challenging curriculum than her school could provide. It was she who then tracked down the private Francis W. Parker School, which agreed to give me a scholarship if I passed the admissions test.

Had I been born a few years earlier, or a decade later, I might now be living on welfare in the Robert Taylor Homes or working as a hospital nurse's aide for $6.67 an hour. People who think such things could never have happened to me haven't met enough poor people to know better. The avenue of escape can be very narrow indeed. The hope and energy of the 1960s — fueled not only by a growing economy but by all the passions of a great national quest — is long gone. The sense of possibility I knew has been replaced with the popular cultural currency that money and those who have it are everything and those without are nothing.

Much has been made of the culture of the underclass, the culture of poverty, as though they were the free-floating illnesses of the African-American poor, rendering them immune to other influences: the widespread American culture of greed, for example, or cynicism. It is a thinly veiled continuation of the endless projection of "disease" onto black life, a convenient way to sidestep a more painful debate about the loss of meaning in American life that has made our entire nation depressed and dispirited. The malaise that has overtaken our country is hardly confined to African-Americans or the poor, and if both groups should disappear tomorrow, our nation would still find itself in crisis. To talk of the black "underclass threat" to the public sphere, as Mickey Kaus does, to demonize the poor among us and thus by association all of us — ultimately this does more damage to the body politic than do a dozen welfare queens.

When I walk down the streets of my Harlem neighborhood, I see women like my mother hustling, struggling, walking their children to school, and walking them back home. And I also see women who have lost both energy and faith, talking loud, hanging out. I see the shadow of men of a new generation, floating by with a few dollars and a toy, then drifting away to the shelters they call home. And I see, a dozen times a day, the little girls my sister and I used to be, the little boys my brothers once were.

Even the grudging, inadequate public help I once had is fading fast for them. The time and patience they will need to re-create themselves is vanishing under pressure for the big, quick fix and the crushing load of blame being heaped upon them. In the big cities and the small towns of America, we have let theory, ideology, and mythology about welfare and poverty overtake these children and their parents.

FROM: *The New York Times Magazine*, November 8, 1992.

In 1
equivale
annually in
percent of the
federal income ta
percentage of federa
for the richest 1 percen
down to 21.5 percent.

(Source: *New York Times*, August 28, 199

PROGRAM PROFILE

AFDC, in addition to providing cash, requires recipients to seek out job training and work experience; it provides child care and transportation to facilitate the move toward financial independence.

To be eligible, families must have a child that is a U.S. citizen under the age of 18 year, who is deprived of parental support due to death, injury, unemployment, or abandonment. The states establish income and asset standards for recipients.

In 1988, AFDC created a subsidiary program for unemployed parents that enables two-parent families to receive assistance when the principal wage earner is laid off. It also sought to shift the priorities of welfare from a hand-out to a hand-up by promoting job-skills training. State welfare agencies must provide job training, education, and employment services as well as cash assistance.

AFDC is managed by the U.S. Department of Health and Human Services. Individual states match the federal allocation. To learn more about AFDC, write the Department of Health and Human Services, Administration for Children and Families, 370 L'Enfant Promenade, SW, Washington DC 20447; (202) 401-9215.

mean
935 as
Aid to Dependent Children (ADC). Its intent was to help poor widows stay at home and care for their children. Today AFDC is the nation's largest cash assistance program for poor families, distributing $22.5 billion to over 5 million families in fiscal 1993. The program is intended to help families meet immediate financial needs and to become economically self-sufficient.

FACT

43, Americans who earned the
t of at least $1 million
modern dollars paid 78
ir total incomes in
es. As of 1990, the
ly taxed income
r had gone

Sharers

CONNIE PORTER

*It is a myth that people living in poverty spend more on alcohol
than do the nonpoor. In fact, out of every dollar spent on food or
alcohol in 1992, alcohol accounted for approximately five cents
of the dollar for the poorest one-fifth of U.S. households, seven
cents for the middle, and eight cents for the wealthiest. Nevertheless, like most widespread social problems, addiction to alcohol makes even more complex the issues of welfare, job training,
nutrition, and basic health care. In this excerpt from Connie
Porter's novel* All-Bright Court, *we get a glimpse of these complexities as they affect Dennis, the son of an alcoholic mother.*

Somewhere in the field, hidden among the tall weeds, was
a hungry boy. He was lying on his stomach, stuffing slices of
bologna in his mouth. He put so many pieces in his mouth that
he gagged, and a ball of pink flesh fell out into the weeds.

"Kiss it up to God," he said, and kissed the meat. He began
eating it, pulling off a few twigs and an ant as he ate. "Dennis,"
a voice called from somewhere in the field. "Where you at,
Dennis? My mama want to talk to you."

The boy stopped eating. He pitched the half-eaten meat over
his shoulder and lay still. He would not come out of hiding
because the pack of bologna he was lying on, he had stolen
from the Red Store.

He had put the cold package inside his pants, but before he
could get to the door, Mr. Jablonski was shouting, "Hey you,
hey boy," coming from behind the counter with a bat in his
hand. Dennis beat him to the door just as Mrs. Taylor, Mikey,
and the baby, Dorene, were coming in. He knocked Dorene to
the ground and escaped.

"Don't ever come back in my store! If I see you again, I'll
beat your brains out," Mr. Jablonski screamed.

Connie Porter is the author of *All-Bright
Court*, her first novel. She has taught
creative writing at Milton Academy and
Emerson College in Massachusetts, and
is currently on the faculty of Southern
Illinois University at Carbondale where
she teaches English.

Mrs. Taylor bent to pick up Dorene.

"No, I'll get her," Mr. Jablonski said as he picked up the crying child. "You're in no shape to be bending like that."

"Don't his mama got credit with you?" Mrs. Taylor asked.

"I cut her off. She never pays me. Every time she gets her check she has a story, or she doesn't show up at all. I'm in business here, you know."

"The boy hungry. It's a shame."

"It's a shame, but what can you do?" Mr. Jablonski said as he returned behind the counter.

At one time, Mary Kate thought there was something she could do. The boy had begun showing up on her doorstep not long after Mikey started kindergarten. Before she ever saw him, Mikey had come home with stories of Dennis.

"He never be having milk money. He always be a sharer, Mama."

"What's a sharer?"

"When you don't bring in milk money, Mrs. Franco split a milk and let you have some."

"That's nice of her," Mikey's mother said.

"Yeah, Mama, but the kids that be sharing all the time be nasty. This boy Dennis, he colored, and he stink. This little white girl be so dirty. Them two always be sharing. Kids be picking on them."

"I hope you not one of them, Mikey. They can't help the way they is."

Mikey was silent. Once he had stuck out his tongue at them when Mrs. Franco wasn't looking. The other children laughed. It was fun. But one Monday toward the end of October, the fun stopped.

Mikey left home with five pennies knotted in a handkerchief, but when he arrived at school, they were gone. He had to share a milk that day with Dennis.

The little white girl shared one with a Puerto Rican girl. All four of them sat at a small table and had their milk in Dixie cups. Mikey did not want to drink his. He didn't even want the windmill cookies Mrs. Franco passed out. He sat staring at the three others at his table.

The white girl drank all her chocolate milk with one lifting of her cup, and there was a brown mustache on her face. Mikey stared at her whiteness. Tiny green veins pulsed around her gray eyes. Thin streams of dirt ran down her arms. She didn't say anything to Mikey, but when she saw him staring, she opened her mouth full of cookies. Mikey turned from her and looked at the Puerto Rican girl.

She looked clean. Her black hair was swept up in a single ponytail and curled in a tight corkscrew. There were gold hoops in her ears. She never looked up from the table, though. She ate slowly, taking careful bites and cautious sips.

Mikey glanced to his side, at Dennis. He had already finished and was licking the crumbs from his napkin.

"Dennis, stop that," Mrs. Franco said.

Dennis smiled. "Them some good cookies, Mike. Don't you like 'em?"

"I had milk money," Mikey said.

"Don't you like them cookies?" Dennis asked.

Mikey stared at the boy's hair. It was uncombed and matted. "You eat 'em."

Dennis grabbed the cookies and stuffed both of them into his mouth, hardly bothering to chew them.

"I'm glad you here, 'cause they don't talk. That one stupid," Dennis said, pointing at the white girl. "The other one stupid too. She can't even speak no English. You hear her in class? 'Monita conita Frito corn chips.'"

Mikey wanted to laugh, but he remembered why he was at the table with the sharers. "I ain't supposed to be here. I lost my money. I ain't going sit here tomorrow."

"Oh," Dennis said. "You want your milk?"

Mikey did not sit with the sharers the next day. His mother had money to send, four pennies knotted in a handkerchief, pinned in his pocket. He had his own milk, in a carton, the way milk was supposed to be. He had a straw and blew bubbles. Sharers never got straws. He did not want to look over to where they sat, but he did, and each time he looked over, Dennis smiled or waved. "Mike," he silently mouthed. Mikey smiled.

Summary

In 1992, 12 million children in the United States received free or reduced-price school lunches, over 3 million more than were considered poor.

School Lunch Programs

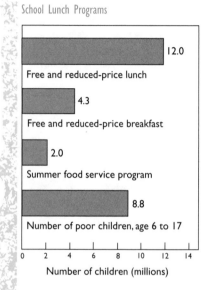

Source: U.S. Department of Agriculture; Bureau of the Census.

Mikey had found a friend. Dennis began following him home from school. He and Mikey would play until it was time for dinner.

"You got to go home now," Mikey's mother or father would say.

The boy would leave Mikey's house, but he wouldn't go home. He would play by himself out back or disappear around the end of the row, only to return in ten or fifteen minutes, asking, "Can Mike come out?"

One Friday night in late November, Mr. Taylor went out to empty the trash and found Dennis squatting next to the back step.

"Boy, you crazy? What you doing out in the snow?"

"Can Mike come out?"

"No, Mike can't come out. It's seven o'clock. You better get on home."

"My mama ain't home."

Mr. Taylor put the garbage in the can and stared at the boy. The boy did not head for home. He stood there looking at the ground until Mr. Taylor invited him in and then went up to bed.

Mrs. Taylor fed him a bowl of black-eyed peas and a piece of corn bread. Dennis ate the bread and peas, and licked the bowl.

"You want some more?" Mrs. Taylor asked.

"Yeah. Them good beans."

"You got a good appetite, Dennis. Mikey won't eat peas. He had peanut butter and jelly for dinner."

Dennis did not say anything. He ate.

At nine Mrs. Taylor woke up her husband. "Sam, take Dennis home."

Mr. Taylor walked Dennis around to 125 to find the front door sitting wide open. There were no lights on in the house.

"My mama not back."

"Well, I'll take you on in and you can turn on the lights and wait for her."

"We don't got no electric. Mama say we going get it back on when she get her check."

34

Mr. Taylor let out a big blast of white steam through his nose. He did not know what to do, so he brought the boy back home with him.

"You just couldn't leave him there," Mrs. Taylor said. "He just a baby."

"I don't know about all that. I don't want to get in no trouble keeping him here, Mary Kate."

"My mama don't care," Dennis said.

Mr. Taylor let out a blow like he did outside. "I just didn't know what to do. I guess he can stay. I'm tired now, Kate. I'm pulling that double tomorrow. Just put him to bed," Mr. Taylor said, and he went upstairs.

Mrs. Taylor ran a bath for Dennis and told him to get in the tub. When she returned to the bathroom a few minutes later, Dennis was playing in the water, and his pants, shirt, and socks were on the floor. They all smelled of urine.

"Where your underclothes?"

"I don't got none clean."

"Hand me that rag, boy. I'm going to bathe you 'cause you not doing nothing but playing."

"My mama let me wash myself."

"It seem your mama let you do a lot of things," Mrs. Taylor said, and she descended on Dennis with the rough white cloth. "Stand up."

Dennis stood while Mrs. Taylor scrubbed every inch of his body. "You a dirty boy," she said. "Stand right there while I get some alcohol."

She went to the hall closet while Dennis stood shaking in the tub. Where was it Mrs. Taylor thought he would go?

She returned and poured half the bottle over his body and the other half in the tub. She continued to wash the boy and talk to him. "Look at this. Look at this." Dennis looked. It was dirt. He did not know if he was supposed to say something.

After the bath, Mrs. Taylor rubbed Vaseline into his cold, raw skin. She dressed him in a pair of Mikey's pajamas and put him to bed. In the morning she made fried eggs, grits with redeye gravy, and buttered toast with grape jelly. She dressed Dennis, Mikey, and Dorene, and they walked to Dennis's house.

On the way, she rehearsed her speech: What kind of mother is you? Leaving a boy alone. Your child hungry and dirty. You send him out with no drawers on. What if something happen to him? What people going to think? You should…

Dennis led them to the front door. It was closed. "My mama home."

She was lying on the couch, sleeping. She opened her eyes. Mrs. Taylor thought she looked like a lizard in a dress. Her eyes were yellow, and the skin on her thin legs was dry and cracked. Her short, reddish hair was standing straight up on her head.

"I'm home, Mama."

"Where you was at?"

"Mike's house. This here his mama," Dennis said, gently pushing Mrs. Taylor closer to the couch.

"Hey," the woman said. "Dennis, go get me some water. You want some water, some water…What your name?"

"Mary Kate."

"I'm Cynthia. Want some water?"

"No, I got to be going. I got some wash to do," Mary Kate said, and began backing toward the door, Dorene on her hip. "Let's go, children."

She saved her speech for Samuel. He was so tired that he only half listened.

"You can't save the world, Kate," he said.

Dennis continued to come around. Sometimes he would show up three or four days in a row, and sometimes a week or more would pass without his coming by. The last time he had come, the Taylors were on their way to the circus in Buffalo. "Go home," Mr. Taylor had told him. "You ain't going to the circus with us."

Mikey's father did not understand. He and Dennis were going to be bareback riders. Mrs. Taylor had taken the boys up to Ridge Road, to the Jubilee, to see *Toby Tyler*. In a few years they would run away and join a circus. They would ride on the backs of horses, and have a clever monkey for a pet. They would wear tights and do tricks and eat candy apples and cotton candy. Toby Tyler would be at the circus tonight, and Dennis would miss it.

Dennis did not move. He stood in the living room staring at the floor. His voice was just a whisper. "My mama say don't be letting ya'll clean me up. I'm clean enough. Ya'll got to take me the way I is."

Mr. Taylor opened the front door to put the boy out, but Mikey ran to him and clung to the boy. He grabbed Dennis around the waist. He held on while his father tried to pull them apart.

"Stop, Mikey. I'm going to whip your ass. Stop."

Mikey and Dennis fell to the floor, and Mrs. Taylor ran downstairs with Dorene in her arms.

"Samuel, what you doing?"

"Ya'll stop," he yelled at the boys. He finally pulled them apart and hurled Dennis out the door. "Don't you come back 'round here, hear me? I don't want you 'round my boy, you goddamn piss pot."

"Sam, he just a boy. He ain't much more than a baby."

"He ain't no baby. Him and Mikey the same age. And you, Michael, I don't want the boy 'round this house. I don't want you talking to a boy like that. He trash. That nasty boy coming here and telling me his whore of a mammy say don't clean him up, we got to take him like he is. So white people be saying, 'See, you smell that? They all stink. They all nasty.'"

"His mama say that? As good as we been to that boy, as many nights he done sat at our table and ate like he lived here?"

"What you expect? The woman a alcoholic. She ain't got sense enough to pay her bills. We done all we can do for that boy. You feed him one day, he hungry the next. You clean him up today, he dirty tomorrow. This thing done gone too far. And you expecting! It's too much, Kate. Too much."

"I'm not going to the stupid circus," Mikey said. "I don't want to go without Dennis."

"Oh yeah, you going, and you going to like it, too. I could've been putting in some overtime today, but I didn't so ya'll could go to the circus. You get on upstairs till your mama call you, 'cause I'm this close to setting a fire to your ass."

Summary

Between 1989 and 1992 the number of children receiving food stamps increased by 41 percent, to 13.3 million.

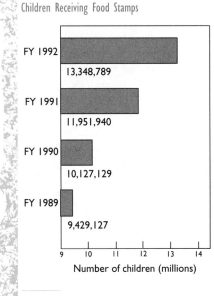

Children Receiving Food Stamps

FY 1992 — 13,348,789
FY 1991 — 11,951,940
FY 1990 — 10,127,129
FY 1989 — 9,429,127

Number of children (millions)

Source: Department of Agriculture.

FACT

American children are twice as likely to
be poor as Canadian children, 3 times
as likely to be poor as British children,
4 times as likely to be poor as French
children, and 7 to 13 times more likely
to be poor than German, Dutch, and
Swedish children.

(Source: Children's Defense Fund, 1994.)

TOBY TYLER WAS not at the circus. Mikey did not care. He had a good time without him, and without Dennis. He ate cotton candy and a candy apple. There was a clown who fascinated Mikey.

The clown coughed and a bright red silk scarf came from his mouth. He pulled on it and a yellow one appeared next, then a green, a blue, an orange. The clown kept pulling, the colors repeating, until a pile of scarves lay curled at his feet. Mikey thought the clown must have been filled with scarves, that they were coiled up inside him.

He did bring back a program and some cotton candy for Dennis. The candy hardened, though, and Dennis was not at school next Monday anyway. When he finally did show up later that week, he wouldn't walk home with Mikey, and he refused the program. He took off running.

Mrs. Taylor worried about him, but she rarely saw him. Now here he was knocking down Dorene in his rush to get out of the Red Store.

She bought her bread quickly. She wanted to catch up with the boy before he headed for home. This was why her son was calling to him through the weeds in the field while he was eating stolen bologna.

Dennis would not answer. He thought Mrs. Taylor might try to take him back to the Red Store. He wouldn't go back. He would never go there again. He would go up to Ridge Road, to the A & P. He would go up Steelawanna Avenue. He would get up the courage to cross all those streets.

"Ma, he gone," Mikey said.

"I guess so, but it don't seem like he could get 'cross the field that quick. Let's get on home. Ya'll daddy be home soon."

And they walked on, leaving the hungry boy lost among the weeds.

EXCERPTED FROM: *All-Bright Court*, 1991.

SHARE enables people of goodwill to exchange two hours of community service for a low-cost bag of groceries. The program, founded in Southern California in 1983, has spread throughout the nation and now serves more than 30,000 people in 17 states.

SHARE works like a food cooperative with a service component. Participants buy into the organization by paying a $14 monthly membership fee and pledging to complete two hours of community service in exchange for a hefty bag of groceries. Because the agency buys the food in bulk, it's able to distribute a lot for a little.

Community service can range from relief agencies to nonprofit fundraising to neighborhood and highway clean-ups. The two hours can be split up into increments for time-pressed volunteers. At the completion of the service, participants receive a bag of food worth $35 in the supermarket. The bags normally contain 6 to 10 pounds of meat, 4 to 7 pounds of vegetables, 2 to 4 pounds of fruits, and such staples as pasta or rice.

"By pooling our efforts, by working together rather than singly, our accomplishments can be vastly greater," said one participant.

Across America, SHARE volunteers contribute more than 70,000 hours of community service each month. For more information or for the location of host organizations near you, contact World SHARE, 6950 Friars Road, San Diego, CA 92108-1137; (619) 686-5818.

World SHARE

Self-Help And Resource Exchange

SHARE

PAT

Parents as Teachers

Parents as Teachers (PAT) is a family support program begun in Missouri in 1981. Recognizing that parents are a child's first teachers — and that the first years of life lay the groundwork for later success — the program seeks to enhance parents' effectiveness in this crucial role.

Through PAT, a certified parent educator visits parents at home during the child's first three years, providing advice on child development and parenting skills, suggestions for activities to enhance learning, and moral support. The home curriculum is based on the work of child-development experts T. Berry Brazelton and Burton White.

Additional components of the program include group meetings for parents, periodic monitoring of children's health and development, and referral to other social services as needed.

PAT operates through the public school system in Missouri and is offered by every school district in the state, serving some 60,000 families. An independent evaluation study found that three-year-

olds whose families had participated in the program showed superior language development, problem-solving skills, and other cognitive abilities as compared to a control group. They also demonstrated better coping skills and more positive relationships with adults. By the end of first grade, PAT children performed better in school than did nonparticipants.

Photo: Cathy Lander-Goldberg

The program's success has led to its replication in 36 states, as well as England and Australia. In 1987, a PAT National Center was set up in St. Louis to facilitate the program's expansion.

For more information, contact Parents as Teachers National Center, Inc., 9374 Olive Boulevard, St. Louis, MO 63132; (314) 432-4330.

AN EXCERPT FROM

Bastard Out of Carolina

DOROTHY ALLISON

At least 5.5 million children younger than 12 experience hunger each year. As of 1993, 10 percent of the American public participated in the nation's food stamp program. This excerpt from Dorothy Allison's 1992 novel offers a child's eye view of being hungry.

Hunger makes you restless. You dream about food — not just any food, but perfect food, the best food, magical meals, famous and awe-inspiring, the one piece of meat, the exact taste of buttery corn, tomatoes so ripe they split and sweeten the air, beans so crisp they snap between the teeth, gravy like mother's milk singing to your bloodstream. When I got hungry my hands would not stay still. I would pick at the edges of scabs, scratch at chigger bites and old scars, and tug at loose strands of my black hair. I'd rock a penny in my palm, trying to learn to roll it one-handed up and around each finger without dropping it, the way my cousin Grey could. I'd chew my fingernails or suck on toothpicks and read everything I hadn't read more than twice already. But when Reese got hungry and there was nothing to eat, she would just sob, shiny fat tears running down her pink cheeks. Nothing would distract her.

We weren't hungry too often. There was always something that could be done. Reese and I walked the side of the highway, picking up return deposit bottles to cash in and buy Mama's cigarettes while she gave home permanents to the old ladies she knew from the lunch counter. Reese would wrinkle her nose and giggle as she slipped the pack of Pall Malls into Mama's pocket, while I ran to get us a couple of biscuits out of the towel-wrapped dish on the stove.

Dorothy Allison is the author of *Trash*, a collection of short stories, and *Bastard Out of Carolina*, which was a finalist for the 1992 National Book Award. *Skin: Talking About Sex, Class and Literature*, a collection of essays, speeches, and performance pieces, was published by Firebrand Books in 1994. *Two or Three Things I Know About Her*, a theater piece about family, sex, and class, will be published by Dutton in spring 1995. Her second novel, *CaveDweller*, is forthcoming from Dutton in 1996.

"Such fine little ladies," the women would tell her, and Mama would pat her pocket and agree.

Mama knew how to make a meal of biscuits and gravy, flour-and-water biscuits with bacon-fat gravy to pour over them. By the time I started the fourth grade, we were eating biscuit dinners more often than not. Sometimes with the biscuits Mama would serve a bowl of tomato soup or cold pork and beans. We joked about liking it right out of the can, but it was cold because the power company had turned the house off — no money in the mail, no electricity. That was hunger wrapped around a starch belly.

One afternoon there was not even flour to make up the pretense of a meal. We sat at the kitchen table, Reese and I grumbling over our rumbling bellies. Mama laughed but kept her face turned away from us. "Making so much noise over so little. You'd think you girls hadn't been fed in a week."

She got out soda crackers and began to spread them with a layer of dark red ketchup spotted with salt and pepper. She poured us glasses of cold tea and told us stories about real hunger, hunger of days with no expectation that there would ever be biscuits again, how when she was a kid she'd wrestled her sisters for the last bacon rind.

"We used to pass the plates around the table, eight plates for eight kids, pretending there was food gonna come off the stove to fill those plates, talking about food we'd never seen, just heard about or imagined, making up stories about what we'd cook if we could. Earle liked the idea of parboiled puppies. Your aunt Ruth always talked about frogs' tongues with dew-berries. Beau wanted fried rutabagas, and Nevil cried for steamed daffodils. But Raylene won the prize with her recipe for sugar-glazed turtle meat with poison greens and hot piss dressing."

After a while Reese and I started making up our own pretend meals. "Peanut butter and Jell-O. Mashed bug meat with pickles." Mama made us laugh with her imitations of her brothers and sisters fighting over the most disgusting meals they could dream up. She filled our stomachs with soda crackers and ketchup, soda crackers and mayonnaise, and more big glasses of tea, all the time laughing and teasing and tickling our shoulders with her long nails as she walked back and forth. Reese

42

finally went outside to chase the dogs from next door and yell insults at the boys who ran them. But I stayed back to watch Mama through the kitchen window, to see her fingers ridge up into fists and her chin stand out in anger. When Daddy Glen came back from fishing with my uncles, she was just like a big angry mama hen, feathers up and eyes yellow.

"Soda crackers and ketchup," she hissed at him. "You so casual about finding another job, but I had to feed my girls that shit while you sat on your butt all afternoon, smoking and telling lies." She shoved her hands under her arms and sucked her lips in tight so that her mouth looked flat and hard.

"Now, Anney …" Daddy Glen reached out to touch her arm. She slapped his hand down and jumped back like a snake that's caught a rat. I backed away from the window and ran around to the side of the house to watch from the open door to the driveway. I had never seen Mama like that. It was scary but wonderful too. She didn't seem to be afraid of anything.

"Not my kids," she told Daddy Glen, her voice carrying like a shout, though she was speaking in a hoarse whisper. "I was never gonna have my kids know what it was like. Never was gonna have them hungry or cold or scared. Never, you hear me? Never!"

The difference between a rich man and a poor man, is this — the former eats when he pleases, and the latter when he can get it.

SIR WALTER RALEIGH
Explorer, Author, Courtier

Head Start

An early childhood enrichment program

Project Head Start was established in 1965 by the federal Office of Economic Opportunity with the aim of enriching the social and cognitive skills — and thus the future life prospects — of low-income preschoolers. Launched during President Lyndon Johnson's "War on Poverty," it is widely considered to be one of the most successful programs from that era. With a $2.8 billion annual budget, Head Start now funds 37,000 classrooms preparing more than 700,000 young children for the world of school. Studies have shown that Head Start participants later reap such benefits as higher scores on school achievement tests, fewer grade retentions and placements in special education classes in elementary school, lower absenteeism, and better overall health.

Since its inception, Head Start has served close to 14 million children in locally run programs throughout the country. The program's innovative family focus recognizes that the parent is the child's "first and best teacher." One-third of the paid staff are parents of current or former Head Start students, and thousands more parents lend a hand as volunteers, acquiring job skills and self-confidence in the process. Head Start's information and referral component links families to job-training programs and other social services, giving parents a boost to economic self-sufficiency.

"Head Start children are more ready for the 'educational whirl' system," said Veronika Shepherd of Columbus, Ohio, whose five children went through the program. "Parents' involvement in the program has given more structure to their expectations for their children. You used to have to convince people to put their children in Head Start. Now there's a waiting list."

For more information, contact Head Start Bureau, Administration for Children, Youth and Families, Department of Health and Human Services, P.O. Box 1182, Washington, DC 20201-0001; (202) 205-8572.

The Circuit

FRANCISCO JIMÉNEZ

Our academic calendar was developed around the agricultural calendar. If children were in the fields, they could not be in a classroom. According to a 1989 report in the Boston Globe, *as many as four million migrants work in American fields and an additional one to one-and-a-half million children accompany them. The high school dropout rate for migrant children is over 90 percent in both Texas and California. In this short story by Francisco Jiménez we see some of the effects of migration on a child's education.*

It was that time of year again. Ito, the strawberry sharecropper, did not smile. It was natural. The peak of the strawberry season was over and the last few days the workers, most of them braceros, were not picking as many boxes as they had during the months of June and July.

As the last days of August disappeared, so did the number of braceros. Sunday, only one — the best picker — came to work. I liked him. Sometimes we talked during our half-hour lunch break. That is how I found out he was from Jalisco, the same state in Mexico my family was from. That Sunday was the last time I saw him.

When the sun had tired and sunk behind the mountains, Ito signaled us that it was time to go home. "Ya esora," he yelled in his broken Spanish. Those were the words I waited for twelve hours a day, every day, seven days a week, week after week. And the thought of not hearing them again saddened me.

As we drove home Papá did not say a word. With both hands on the wheel, he stared at the dirt road. My older brother, Roberto, was also silent. He leaned his head back and closed his eyes. Once in a while he cleared from his throat the dust that blew in from outside.

Francisco Jiménez is professor of Spanish and Director of Arts and Humanities at the University of Santa Clara. He has edited several anthologies and his writing has appeared in the anthology *Cuentos Chicanos*.

Yes, it was that time of year. When I opened the front door
to the shack, I stopped. Everything we owned was neatly packed
in cardboard boxes. Suddenly I felt even more the weight of
hours, days, weeks, and months of work. I sat down on a box.
The thought of having to move to Fresno and knowing what
was in store for me there brought tears to my eyes.

That night I could not sleep. I lay in bed thinking about how
much I hated this move.

A little before five o'clock in the morning, Papá woke everyone up. A few minutes later, the yelling and screaming of my
little brothers and sisters, for whom the move was a great adven-
ture, broke the silence of dawn. Shortly, the barking of the dogs
accompanied them.

While we packed the breakfast dishes, Papá went outside to
start the "Carcanchita." That was the name Papá gave his old
'38 black Plymouth. He bought it in a used-car lot in Santa Rosa
in the winter of 1949. Papá was very proud of his little jalopy.
He had a right to be proud of it. He spent a lot of time looking
at other cars before buying this one. When he finally chose the
"Carcanchita," he checked it thoroughly before driving it out
of the car lot. He examined every inch of the car. He listened
to the motor, tilting his head from side to side like a parrot, trying to detect any noises that spelled car trouble. After being satisfied with the looks and sounds of the car, Papá then insisted
on knowing who the original owner was. He never did find out
from the car salesman, but he bought the car anyway. Papá figured the original owner must have been an important man
because behind the rear seat of the car he found a blue necktie.

Papá parked the car out in front and left the motor running.
"Listo," he yelled. Without saying a word, Roberto and I began
to carry the boxes out to the car. Roberto carried the two big
boxes and I carried the two smaller ones. Papá then threw the
mattress on top of the car roof and tied it with ropes to the front
and rear bumpers.

Everything was packed except Mamá's pot. It was an old large
galvanized pot she had picked up at an army surplus store in
Santa María the year I was born. The pot had many dents and
nicks, and the more dents and nicks it acquired the more Mamá
liked it. "Mi olla," she used to say proudly.

46

I held the front door open as Mamá carefully carried out her pot by both handles, making sure not to spill the cooked beans. When she got to the car, Papá reached out to help her with it. Roberto opened the rear car door and Papá gently placed it on the floor behind the front seat. All of us then climbed in. Papá sighed, wiped the sweat off his forehead with his sleeve, and said wearily: "Es todo."

As we drove away, I felt a lump in my throat. I turned around and looked at our little shack for the last time.

At sunset we drove into a labor camp near Fresno. Since Papá did not speak English, Mamá asked the camp foreman if he needed any more workers. "We don't need no more," said the foreman, scratching his head. "Check with Sullivan down the road. Can't miss him. He lives in a big white house with a fence around it."

When we got there, Mamá walked up to the house. She went through a white gate, past a row of rose bushes, up the stairs to the front door. She rang the doorbell. The porch light went on and a tall husky man came out. They exchanged a few words. After the man went in, Mamá clasped her hands and hurried back to the car. "We have work! Mr. Sullivan said we can stay there the whole season," she said, gasping and pointing to an old garage near the stables.

The garage was worn out by the years. It had no windows. The walls, eaten by termites, strained to support the roof full of holes. The dirt floor, populated by earth worms, looked like a gray road map.

That night, by the light of a kerosene lamp, we unpacked and cleaned our new home. Roberto swept away the loose dirt, leaving the hard ground. Papá plugged the holes in the walls with old newspapers and tin can tops. Mamá fed my little brothers and sisters. Papá and Roberto then brought in the mattress and placed it on the far corner of the garage. "Mamá, you and the little ones sleep on the mattress. Roberto, Panchito, and I will sleep outside under the trees," Papá said.

Early next morning Mr. Sullivan showed us where his crop was, and after breakfast, Papá, Roberto, and I headed for the vineyard to pick.

Summary

In 1988 the average income for a migrant farmworker family was only about one-fifth of the median income for the average American family.

Migrant Farmworkers and Poverty

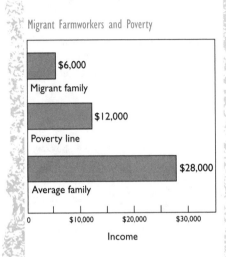

Source: Centers for Disease Control; National Center for Health Statistics (1988).

Education is not just another consumer item. It is the bedrock of our democracy.

MARY HATWOOD FUTRELL
President, Education International

Around nine o'clock the temperature had risen to almost one hundred degrees. I was completely soaked in sweat and my mouth felt as if I had been chewing on a handkerchief. I walked over to the end of the row, picked up the jug of water we had brought, and began drinking. "Don't drink too much; you'll get sick," Roberto shouted. No sooner had he said that than I felt sick to my stomach. I dropped to my knees and let the jug roll off my hands. I remained motionless with my eyes glued on the hot sandy ground. All I could hear was the drone of insects. Slowly I began to recover. I poured water over my face and neck and watched the dirty water run down my arms to the ground.

I still felt a little dizzy when we took a break to eat lunch. It was past two o'clock and we sat underneath a large walnut tree that was on the side of the road. While we ate, Papá jotted down the number of boxes we had picked. Roberto drew designs on the ground with a stick. Suddenly I noticed Papá's face turn pale as he looked down the road. "Here comes the school bus," he whispered loudly in alarm. Instinctively, Roberto and I ran and hid in the vineyards. We did not want to get in trouble for not going to school. The neatly dressed boys about my age got off. They carried books under their arms. After they crossed the street, the bus drove away. Roberto and I came out from hiding and joined Papá. "Tienen que tener cuidado," he warned us.

After lunch we went back to work. The sun kept beating down. The buzzing insects, the wet sweat, and the hot dry dust made the afternoon seem to last forever. Finally the mountains around the valley reached out and swallowed the sun. Within an hour it was too dark to continue picking.

The vines blanketed the grapes, making it difficult to see the bunches. "Vámonos," said Papá, signaling to us that it was time to quit work. Papá then took out a pencil and began to figure out how much we had earned our first day. He wrote down numbers, crossed some out, wrote down some more. "Quince," he murmured.

When we arrived home, we took a cold shower underneath a waterhose. We then sat down to eat dinner around some wooden crates that served as a table. Mamá had cooked a special meal for us. We had rice and tortillas with "carne con chile," my favorite dish.

The next morning I could hardly move. My body ached all over. I felt little control over my arms and legs. This feeling went on every morning for days until my muscles finally got used to the work.

It was Monday, the first week of November. The grape season was over and I could now go to school. I woke up early that morning and lay in bed, looking at the stars and savoring the thought of not going to work and of starting sixth grade for the first time that year. Since I could not sleep, I decided to get up and join Papá and Roberto at breakfast. I sat at the table across from Roberto, but I kept my head down. I did not want to look up and face him. I knew he was sad. He was not going to school today. He was not going tomorrow, or next week, or next month. He would not go until the cotton season was over, and that was sometime in February. I rubbed my hands together and watched the dry, acid-stained skin fall to the floor in little rolls.

When Papá and Roberto left for work, I felt relief. I walked to the top of a small grade next to the shack and watched the "Carcanchita" disappear in the distance in a cloud of dust.

Two hours later, around eight o'clock, I stood by the side of the road waiting for school bus number 20. When it arrived I climbed in. Everyone was busy either talking or yelling. I sat in an empty seat in the back.

When the bus stopped in front of the school, I felt very nervous. I looked out the bus window and saw boys and girls carrying books under their arms. I put my hands in my pant pockets and walked to the principal's office. When I entered I heard a woman's voice say: "May I help you?" I was startled. I had not heard English for months. For a few seconds I remained speechless. I looked at the lady who waited for an answer. My first instinct was to answer her in Spanish, but I held back. Finally, after struggling for English words, I managed to tell her that I wanted to enroll in the sixth grade. After answering many questions, I was led to the classroom.

Mr. Lema, the sixth grade teacher, greeted me and assigned me a desk. He then introduced me to the class. I was so nervous and scared at that moment when everyone's eyes were on me that I wished I were with Papá and Roberto picking cotton. After taking roll, Mr. Lema gave the class the assignment for

Summary

The dropout rate for migrants (45 percent) is 50 percent higher than the U.S. average for low-income families.

Migrant Dropouts

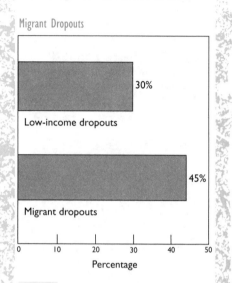

Source: *Migrant Attrition Project, Testimony before the National Commission on Migrant Education* (February 1991); *The Condition of Education, 1993.*

the first hour. "The first thing we have to do this morning is finish reading the story we began yesterday," he said enthusiastically. He walked up to me, handed me an English book, and asked me to read. "We are on page 125," he said politely. When I heard this, I felt my blood rush to my head; I felt dizzy. "Would you like to read?" he asked hesitantly. I opened the book to page 125. My mouth was dry. My eyes began to water. I could not begin. "You can read later," Mr. Lema said understandingly.

For the rest of the reading period I kept getting angrier and angrier with myself. I should have read, I thought to myself.

During recess I went into the restroom and opened my English book to page 125. I began to read in a low voice, pretending I was in class. There were many words I did not know. I closed the book and headed back to the classroom.

Mr. Lema was sitting at his desk correcting papers. When I entered he looked up at me and smiled. I felt better. I walked up to him and asked if he could help me with the new words. "Gladly," he said.

The rest of the month I spent my lunch hours working on English with Mr. Lema, my best friend at school.

One Friday during lunch hour Mr. Lema asked me to take a walk with him to the music room. "Do you like music?" he asked me as we entered the building.

"Yes, I like corridos," I answered. He then picked up a trumpet, blew on it and handed it to me. The sound gave me goose bumps. I knew that sound. I had heard it in many corridos. "How would you like to learn how to play it?" he asked. He must have read my face because before I could answer, he added: "I'll teach you how to play it during our lunch hours."

That day I could hardly wait to get home to tell Papá and Mamá the great news. As I got off the bus, my little brothers and sisters ran up to meet me. They were yelling and screaming. I thought they were happy to see me, but when I opened the door to our shack, I saw that everything we owned was neatly packed in cardboard boxes.

FROM: *The Arizona Quarterly,* 1973.

Farmworker Justice Fund, Inc.

The Farmworker Justice Fund (FJF) is a national nonprofit organization working to improve the lives and working conditions of migrant and seasonal farmworkers. Based in Washington, DC, FJF advocates for farmworkers' rights by monitoring government policies that affect them, by educating policymakers and the public, and by litigating court cases to press for better wages and better working conditions. FJF also focuses on immigration rights, issues affecting women farmworkers, and occupational health and safety, with an emphasis on pesticide exposure.

In monitoring federal legislation and policy, FJF pays particular attention to the departments of Labor and Agriculture, the Immigration and Naturalization Service, and the Environmental Protection Agency (EPA). FJF's attorneys and staff specialists speak up for farmworkers' rights by meeting with policymakers and submitting comments on proposed regulations. For example, FJF led a successful eight-year campaign to convince the EPA to issue regulations protecting farmworkers from exposure to pesticides.

In a federal court case, the FJF persuaded the court to order the Department of Labor to determine and enforce a prevailing wage for seed cane cutters in the Florida sugar cane industry. The farm employers eventually agreed to pay the farmworkers more than $500,000 in back wages.

For more information, contact Farmworker Justice Fund, Inc., 2001 S Street N.W., Suite 210, Washington, DC 20009; (202) 462-8192.

BOCES

Geneseo Migrant Center

"Migrant workers feed the nation, and yet they can barely afford to feed themselves," said Robert Lynch, director of the BOCES Geneseo Migrant Center, to a reporter in 1993. With an average annual family income of just $6,500, putting food on the table is but one of many tough challenges faced by migrant farmworkers today. Moving frequently from place to place in search of work, they have no stable community to call their own. Ninety percent of the children become school dropouts, and adult illiteracy is common. Migrants are also prone to a host of medical problems, from tuberculosis to pesticide poisoning, and their average life expectancy is just 49 years.

The Geneseo Migrant Center, serving twelve migrant worker camps in rural New York, exists to address these ills. Founded in 1968 and operated by the Board of Cooperative Educational Services (BOCES), the Center has become a national model for service to migrant families. Among its programs are: in-camp adult basic education and English as a second language; medical and dental care; and several creative arts programs, including CAMPS — Creative Artists Migrant Program Services — which brings poets and fiction writers into the camps to conduct readings and workshops.

The Center is located on the campus of Geneseo State University and draws on the college's resources and students, many of whom are involved in the Center as interns, volunteers, and paid workers. The Geneseo Center also maintains a comprehensive collection of resource materials on migrant farmworker issues and coordinates other projects of regional and national scope.

For more information, contact BOCES Geneseo Migrant Center, Holcomb Building 210-211, Geneseo, NY 14454; (800) 245-5681.

The Manful Life of Nicholas, 10

ISABEL WILKERSON

One of the most common myths about poverty is that it is a pre-dominantly African-American and urban phenomenon. As the Children's Defense Fund pointed out in 1994, more white than black children are poor and more poor children live outside central cities than in them. Nevertheless, urban poverty is an urgent problem in the United States. Nearly one-third of all children living in our nation's cities are poor and the majority of those children are either African American or Latino. In this article by New York Times *writer Isabel Wilkerson, we meet Nicholas Whitiker, a child who assumes a great deal of responsibility helping keep his family healthy and growing.*

Chicago, April 3 — A fourth-grade classroom on a forbidding stretch of the South Side was in the middle of multiplication tables when a voice over the intercom ordered Nicholas Whitiker to the principal's office. Cory and Darnesha and Roy and Delron and the rest of the class fell silent and stared at Nicholas, sitting sober-faced in the back.

"What did I do?" Nicholas thought as he gathered himself to leave.

He raced up the hall and down the steps to find his little sister, Ishtar, stranded in the office, nearly swallowed by her purple coat and hat, and the principal's aides wanting to know why no one had picked her up from kindergarten.

"I Don't Know"

It was yet another time that the adult world called on Nicholas, a gentle, brooding 10-year-old, to be a man, to answer for the complicated universe he calls family.

Isabel Wilkerson is a journalist for *The New York Times*. She won the Pulitzer prize for "First Born, Fast Grown: The Manful Life of Nicholas" in 1994. She has served as bureau chief of *The New York Times* in Chicago since 1991.

Summary

Between 1975 and 1990, birthrates for unmarried minority women 20 to 24 years old increased by 22 percent; for 15- to 19-year-olds by 2 percent. At the same time, birthrates for unmarried white women in those same age groups increased by 320 percent and 250 percent respectively (although the per capita birthrate for unmarried whites remains low relative to minority women).

Births to Unmarried Women

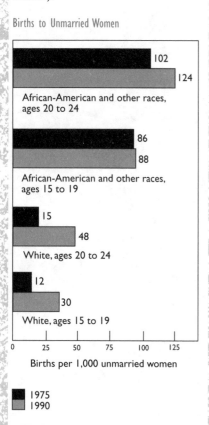

African-American and other races, ages 20 to 24 — 102, 124

African-American and other races, ages 15 to 19 — 86, 88

White, ages 20 to 24 — 15, 48

White, ages 15 to 19 — 12, 30

Births per 1,000 unmarried women

■ 1975
▨ 1990

Source: Bureau of the Census, *Historical Statistics of the United States to 1975* and National Center for Health Statistics, *Monthly Vital Statistics Report* (various years).

How could he begin to explain his reality — that his mother, a welfare recipient rearing five young children, was in college trying to become a nurse and so was not home during the day; that Ishtar's father was separated from his mother and in a drug-and-alcohol haze most of the time; that the grandmother he used to live with was at work; and that, besides, he could not possibly account for the man who was supposed to take his sister home — his mother's companion, the father of her youngest child?

"My stepfather was supposed to pick her up," he said for simplicity's sake. "I don't know why he's not here."

Nicholas gave the school administrators the name and telephone numbers of his grandmother and an aunt, looked back at Ishtar with a big brother's reassuring half-smile and rushed back to class still worried about whether his sister would make it home O.K.

Of all the men in his family's life, Nicholas is perhaps the most dutiful. When the television picture goes out again, when the 3-year-old scratches the 4-year-old, when their mother, Angela, needs ground beef from the store or the bathroom cleaned or can't find her switch to whip him or the other children, it is Nicholas's name that rings out to fix whatever is wrong.

He is nanny, referee, housekeeper, handyman. Some nights he is up past midnight, mopping the floors, putting the children to bed, and washing their school clothes in the bathtub. It is a nightly chore: the children have few clothes and wear the same thing every day.

Curbside Service

He pays a price. He stays up late and goes to school tired. He brings home mostly mediocre grades. But if the report card is bad, he gets a beating. He is all boy — squirming in line, sliding down banisters, shirt-tail out, shoes untied, dreaming of becoming a fireman so he can save people — but his walk is the stiff slog of a worried father behind on the rent.

He lives with his four younger half-siblings, his mother, and her companion, John Mason, on the second floor of a weathered three-family walkup in the perilous and virtually all black Englewood section of Chicago.

It is a forlorn landscape of burned-out tenements and long-shuttered storefronts where drunk men hang out on the corner, where gang members command more respect than police officers, and where every child can tell you where the crack houses are.

The neighborhood is a thriving drug mart. Dealers provide curbside service and residents figure that any white visitor must be a patron or a distributor. Gunshots are as common as rainfall. Eighty people were murdered in the neighborhood last year, more than in Omaha and Pittsburgh combined.

Living with fear is second nature to the children. Asked why he liked McDonald's, Nicholas's brother, Willie, described the restaurant playground with violence as his yardstick. "There's a giant hamburger, and you can go inside of it," Willie said. "And it's made out of steel, so no bullets can't get through."

The Family: Many Eyes, Many Hands

It is in the middle of all this that Angela Whitiker is rearing her children and knitting together a new life from a world of fast men and cruel drugs. She is a strong-willed, 26-year-old onetime waitress who has seen more than most 70-year-olds ever will. A 10th-grade dropout, she was pregnant at 15, bore Nicholas at 16, had her second son at 17, was married at 20, separated at 21, and was on crack at 22.

In the depths of her addiction, she was a regular at nearby crack houses; doing drugs with gang members, businessmen, and, she said, police detectives; sleeping on the floors some nights. In a case of mistaken identity, she once had a gun put to her head. Now she feels she was spared for a reason.

She has worked most of her life, picking okra and butter-beans and cleaning white people's houses as a teenager in Louisiana, bringing home big tips from businessmen when she waited tables at a restaurant in downtown Chicago, selling Polish sausages from a food truck by the Dan Ryan Expressway and snow cones at street fairs.

She is a survivor who has gone from desperation to redemption, from absent mother to nurturing one, and who now sees

FACT

Every day over 500 children ages 10 to 14 begin using illegal drugs, and over 1,000 start drinking alcohol. Nearly half of all middle-schoolers abuse drugs or alcohol.

(Source: *Fortune*, August 10, 1992.)

FACT

As of 1992, homicide by firearms was the third leading cause of death (after motor vehicles and suicide) for whites ages 15- to 19-years-old, and the leading cause of death for African-Americans in the same age bracket.

(Source: *Fortune*, August 10, 1992.)

economic salvation in nursing. Nicholas sees brand-name gym shoes and maybe toys and a second pair of school pants once she gets a job.

Studying for Midterms

She went through treatment and has stayed away from drugs for two years. Paperback manuals from Alcoholics and Narcotics Anonymous sit without apology on the family bookshelf. A black velvet headdress from church is on the windowsill and the Bible is turned to Nehemiah — emblems of her new life as a regular at Faith Temple, a Coptic Christian church on a corner nearby.

For the last year, she has been studying a lot, talking about novels and polynomials, and shutting herself in her cramped bedroom to study for something called midterms.

That often makes Nicholas the de facto parent for the rest of the children. There is Willie, the 8-year-old with the full-moon face and wide grin who likes it when adults mistake him for Nicholas. There is Ishtar, the dainty 5-year-old. There is Emmanuel, 4, who worships Nicholas and runs crying to him whenever he gets hurt. And there is Johnathan, 3, who is as bad as he is cute and whom everyone calls John-John.

That is just the beginning of the family. There are four fathers in all: Nicholas's father, a disabled laborer who comes around at his own rhythm to check on Nicholas, give him clothes, and whip him when he gets bad grades. There is Willie's father, a construction worker whom the children like because he lets them ride in his truck.

There is the man their mother married and left, a waiter at a soul-food place. He is the father of Ishtar and Emmanuel and is remembered mostly for his beatings and drug abuse.

The man they live with now is Mr. Mason, a truck driver on the night shift, who met their mother at a crack house and bears on his neck the thick scars of a stabbing, a reminder of his former life on the streets. He gets Nicholas up at 3 A.M. to sweep the floor or take out the garbage and makes him hold onto a bench to be whipped when he disobeys.

Unemployment and drugs and violence mean that men may come and go, their mother tells them. "You have a father, true

Poverty is an awful, eventually a degrading thing, and it is rare that anything good comes from it. We rise, old friend, in spite of adversity, not because of it.

THOMAS WOLFE
Novelist, Short Story Writer

enough, but nothing is guaranteed," she says. "I tell them no man is promised to be in our life forever."

There is an extended family of aunts, an uncle, cousins and their maternal grandmother, Deloris Whitiker, the family lifeboat, whom the children moved in with when drugs took their mother away.

To the children, life is not the neat, suburban script of sitcom mythology with father, mother, two kids, and golden retriever. But somehow what has to get done gets done.

When Nicholas brings home poor grades, sometimes three people will show up to talk to the teacher — his mother, his father and his mother's companion. When Nicholas practices his times tables, it might be his mother, his grandmother, or Mr. Mason asking him what 9 times 8 is.

But there is a downside. The family does not believe in sparing the rod and when Nicholas disobeys, half a dozen people figure they are within their rights to whip or chastise him, and do. But he tries to focus on the positive. "It's a good family," he says. "They care for you. If my mama needs a ride to church, they pick her up. If she needs them to babysit, they babysit."

The Rules: Ready to Run, Quick to Pray

It is a gray winter's morning, zero degrees outside, and school starts for everybody in less than half an hour. The children line up, all scarves and coats and legs. The boys bow their heads so their mother, late for class herself, can brush their hair one last time. There is a mad scramble for a lost mitten.

Then she sprays them. She shakes an aerosol can and sprays their coats, their heads, their tiny outstretched hands. She sprays them back and front to protect them as they go off to school, facing bullets and gang recruiters and a crazy, dangerous world. It is a special religious oil that smells like drugstore perfume, and the children shut their eyes tight as she sprays them long and furiously so they will come back to her, alive and safe, at day's end.

These are the rules for Angela Whitiker's children, recounted at the Formica-top dining-room table:

"Don't stop off playing," Willie said.

Summary

During the 1980s, the number of firearm homicide victims among young African-American males (ages 15 to 24) as a percentage of total homicides went up 10 percent to 88 percent.

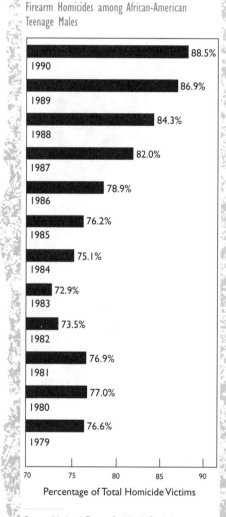

Firearm Homicides among African-American Teenage Males

Year	Percentage
1990	88.5%
1989	86.9%
1988	84.3%
1987	82.0%
1986	78.9%
1985	76.2%
1984	75.1%
1983	72.9%
1982	73.5%
1981	76.9%
1980	77.0%
1979	76.6%

Percentage of Total Homicide Victims

Source: National Center for Health Statistics.

Summary

More than one in three African-American children (ages 1 to 10) live in poverty for at least 7 to 10 years, while only one in five—compared to almost four in five white children—never know poverty.

Living in Poverty

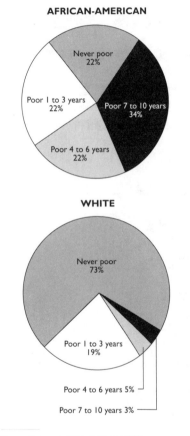

Source: Economic Policy Institute (1993).

"When you hear shooting, don't stand around — run," Nicholas said.

"Why do I say run?" their mother asked.

"Because a bullet don't have no eyes," the two boys shouted.

"She pray for us every day," Willie said.

The Walk to School

Each morning, Nicholas and his mother go in separate directions. His mother takes the two little ones to day-care on the bus and then heads to class at Kennedy-King College nearby, while Nicholas takes Willie and Ishtar to Banneker Elementary School.

The children pass worn apartment buildings and denuded lots with junked cars to get to Banneker. Near an alley, unemployed men warm themselves by a trash-barrel fire under a plastic tent. There is a crack house across the street from school.

To Nicholas it is not enough to get Ishtar and Willie to school. He feels he must make sure they're in their seats. "Willie's teacher tell me, 'You don't have to come by here,' Nicholas said. "I say, 'I'm just checking.'"

Mornings are so hectic that the children sometimes go to school hungry or arrive too late for the free school breakfast that Nicholas says isn't worth rushing for anyway.

One bitter cold morning when they made it to breakfast, Nicholas played the daddy as usual, opening a milk carton for Ishtar, pouring it over her cereal, handing her the spoon, and saying sternly, "Now eat your breakfast."

He began picking over his own cardboard bowl of Corn Pops sitting in vaguely sour milk and remembered the time Willie found a cockroach in his cereal. It's been kind of hard to eat the school breakfast ever since.

The Children: When Brothers Are Friends

Nicholas and Willie on brotherhood:

"He act like he stuck to me," Nicholas said of Willie. "Every time I move somewhere, he want to go. I can't even breathe."

"Well, what are brothers for?" Willie asked.

"To let them breathe and live a long life," Nicholas said. "Everytime I get something, they want it. I give them what they want after they give me a sad face."

"He saves me all the time," Willie said. "When I'm getting a whooping he says he did it."

"Then I get in trouble," Nicholas said.

"Then I say I did it, too, and we both get a whooping," Willie said. "I save you, too, don't I, Nicholas?"

"Willie's my friend," Nicholas said.

"I'm more than your friend," Willie shot back, a little hurt.

Once Willie almost got shot on the way home from school. He was trailing Nicholas, as he usually does, when some sixth-grade boys pulled out a gun and started shooting.

"They were right behind Willie," Nicholas said. "I kept calling him to get across the street. Then he heard the shots and ran."

Nicholas shook his head. "I be pulling on his hood, but he be so slow," he said.

"Old slowpoke," Ishtar said, chiming in.

No Friends, One Toy

In this neighborhood, few parents let their children outside to play or visit a friend's house. It is too dangerous. "You don't have any friends," Nicholas's mother tells him. "You don't have no homey. I'm your homey."

So Nicholas and his siblings usually head straight home. They live in a large barren apartment with chipped tile floors and hand-me-down furniture, a space their mother tries to spruce up with her children's artwork.

The children spend their free time with the only toy they have — a Nintendo game that their mother saved up for and got them for Christmas. The television isn't working right, though, leaving a picture so dark that the children have to turn out all the lights and sit inches from the set to see the cartoon Nintendo figure flicker over the walls to save the princess.

Dinner is what their mother has time to make between algebra and Faith Temple. Late for church one night, she pounded on the stove to make the burners fire up, set out five plastic blue plates, and apportioned the canned spaghetti and pan-fried bologna.

"Come and get your dinner before the roaches beat you to it!" she yelled with her own urban gallows humor.

Rhinestones in Church

Faith Temple is a tiny storefront church in what used to be a laundry. It is made up mostly of two or three clans, including Nicholas's, and practices a homegrown version of Ethiopian-derived Christianity.

At the front of the spartan room with white walls and metal folding chairs, sits a phalanx of regal, black-robed women with foot-high, rhinestone-studded headdresses. They are called empresses, supreme empresses, and imperial empresses. They include Nicholas's mother, aunt, and grandmother, and they sing and testify and help calm flushed parishioners, who sometimes stomp and wail with the holy spirit.

The pastor is Prophet Titus. During the week he is Albert Lee, a Chicago bus driver, but on Sundays he dispenses stern advice and $35 blessings to his congregation of mostly single mothers and their children. "Just bringing children to the face of the earth is not enough," Prophet Titus intones. "You owe them more."

Nicholas's job during church is to keep the younger children quiet, sometimes with a brother asleep on one thigh and a cousin on the other. Their mother keeps watch from her perch up front where she sings. When the little ones get too loud, their mother shoots them a threatening look from behind the microphone that says, "You know better."

Grandmother Empress

On this weeknight, Nicholas and Willie are with cousins and other children listening to their grandmother's Bible lesson.

She is a proud woman who worked for 22 years as a meat wrapper at a supermarket, reared five children of her own, has stepped in to help raise some of her grandchildren, and packs a .38 in her purse in case some stranger tries to rob her again. On Sundays and during Bible class, she is not merely Nicholas's grandmother but Imperial Empress Magdala in her velvet-collared cape.

The children recite Bible verses ("I am black but beautiful," from Solomon, or "My skins is black," from Job), and then Mrs. Whitiker breaks into a free-form lecture that seems a mix of black pride and Dianetics.

"Be dignified," she told the children. "Walk like a prince or princess. We're about obeying our parents and staying away from people who don't mean us any good."

The boys got home late that night, but their day was not done. "Your clothes are in the tub," their mother said, pointing to the bathroom, "and the kitchen awaits you."

"I know my baby's running out of hands," she said under her breath.

This is not the life Nicholas envisions for himself when he grows up. He has thought about this, and says he doesn't want any kids. Well, maybe a boy, one boy he can play ball with and show how to be a man. Definitely not a girl. "I don't want no girl who'll have four or five babies," he said. "I don't want no big family with 14, 20 people, all these people to take care of. When you broke, they still ask you for money, and you have to say, 'I'm broke. I don't have no money.'"

A Sister Safe

Ishtar made it home safely the afternoon Nicholas was called to the principal's office. Mr. Mason was a couple of hours late picking her up, but he came through in the end.

Nicholas worries anyway, the way big brothers do. He worried the morning his mother had an early test and he had to take the little ones to day-care before going to school himself.

John-John began to cry as Nicholas walked away. Nicholas bent down and hugged him and kissed him. Everything, Nicholas assured him, was going to be O.K.

FROM: a ten-part series, "Children of the Shadows" in *The New York Times*, 1993.

Summary

Between 1984 and 1987, the United States had the lowest success rate in lifting children out of poverty among a sample of industrialized nations, with a rate nine times smaller than countries like the United Kingdom and France.

Lifted Out of Poverty

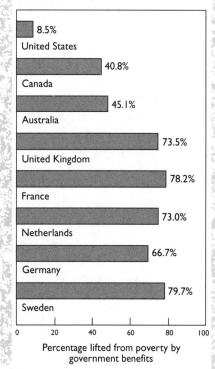

United States	8.5%
Canada	40.8%
Australia	45.1%
United Kingdom	73.5%
France	78.2%
Netherlands	73.0%
Germany	66.7%
Sweden	79.7%

Percentage lifted from poverty by government benefits

Source: *Cross National Perspectives on Income Security Program*, Timothy M. Smeeding (testimony before the U.S. Congress Joint Economic Committee, September 25, 1991).

STAR

Serious Teens Acting Responsibly

The Serious Teens Acting Responsibly (STAR) program aims to prevent teen pregnancy, youth violence, and drug abuse by channeling young people's energies into community service. The program is managed and run by the young people themselves, with the support of adult advisers.

Now under the sponsorship of Save the Children, an international development agency, STAR was born in 1984 in South Carolina's rural Jasper County, one of the poorest areas in the state. Here, crack cocaine use among teens was rampant. The number of adults without a high school diploma stood at 44 percent, the pregnancy rate for teenage girls at 38 percent.

These issues galvanized a group of Jasper County adults called TASC (Taxpayers' Advocacy and Support Coalition). What they began as a pregnancy prevention group for young girls grew into a more comprehensive program. Through STAR, teenagers identify community problems and the ways in which they might help to alleviate them. Projects have included setting up a recycling center, tutoring younger children, and counseling peers. STAR members plan the group's projects and allocate its resources. The decision-making and leadership skills gained in the process pave the way for future success.

STAR has been highly effective in reducing teen pregnancy, youth violence, and drug abuse in Jasper County. Among 400 STAR participants, only four pregnancies and two incidences of drug abuse were recorded in four years; school attendance climbed to 100 percent. STAR has now spread to Georgia, Virginia, and Connecticut, and Save the Children plans to introduce it elsewhere.

For more information, contact STAR, c/o Veronica Thomas, Save the Children, P.O. Box 1100, Hardeeville, SC 29927; (803) 726-3461.

Linking Lifetimes

Linking Lifetimes provides youths from disadvantaged backgrounds with the benefits of the professional experience and maturity of older mentors — with an eye toward matching youths and mentors who come from similar socioeconomic backgrounds.

Project coordinators introduce the youths to mentors aged 55 years and older. Mentors are recommended to participate in 10 hours of training and to attend 10 regular workshops and group meetings thereafter. At the same time, the youths develop their goals with the help of parents, program coordinators, and mentors, and learn the expectations of the mentors and coordinators.

After the training period, the youths and mentors are brought together with a better sense of how to benefit from one another's knowledge, skills, and experiences. Both mentors and youths periodically meet in separate groups to discuss their experiences and the program.

Washington Post columnist William Raspberry, mentor to a young man in Washington, DC, writes: "I wanted one more young black man to have a glimpse of a bigger world, to have a sense of the possibilities that exist for those who get ready for them."

Linking Lifetimes is a national demonstration project involving nine social service agencies nationwide and is coordinated by the Center for Intergenerational Learning at Temple University.

For more information, write the Center for Intergenerational Learning, Temple University, 1601 N. Broad Street, Suite 206, Philadelphia, PA 19122; (215) 787-3767.

YouthBuild

In 15 cities across the United States, teens are learning construction skills and putting them to use, rehabilitating abandoned buildings to provide housing for homeless or low-income people.

The 12-to 18-month training program stresses personal development and leadership training, in addition to mastery of basic construction skills and general preparation for a high school equivalency diploma. The program enhances the self-esteem of young men who have dropped out of school by teaching them a useful and respected role in their community; it also attracts young women into nontraditional careers.

"Working with their hands and building something creates a sense of accomplishment that contributes to self-esteem," Joyce Sonn, Director of YouthBuild in St. Louis, told *Historic Preservation* magazine. "People who may not have been very successful in school can learn how very successful they can be."

The program's strong counseling and leadership training helps youths who have even long histories with gangs learn to manage problems and conquer obstacles that otherwise would derail them into marginal lives.

Pioneered by the Youth Action Program of the East Harlem Block Schools between 1978 and 1984, the program is now replicated in 14 U.S. cities, supported by private and public funds. Youth-Build, which counts 496 organizational members

and 232 youth members, was selected by the Corporation for National and Community Service for multistate replication. Recent federal funding of $20 million to $40 million, to be administered by the U.S. Department of Housing and Urban Development, ensures that the effort will reach more teens and homeless families across the country.

Photo: William Moree, 1994

For more information, contact YouthBuild USA, 58 Day Street, P.O. Box 440322, Somerville, MA 02144; (617) 623-9900.

The Lesson

TONI CADE BAMBARA

Economic inequality in the United States increased dramatically over the last several decades. In 1959, the top 4 percent of American families earned as much as the bottom 35 percent. By 1989, that number increased to 51 percent — that is, the top 4 percent of American families earned more than half of the entire nation. In this short story, Toni Cade Bambara portrays a child being made aware of inequality.

Back in the days when everyone was old and stupid or young and foolish and me and Sugar were the only ones just right, this lady moved on our block with nappy hair and proper speech and no makeup. And quite naturally we laughed at her, laughed the way we did at the junk man who went about his business like he was some big-time president and his sorry-ass horse his secretary. And we kinda hated her too, hated the way we did the winos who cluttered up our parks and pissed on our handball walls and stank up our hallways and stairs so you couldn't halfway play hide-and-seek without a goddamn gas mask. Miss Moore was her name. The only woman on the block with no first name. And she was black as hell, cept for her feet, which were fish-white and spooky. And she was always planning these boring-ass things for us to do, us being my cousin, mostly, who lived on the block cause we all moved North the same time and to the same apartment then spread out gradual to breathe. And our parents would yank our heads into some kinda shape and crisp up our clothes so we'd be presentable for travel with Miss Moore, who always looked like she was going to church, though she never did. Which is just one of things the grownups talked about when they talked behind her back like a dog. But when she came calling with some sachet she'd sewed up or some gingerbread she'd made or some

Summary

The richest 5 percent of Americans saw their share of total income rise sharply in the 1980s, while the poorest 20 percent saw their share decline.

Income Disparity

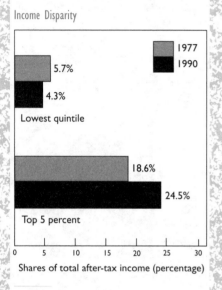

| | 1977 |
| | 1990 |

5.7%

4.3%

Lowest quintile

18.6%

24.5%

Top 5 percent

0   5   10   15   20   25   30

Shares of total after-tax income (percentage)

Source: Congressional Budget Office

book, why then they'd all be too embarrassed to turn her down and we'd get handed over all spruced up. She'd been to college and said it was only right that she should take responsibility for the young ones' education, and she not even related by marriage or blood. So they'd go for it. Specially Aunt Gretchen. She was the main gofer in the family. You got some ole dumb shit foolishness you want somebody to go for, you send for Aunt Gretchen. She been screwed into the go-along for so long, it's a blood-deep natural thing with her. Which is how she got saddled with me and Sugar and Junior in the first place while our mothers were in a la-de-da apartment up the block having a good ole time.

So this one day Miss Moore rounds us all up at the mailbox and it's puredee hot and she's knockin herself out about arithmetic. And school suppose to let up in summer I heard, but she don't never let up. And the starch in my pinafore scratching the shit outta me and I'm really hating this nappyhead bitch and her goddamn college degree. I'd much rather go to the pool or to the show where it's cool. So me and Sugar leaning on the mailbox being surly, which is a Miss Moore word. And Flyboy checking out what everybody brought for lunch. And Fat Butt already wasting his peanut-butter-and-jelly sandwich like the pig he is. And Junebug punchin on Q.T.'s arm for potato chips. And Rosie Giraffe shifting from one hip to the other waiting for somebody to step on her foot or ask her if she from Georgia so she can kick ass, preferably Mercedes'. And Miss Moore asking us do we know what money is, like we a bunch of retards. I mean real money, she say, like it's only poker chips or monopoly papers we lay on the grocer. So right away I'm tired of this and say so. And would much rather snatch Sugar and go to the Sunset and terrorize the West Indian kids and take their hair ribbons and their money too. And Miss Moore files that remark away for next week's lesson on brotherhood, I can tell. And finally I say we oughta get to the subway cause it's cooler and besides we might meet some cute boys. Sugar done swiped her mama's lipstick, so we ready.

So we heading down the street and she's boring us silly about what things cost and what our parents make and how much goes for rent and how money ain't divided up right in this country. And then she gets to the part about we all poor and live in the slums, which I don't feature. And I'm ready to speak on that, but she steps out in the street and hails two cabs just like that. Then she hustles half the crew in with her and hands me a five-dollar bill and tells me to calculate 10 percent tip for the driver. And we're off. Me and Sugar and Junebug and Flyboy hangin out the window and hollering to everybody, putting lipstick on each other cause Flyboy a faggot anyway, and making farts with our sweaty armpits. But I'm mostly trying to figure how to spend this money. But they all fascinated with the meter ticking and Junebug starts laying bets as to how much it'll read when Flyboy can't hold his breath no more. Then Sugar lays bets as to how much it'll be when we get there. So I'm stuck. Don't nobody want to go for my plan, which is to jump out at the next light and run off to the first bar-b-que we can find. Then the driver tells us to get the hell out cause we there already. And the meter reads 85 cents. And I'm stalling to figure out the tip and Sugar say give him a dime. And I decide he don't need it bad as I do, so later for him. But then he tries to take off with Junebug foot still in the door so we talk about his mama something ferocious. Then we check out that we on Fifth Avenue and everybody dressed up in stockings. One lady in a fur coat, hot as it is. White folks crazy.

"This is the place," Miss Moore say, presenting it to us in the voice she uses at the museum. "Let's look in the windows before we go in."

"Can we steal?" Sugar asks very serious like she's getting the ground rules squared away before she plays. "I beg your pardon," say Miss Moore, and we fall out. So she leads us around the windows of the toy store and me and Sugar screamin, "This is mine, that's mine, I gotta have that, that was made for me, I was born for that," till Big Butt drowns us out.

"Hey, I'm goin to buy that there."

"That there? You don't even know what it is, stupid."

"I do so," he say punchin on Rosie Giraffe. "It's a microscope."

"Whatcha gonna do with a microscope, fool?"

"Look at things."

"Like what, Ronald?" ask Miss Moore. And Big Butt ain't got the first notion. So here go Miss Moore gabbing about the thousands of bacteria in a drop of water and the somethinorother in a speck of blood and the million and one living things in the air around us is invisible to the naked eye. And what she say that for? Junebug go to town on that "naked" and we rolling. Then Miss Moore ask what it cost. So we all jam into the window smudgin it up and the price tag say $300. So then she ask how long'd take for Big Butt and Junebug to save up their allowances. "Too long," I say. "Yeh," adds Sugar, "outgrown it by that time." And Miss Moore say no, you never outgrow learning instruments. "Why, even medical students and interns and," blah, blah, blah. And we ready to choke Big Butt for bringing it up in the first damn place. "This here costs four hundred eighty dollars," say Rosie Giraffe. So we pile up all over her to see what she pointin out. My eyes tell me it's a chunk of glass cracked with something heavy, and different-color inks dripped into the splits, then the whole thing put into a oven or something. But for $480 it don't make sense.

"That's a paperweight made of semi-precious stones fused together under tremendous pressure," she explains slowly, with her hands doing the mining and all the factory work.

"So what's a paperweight?" asks Rosie Giraffe.

"To weigh paper with, dumbbell," say Flyboy, the wise man from the East.

"Not exactly," say Miss Moore, which is what she say when you warm or way off too. "It's to weigh paper down so it won't scatter and make your desk untidy." So right away me and Sugar curtsy to each other and then to Mercedes who is more the tidy type.

"We don't keep paper on top of the desk in my class," say Junebug, figuring Miss Moore crazy or lyin one.

"At home, then," she say. "Don't you have a calendar and a pencil case and a blotter and a letter-opener on your desk at home where you do your homework?" And she know damn well what our homes look like cause she nosys around in them every chance she gets.

"I don't even have a desk," say Junebug. "Do we?"

"No. And I don't get no homework neither," say Big Butt.

68

"And I don't even have a home," say Flyboy like he do at school to keep the white folks off his back and sorry for him. Send this poor kid to camp posters, is his specialty.

"I do," says Mercedes. "I have a box of stationery on my desk and a picture of my cat. My godmother bought the stationery and the desk. There's a big rose on each sheet and the envelopes smell like roses."

"Who wants to know about your smelly-ass stationery," say Rosie Giraffe fore I can get my two cents in.

"It's important to have a work area all your own so that…"

"Will you look at this sailboat, please," say Flyboy, cuttin her off and pointin to the thing like it was his. So once again we tumble all over each other to gaze at this magnificent thing in the toy store which is just big enough to maybe sail two kittens across the pond if you strap them to the posts tight. We all start reciting the price tag like we in assembly. "Handcrafted sailboat of fiberglass at one thousand one hundred ninety-five dollars."

"Unbelievable," I hear myself say and am really stunned. I read it again for myself just in case the group recitation put me in a trance. Same thing. For some reason this pisses me off. We look at Miss Moore and she lookin at us, waiting for I dunno what.

"Who'd pay all that when you can buy a sailboat set for a quarter at Pop's, a tube of glue for a dime, and a ball of string for eight cents? It must have a motor and a whole lot else besides," I say. "My sailboat cost me about fifty cents."

"But will it take water?" say Mercedes with her smart ass.

"Took mine to Alley Pond Park once," say Flyboy. "String broke, lost it. Pity."

"Sailed mine in Central Park and it keeled over and sank. Had to ask my father for another dollar."

"And you got the strap," laugh Big Butt. "The jerk didn't even have a string on it. My old man wailed on his behind."

Little Q.T. was staring hard at the sailboat and you could see he wanted it bad. But he too little and somebody'd just take it from him. So what the hell. "This boat for kids, Miss Moore?"

"Parents silly to buy something like that just to get all broke up," say Rosie Giraffe.

*In a morally adjusted society...
the rich should not get richer
if the poor get poorer.*

MALACHI MARTIN
Author, Theologian

"That much money it should last forever," I figure.

"My father'd buy it for me if I wanted it."

"Your father, my ass," say Rosie Giraffe getting a chance to finally push Mercedes.

"Must be rich people shop here," say Q.T.

"You are a very bright boy," say Flyboy. "What was your first clue?" And he rap him on the head with the back of his knuckles, since Q.T. the only one he could get away with. Though Q.T. liable to come up behind you years later and get his licks in when you half expect it.

"What I want to know is," I says to Miss Moore though I never talk to her, I wouldn't give the bitch that satisfaction, "is how much a real boat costs? I figure a thousand'd get you a yacht any day."

"Why don't you check that out," she says, "and report back to the group?" Which really pains my ass. If you gonna mess up a perfectly good swim day least you could do is have some answers. "Let's go in," she say like she got something up her sleeve. Only she don't lead the way. So me and Sugar turn the corner to where the entrance is, but when we get there I kinda hang back. Not that I'm scared, what's there to be afraid of, just a toy store. But I feel funny, shame. But what I got to be shamed about? Got as much right to go in as anybody. But somehow I can't seem to get hold of the door, so I step away for Sugar to lead. But she hangs back too. And I look at her and she looks at me and this is ridiculous. I mean, damn, I have never ever been shy about doing nothing or going nowhere. But then Mercedes steps up and then Rosie Giraffe and Big Butt crowd in behind and shove, and next thing we all stuffed into the doorway with only Mercedes squeezing past us, smoothing out her jumper and walking right down the aisle. Then the rest of us tumble in like a glued-together jigsaw done all wrong. And people lookin at us. And it's like the time me and Sugar crashed into the Catholic church on a dare. But once we got in there and everything so hushed and holy and the candles and the bowin and the handkerchiefs on all the drooping heads, I just couldn't go through with the plan. Which was for me to run up to the altar and do a tap dance while Sugar played the nose flute and messed around in the holy water. And Sugar kept givin me the elbow. Then later teased me so bad I tied her up in the shower and turned it on and locked her in. And she'd be there till this day if Aunt Gretchen hadn't finally figured I was lyin about the boarder takin a shower.

Same thing in the store. We all walkin on tiptoe and hardly touchin the games and puzzles and things. And I watched Miss Moore who is steady watchin us like she waitin for a sign. Like Mama Drewery watches the sky and sniffs the air and takes note of just how much slant is in the bird formation. Then me and Sugar bump smack into each other, so busy gazing at the toys, 'specially the sailboat. But we don't laugh and go into our fat-lady bump-stomach routine. We just stare at that price tag. Then Sugar run a finger over the whole boat. And I'm jealous and want to hit her. Maybe not her, but I sure want to punch somebody in the mouth.

"Watcha bring us here for, Miss Moore?"

"You sound angry, Sylvia. Are you mad about something?" Givin me one of them grins like she tellin a grown-up joke that never turns out to be funny. And she's lookin very closely at me like maybe she plannin to do my portrait from memory. I'm mad, but I won't give her that satisfaction. So I slouch around the store bein very bored and say, "Let's go."

Me and Sugar at the back of the train watchin the tracks whizzin by large then small then gettin gobbled up in the dark. I'm thinkin about this tricky toy I saw in the store. A clown that somersaults on a bar then does chin-ups just cause you yank lightly at his leg. Cost $35. I could see me askin my mother for a $35 birthday clown. "You wanna who that costs what?" she'd say, cocking her head to the side to get a better view of the hole in my head. Thirty-five dollars could buy new bunk beds for Junior and Gretchen's boy. Thirty-five dollars and the whole household could go visit Granddaddy Nelson in the country. Thirty-five dollars would pay for the rent and the piano bill too. Who are these people that spend that much for performing clowns and $1,000 for toy sailboats? What kinda work they do and how they live and how come we ain't in on it? Where we are is who we are, Miss Moore always pointin out. But it don't necessarily have to be that way, she always adds then waits for somebody to say that poor people have to wake up and demand their share of the pie and don't none of us know what kind of pie she talkin about in the first damn place. But she ain't so smart cause I still got her four dollars from the taxi and she sure ain't gettin it. Messin up my day with this shit. Sugar nudges me in my pocket and winks.

Miss Moore lines us up in front of the mailbox where we started from, seem like years ago, and I got a headache for thinkin so hard. And we lean all over each other so we can hold up under the draggy-ass lecture she always finishes us off with at the end before we thank her for borin us to tears. But she just looks at us like she readin tea leaves. Finally she say, "Well, what did you think of F. A. O. Schwartz?"

Rosie Giraffe mumbles, "White folks crazy."

"I'd like to go there again when I get my birthday money," says Mercedes, and we shove her out the pack so she has to lean on the mailbox by herself.

"I'd like a shower. Tiring day," say Flyboy.

Then Sugar surprises me by sayin, "You know, Miss Moore, I don't think all of us here put together eat in a year what that sailboat costs." And Miss Moore lights up like somebody goosed her. "And?" she say, urging Sugar on. Only I'm standin on her foot so she don't continue.

"Imagine for a minute what kind of society it is in which some people can spend on a toy what it would cost to feed a family of six or seven. What do you think?"

"I think," say Sugar pushing me off her feet like she never done before, cause I whip her ass in a minute, "that this is not much of a democracy if you ask me. Equal chance to pursue happiness means an equal crack at the dough, don't it?" Miss Moore is besides herself and I am disgusted with Sugar's treachery. So I stand on her foot one more time to see if she'll shove me. She shuts up, and Miss Moore looks at me, sorrowfully I'm thinkin. And somethin weird is goin on, I can feel it in my chest.

"Anybody else learn anything today?" lookin dead at me. I walk away and Sugar has to run to catch up and don't even seem to notice when I shrug her arm off my shoulder.

"Well, we got four dollars anyway," she says.

"Uh hunh."

"We could go to Hascombs and get half a chocolate layer and then go to the Sunset and still have plenty money for potato chips and ice-cream sodas."

"Uh hunh."

"Race you to Hascombs," she say.

We start down the block and she gets ahead which is O.K. by me cause I'm goin to the West End and then over to the Drive to think this day through. She can run if she want to and even run faster. But ain't nobody gonna beat me at nuthin.

FROM: *Gorillas, My Love,* 1972.

FACT

In 1994 there were 28 millionaires in the U.S. Senate and 50 millionaires in the U.S. House of Representatives.

(Source: Center for Responsive Politics, Reuter News Service, October 19, 1994.)

The Algebra Project

An innovative math literacy program

The Algebra Project seeks to prepare minority students for the civil rights struggle of their generation, a struggle associated not with the denied access to vote, but with the critical thinking skills needed to participate in a high-tech economy.

Founded in 1982, the project is the brainchild of Bob Moses, a math teacher and former civil rights organizer during the 1964 Mississippi Freedom summer: "In those days, the issue was the 'Right to Vote,' the question was 'Political Access.' Now math literacy holds the key. Math literacy and economic access are how we are going to give hope to the young generation."

The Algebra Project is unique because it both empowers students and builds community support. It teaches middle school students to experience an event, draw or model it, write and talk about it, and then translate it into mathematical language. In addition, it creates a supportive network of parents, teachers, administrators, and community leaders around the concept of the necessity of math education for disadvantaged children.

The Algebra Project was spawned in the Martin Luther King, Jr. Middle School in Cambridge, MA. It has since been adopted by an estimated 110 schools in Mississippi, California, Kentucky, and South Carolina, and in the cities of Chicago, Indianapolis, Milwaukee, New Orleans, Boston, and New York. Educators credit the program for helping at-risk students become independent learners.

Photograph of Bob Moses by Doug Mindell © 1994

For more information, contact The Algebra Project, Inc., 99 Bishop Richard Allen Drive, Cambridge, MA 02139; (617) 491-0200.

"I Have a Dream" Foundation

Offering an incentive to finish school

In a 1981 graduation address, a New York businessman made an unusual impromptu offer to a class of East Harlem sixth graders: If they would stay in school long enough to complete high school, he would foot the bill for their college tuition.

Statistically, the children's chances of making it through high school were slim: only about 25 percent of them were predicted to do so. But Eugene Lang's promise to the sixth graders of Public School 121 — which he had attended 50 years earlier — proved a powerful incentive. A full 90 percent of the class graduated, and 60 percent went on to college.

In the years between sixth grade and high school graduation, Lang kept in close contact with the 61 children and hired a social worker to work with them. In 1986, when the class was in eleventh grade, Lang created the "I Have a Dream" (IHAD) Foundation to extend his idea to other low-income communities.

There are now 150 IHAD projects operating in 57 cities and 28 states. Each project "adopts" a class of third or fourth graders — or a comparable age group of children from a public housing project — and provides them with academic, social, and recreational enrichment activities throughout their school years. For those who graduate from high school, the program furnishes tuition assistance for college or vocational school. The $400,000 cost of each 10-year project is underwritten by a local sponsor, either alone or with the aid of grants and donations. Nation-

"I Have a Dream"® Foundation

wide, the program has served some 12,000 children.

For more information, contact Charles Chestnut, Director of Communications, "I Have a Dream" Foundation, 330 Seventh Avenue, 20th Floor, New York, NY 10001; (212) 736-1730, extension 14.

Lessons for a new war on poverty

AN INTERVIEW WITH MARIAN WRIGHT EDELMAN

Excerpts from an interview with Marian Wright Edelman, activist, author, advocate for children, and currently the president of the Children's Defense Fund. The interview was conducted in 1994 by the producers of Blackside, Inc.'s documentary series, America's War on Poverty.

In order to wage an effective war on poverty today, it's going to take sustained leadership and commitment at all levels. Child poverty is at extraordinarily high levels today, and we are going to have to have this country recognize that we cannot afford to have it if we're going to survive as a nation. But it's going to take a mass movement to pick up and finish where Mr. King left off, and to put the social and economic underpinnings under all of our children and families. That's what the Child Development Group of Mississippi (CDGM) was trying to do. That's what Head Start was trying to do. A lot of the leaders and parents that arose through that program are providing continuing leadership today as elected officials and as leaders in their communities. When we looked at some of those students out of Head Start in those early years who are now graduating from law school, I always pointed out how excited I was to meet a young man in Ohio who was in the first CDGM program in that first summer who had just graduated from law school in Ohio, and who was working for the Governor's office. You know, that program has been a breeding ground for new leaders, but we need now to have

every child get a head start, which is what President Clinton has committed himself to doing. We are now debating health insurance this year, and, in fact, 1994 is the year when I hope we're going to pick up where we left off in 1968 with Dr. King's and Robert Kennedy's deaths. It (is) a year when the nation is debating health reform, welfare reform, the re-authorization of Head Start, the re-authorization of the summer food program, the re-authorization of Chapter 1 of the Elementary and Secondary Education Act. You know, this is an enormous, major watershed period in federal policy, which harks back to how do we build on the best of what was begun with the War on Poverty in 1968. We have learned a lot, we have gained a lot,…millions of children, millions of citizens have gained a lot, and now it's time to build on those positive lessons, avoid negative problems, but to really now do the level of investment in all our children that is going to be needed to prepare them for the twenty-first century. If we do not do it, if we do not give every child a high quality head start and a healthy start in life, the country is not going to be the country that we know and want it to be in the competitive arena of the world. So I think that the paths have been built for us, and the issue is whether our leadership and whether our citizens are going to take up the challenge of seeing that no child is left behind in America because, if we don't, the country is going to be left behind.

Children's Defense Fund

An advocacy group for children

Recognizing that the children of America "cannot vote, lobby, or speak for themselves," the Children's Defense Fund (CDF) speaks for them. CDF is a national, nonprofit organization that advocates for the rights of all children, with particular focus on the needs of minorities, the disabled, and the poor.

As America's conscience toward our children, CDF seeks to educate the public and the policymakers about children's needs and the issues that affect them. To that end, CDF gathers and disseminates information on children's issues and monitors federal and state policies that bear on their lives. Crusading to put children's issues at the top of our political priority list, CDF lobbies Congress to enact pro-child legislation and litigates cases of major importance to children.

Photo: © 1994 Jason Miccolo Johnson

CDF stresses the importance of "preventive investment in children before they get sick, drop out of school, suffer family breakdown, or get into trouble." Based in the nation's capital, the organization maintains a staff of specialists in health, education, child welfare, mental health, child development, adolescent pregnancy prevention, and youth employment. CDF is headed by Marian Wright Edelman (see page 76) who began the organization in 1968 as the Washington Research Project. It became the Children's Defense Fund in 1973.

For more information, contact Children's Defense Fund, 122 C Street NW, Washington, DC 20001; (202) 628-8787.

Poverty, Families, and Friends

Home life ceases to be free and beautiful as soon as it is founded on borrowing and debt.

Henrik Ibsen, *A Doll's House*

There is much talk these days about "family values" and the importance of the family unit as the most basic and cohesive building block of society. But, often, the term *family values* is a code phrase implying that some families are "better" than others — and that the ideal family is a 1950s-style nuclear one in which the father is the sole breadwinner and the mother stays home full time with the children. In fact, this family model was never the norm in America, except for a segment of the middle class, and today it is an anachronism, except in the minds of a few highly visible social moralists. Fewer than 27 percent of U.S. households now consist of married couples with children (and, of those, nearly six in ten mothers with children under the age of six are in the labor force). For many reasons, the modern family is very complex — encompassing two-income households, single-parent households, and families who have no household at all to call their own. And families today, particularly those living in poverty, are facing tremendous stress.

The federal government's Aid to Families with Dependent Children (AFDC) program was developed in the 1930s with the aim of helping mothers in poverty to stay home and take care of their young ones. Its purpose was to help keep families intact. Nevertheless, when single mothers of today stay home to take care of their children (either by choice or through lack of opportunity) and are compelled to turn to AFDC for support, they are vilified by politicians, radio talk-show hosts (sometimes termed "data-free analysts"), and television evangelists.

Pundits and politicians may give lip service to families, but their words tend to be the only support that is offered. Affordable health insurance, daycare, a livable minimum wage, good schools, open and well-maintained public libraries (and any number of other public spaces), home care for the elderly — these are but a few of the obvious needs of modern families. As evidenced by the stories and data that follow, when we ignore or deny obvious needs we allow numerous problems to surface elsewhere.

Today, only half of America's children live in nuclear families where both biological parents are present. The remainder live in "blended" families (those with at least one step-parent) or with a single mother (or, increasingly, a single father). In the essays and fiction that follow, the many stresses felt by today's families are apparent. What is less apparent but worthy of note, is the fact that families, in their broadest and ever-changing configurations, remain the cornerstone of our communities. As these writings attest, the family today is under stress as never before, and its members would be better served by support and encouragement than by moralistic lectures.

Getting Nowhere

TONY HORWITZ

*The following article offers a profile of the "working homeless"
— people who, though gainfully employed, are unable to afford
a permanent place to live. The federal minimum wage today is
$4.25 an hour (though some states have taken it upon themselves
to set a higher rate). In 1979, a minimum-wage income was
enough to keep a family of three out of poverty. Today it doesn't even
come close.*

Springfield, MO — After a 10-hour shift scraping white meat
off turkey bone, Nancy Rogers is ready to go home, if only she
had one.

"Don't kiss me, I stink of turkey," she says to her husband,
John, who drives her from a local poultry plant to the Missouri
Hotel, a homeless shelter by the railroad tracks.

In the family's cramped, two-room quarters, the Rogers's four
sons play on a bunk bed beneath naked bulbs. As the 28-year-
old Mrs. Rogers pulls off rubber boots smeared with skin and
gore, her husband smoothes a security-guard uniform. After
dinner at the shelter's soup kitchen, he will start a night shift,
returning at dawn to look after the boys when his wife resumes
work.

"I don't feel like we're 'homeless' because that sounds like
we're winos or moochers," says Mr. Rogers, 39, who earns the
minimum wage, plus a 10-cent-an-hour laundry allowance.
"We're just a working family that can't afford our own place."

Boomtown Rash

The "working homeless" might once have seemed like a contradiction in terms, but today the phrase describes a significant
slice of the American work force. This is particularly true in

Tony Horwitz began contributing to *The
Wall Street Journal* as a free-lance jour-
nalist in 1987 and in 1990 joined the
London Bureau as a reporter covering
the Middle East and other foreign loca-
tions. He is currently at the Pittsburgh
Bureau. He is the author of *One For the
Road*, *Baghdad Without a Map*, and the
producer of the television documentary
"Mississippi Wood."

towns burgeoning with service jobs, as such places often lack the amenities needed to sustain an influx of the working poor.

Over half the adults at the Missouri Hotel, for instance, work at least part time: The shelter even maintains a "day sleeper" room for those who work nights. In the nearby boomtown of Branson, jobs are plentiful but affordable housing so scarce that working families who can't afford permanent shelter crowd into church basements, bunkhouses, campgrounds, condemned buildings, and the back seats of cars.

Boomtowns, whether in the California gold fields of the 1840s or the Texas oil patch of the 1980s, almost always have been raw places with itinerant workers and makeshift accommodations. But in the 1990s, the economic forces are different and in many ways more desperate. Those flocking to Branson are seeking service jobs that typically offer low pay, seasonal work, few if any benefits and even less hope of the sudden prosperity that can come when panning for gold or prospecting for crude. Many have uprooted themselves simply because most jobs start at a dollar or so above the minimum wage — better than where they came from.

Nor is working homelessness confined to towns such as Branson, though it is perhaps most acute here. Interviews with shelter directors, social workers, and homeless experts point to a nationwide trend. "Our growth area isn't alcoholics or the mentally ill. It's working families who can't afford rent on the wages they earn," says Sister Nancy Crowder, head of the Holy Family Shelter in Indianapolis. She and others estimate that about 25 percent of the homeless now work at least part-time, double the rate of five years ago.

To some degree, this rise reflects the growing availability of work as the economy pulls out of recession. But it also speaks to the falling status of low-income workers, due in part to a minimum wage that has badly lagged inflation. According to a Census Bureau report in March, almost one in five Americans works full time but earns a wage below the poverty line of $13,091 for a family of four. This represents a 50 percent increase since 1979 and a trend that the normally muted agency termed "astounding."

Summary

Between 1970 and 1993, there was a 178 percent increase in the number of involuntary part-time workers, while the number of full-time workers went up by only 51 percent.

Part-Time versus Full-Time Work

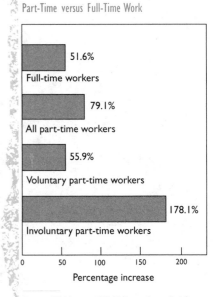

Full-time workers	51.6%
All part-time workers	79.1%
Voluntary part-time workers	55.9%
Involuntary part-time workers	178.1%

Percentage increase

Source: *U.S. News and World Report* (compiled from data from the Employment Benefit Research Institute; U.S. Department of Labor).

FACT

The proportion of Americans with full-time jobs whose incomes were too low to bring a family above the poverty level rose by 50 percent between 1979 and 1992, from 12 percent to 18 percent of all workers.

(Source: Census Bureau, 1994.)

Summary

The percentage of full-time, year-round workers with low earnings (less than $11,570 in 1989 dollars) has increased since 1979.

Barely Getting By

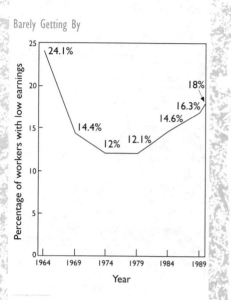

Source: U.S. Census Bureau.

FACT

A full-time worker at the $4.25 minimum wage will earn about $735 a month, before taxes. When the costs of rent, utilities, and child care are deducted, an average family living on the minimum wage in Kansas will be lucky to have $10 for a week of labor.

(Source: *Kansas City Pitch*, February 18, 1991.)

FACT

In 1990, one-third of the homeless were families with children.

(Source: *A Status Report on Hunger and Homelessness in the United States*, 1990.)

One Town's Tale

Another problem: While factory and professional jobs tend to cluster in urban areas, service work — the principal source of recent job creation — often booms in such out-of-the-way towns as St. George, Utah; Pigeon Forge, Tennessee; and Myrtle Beach, South Carolina, where inexpensive housing, daycare, public transport, and other services crucial to the working poor are scarce.

Branson, in the gently rolling Ozarks of southwestern Missouri, provides a stark case in point. Over the past five years, this sleepy railroad stop has blossomed into a country-music mecca, a top bus-tour destination with 5.6 million visitors last year. This influx has, in turn, lured legions of job-seekers, most of whom work on "the Strip," a gaudy, Las Vegas-like ribbon of motels, fast-food restaurants, gift shops, amusement parks, and theaters where performers such as Tony Orlando and the Osmond Brothers appear.

"You're looking at the pioneers of the '90s, in trailers and vans instead of covered wagons," says John Brown, who owns the Oak Hills campground, intended for tourists but crammed with low-wage workers.

Touring the campground is a walk on the dire side of the U.S. economy: busted farmers from Nebraska, laid-off factory workers from Wisconsin, former oil-field hands from Oklahoma, dishwashers, and maids who have never earned more than the minimum wage.

Many have been here for months, lending the sprawling bivouac a curious air of permanence. There are doghouses, wind chimes, and welcome mats. A school bus now stops here and the front office serves as a makeshift post office.

"We've got five jobs, five kids and about five square feet per person," says Don Mullins, a plumber from Austin, Texas, who came here a year ago with his wife, two unemployed sons, their spouses and children.

Like most newcomers, the Mullinses quickly found work but couldn't clear the first hurdle in the housing market: the three months' rent that landlords demand as security. There also are down payments for utilities. Having exhausted their slim savings getting here, and earning an average of $6 an hour, the

Mullinses simply couldn't muster those sums. (Rents for simple two-bedroom accommodations here start at about $700 a month.)

Seasonal Work

The Mullinses soon found another drain on savings: Branson employers lay off their workers in slow times, causing the town's jobless rate last year to jump to 20 percent in December from 3.6 percent in July.

So the family, 11 in all, has spent most of its first year scrunched inside the 28 foot trailer it towed from Texas. For months, they slept side by side on the floor, with a newborn baby perched in the sink. "It's been bearable because we work all different hours," says Mr. Mullins, 51. "Each time someone goes to work, that's a few more inches for the rest of us."

The family recently saved enough to rent an adjoining trailer, but has little hope of better housing. With day-care scarce, the clan needs to stay together so Mrs. Mullins can watch the children while the other adults work. An affordable house is out of reach, so the family now clings to more modest dreams.

"All I really crave," says Audra Mullins, a waitress, who has lived with her in-laws for 14 months, "is one quiet night with my husband. It would be nice just once to close a door and be alone."

Branson's housing crisis is an extreme example of the nationwide gulf between wages and rents. Rent for two-bedroom housing in the United States currently averages $485 a month, which the Washington-based Low Income Housing Information Service says requires hourly earnings more than twice the minimum wage of $4.25. Such housing now is out of reach for 40 percent of rental households, the group says.

This gap forces many workers into overcrowded or substandard housing, and consigns others to no housing at all. "We're seeing a lot of working families that obviously haven't been in this situation before," says Ellie Widmer, co-director of the Missouri Hotel, the homeless shelter in Springfield. "Some start sobbing in the lobby from the shock of it all."

Summary

The minimum wage has not kept pace with inflation. Minimum-wage earnings for a full-time, year-round worker have fallen below the annual poverty line for a family of three.

Minimum Wage

Source: U.S. Department of Labor; U.S. Census Bureau.

A man willing to work, and unable to find work, is perhaps the saddest sight that fortune's inequality exhibits under this sun.

THOMAS CARLYLE
19th-century English Prose Writer

Summary

After 1980, it became more difficult for low-income Americans to move up to the middle class and harder for middle-class Americans to avoid sliding into poverty.

Growing Thinner

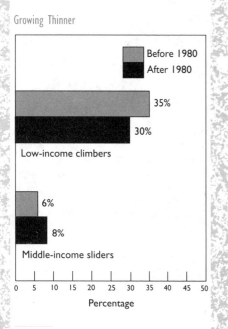

Before 1980	
After 1980	

Low-income climbers
- 35%
- 30%

Middle-income sliders
- 6%
- 8%

Percentage

Source: *American Demographics;* Survey Research Center's Panel Study of Income Dynamics (1992).

Branded as "Losers"

The hotel may offer shelter, but it doesn't often improve job prospects. Listing a shelter or mission as an address on job applications, says Ms. Widmer, "brands people as losers." Also, it makes job-seekers or day laborers hard to reach by telephone —a problem for others in temporary lodgings, too. Transportation often poses another obstacle in burgeoning towns such as Branson, which sprawls for miles and lacks public transport.

"When things start going down, people just get trapped," says Karen Schmit, who runs a $25-a-week bunkhouse, 15 miles by mountain road from Branson. A dozen men live in a basement dormitory with few windows and shared toilet stalls. Most must bum rides to work in Branson.

"I thought this place would be for college students who wanted to save money while working summer jobs," says Ms. Schmit, who opened the place six years ago.

Of course, low wages and high rents rarely tell the whole story. Branson's bunkhouses and campgrounds are filled with tales of heavy drinking, compulsive gambling, and broken homes that sound straight out of the hard-luck ballads sung by the town's country-and-western stars.

Such difficulties can devastate those with few skills and little income, particularly workers on the move. Lacking savings or friends and family nearby to fall back on, workers on the road can see their lives unravel over a costly car repair. Often it is health that causes a crisis. Since Branson began booming several years ago, homeless workers and their families have inundated the hospital emergency room because they lack health insurance and have nowhere else to go for treatment.

Pitching In

Many exhibit flu-like symptoms that doctors say are caused or exacerbated by malnourishment and exposure to the elements from sleeping in tents and cars. Another problem: Once diagnosed, many patients can't afford the medicine prescribed. Hospital staff have passed the hat to help out such patients.

Others in Branson have helped, too, donating food to church groups and aiding projects to build low-income housing. But given the magnitude of the problem, the response so far appears piecemeal. Branson's Chamber of Commerce blames this on the speed of the town's boom, the hilly terrain, sky-high land prices, and the town's appeal as a budget destination. Employers can't afford higher wages or benefits, the chamber says, because tourists demand low prices.

Keith Dunn, one of Branson's biggest employers, feels otherwise, "A lot of people are making millions here while claiming that they can't afford to pay more than $5 an hour or give any benefits," says the owner of McGuffey's restaurants.

The McGuffey's chain, by contrast, pays an average of $8 an hour as well as providing generous health and dental insurance, paid vacations, and promotion from within. Mr. Dunn also plans to provide low-cost housing and day-care for his workers. He says this contributes to better service and a turnover rate about one quarter the industry average. His boast is borne out by the fact that McGuffey's just opened its fifth outlet in Branson.

Few employers, though, have followed Mr. Dunn's lead. And with unions almost nonexistent, few workers appear to know what their rights are. Jessica Carden, 20, who has spent three weeks living in a pup tent with her fiance, says she recently lost a restaurant job after becoming dizzy at work and telling her employer that she was three months pregnant. The assistant general manager says the eatery feared it might be sued if the Dallas native lost her baby after a fall at work. Missouri's labor department says the action is illegal.

Newcomers desperate for housing also are vulnerable. Scams include phony landlords who rent the same house or trailer to several families —then run off with their deposits. Authorities also are investigating allegations that many buildings in Branson have gone up without permits or despite flunking inspections.

"It says something about the level of desperation in the rest of the country," says Jean Mueller, director of a church group that helps distressed newcomers, "that people are still flocking here."

One such new arrival is Stephen Malcolm, a second-generation shoe-factory worker from Massachusetts who hitchhikes

Summary

The share of adults who are middle class declined from 75 percent in 1978 to 67 percent in 1986.

The Disappearing Middle Class

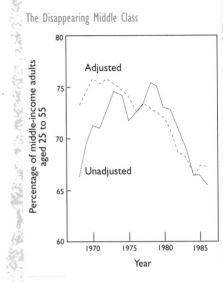

Source: *American Demographics;* Survey Research Center's Panel Study of Income Dynamics.

FACT

Nearly one-third of the households making use of emergency food programs have someone working full- or part-time.

(Source: Second Harvest, 1994.)

Summary

Between 1973 and 1991, real entry-level wages for high school graduates went down by over 25 percent from $8.69 to $6.48.

Low Hopes

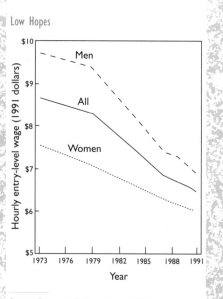

Source: Economic Policy Institute (1993).

into town carrying a change of clothes and a well-thumbed Bible. With no money and no place to stay, he spends his first night walking the Strip, scribbling down the names of restaurants with help-wanted signs. At dawn, after washing up in a gas station restroom, he applies for several jobs and then stops at Ms. Mueller's office to plead for help.

Waiting in the lobby, he overhears three disheveled men talk about where they spent the previous night: beneath a highway overpass, in a "pop-top motel" (slang for a dumpster), and in the back seat of a car. After collecting a bag of food, Mr. Malcolm hurries outside. "I've never been broke before," he says. "It's awkward to feel like a tramp."

After the shoe factory closed in his native Newburyport, Mr. Malcolm worked at a bakery and then fled the recession-ridden Northeast for Florida. In the three years since, he has hopped buses from state to state, slowly realizing "there's no gold out there" for a 36-year-old with a 10th grade education and few skills.

"There's so much romance in America about tilling the road to better yourself," he says. "It's hard to accept that things can get worse."

Now, down to pocket change, he calls his mother back home, then resumes walking. By day's end, he has found a job much like the last one: kitchen work at $6 an hour. All he needs is a place to sleep until his first paycheck, two weeks hence.

As busloads of tourists roar past, Mr. Malcolm spots a dime in the gutter and plucks it from the dust.

"Things are looking up," he says.

FROM: *The Wall Street Journal,* June 14, 1994.

Job Corps

Job training for disadvantaged youth

Hailed as one of the War on Poverty's success stories, Job Corps is a national vocational training program for young people ages 16 to 24.

Created in 1964 by the Economic Opportunity Act under President Lyndon Johnson, Job Corps aims to prepare sorely disadvantaged 16- to 24-year-olds for employment, further education, or enlistment in the armed forces. Eighty percent of the students are high school dropouts.

A distinctive feature of Job Corps is its residential nature. Most students live at the Job Corps center — one of 108 such facilities throughout the country — where they receive hands-on vocational training and basic education in math, reading, and other subjects. The disciplined environment of the centers is designed to instill honesty, responsibility, and good citizenship, as well.

Job Corps is administered by the Department of Labor in partnership with private corporations and agencies, which contract to run the centers, and trade unions and associations, which conduct the vocational training. At a cost of more than $20,000 per year for each student's room, board, and training, the program is expensive. An independent study revealed, however, that for every dollar invested, JobCorps returns $1.46 from added tax revenues and lower expenditures on welfare and incarceration.

A third of the students drop out of Job Corps within the first three months. Still, of the 62,000 students served each year, 61 percent find employment after the program, and 12 percent

continue their education. Among those who stick with Job Corps for at least six months, the success rate is even higher. The program is so successful, in fact, that the Clinton administration has endorsed the "50-50 plan," which calls for the establishment of 50 new Job Corps centers and a 50 percent increase in enrollment over several years' time.

For more information, contact Job Corps, U.S. Department of Labor, Employment and Training Administration, 200 Constitution Avenue, NW, Washington, DC 20210; (202) 219-8550.

Getting the Facts of Life

PAULETTE CHILDRESS WHITE

When her father loses the welding job he's held for 11 years because the company is moving to Indianapolis, the young protagonist of this short story learns about welfare the hard way. In numerous ways, a plant closing can devastate a family. The prospect of uprooting a family — leaving behind relatives and friends — in order to follow a welding job is, for many, an unbearable expense. But remaining in a de-industrialized community often results in relying on welfare. Today, this scenario is replayed with many variations across the nation, as manufacturing jobs move not only out of the state but out of the country as well. Since 1980, over 300,000 U.S. manufacturing jobs have been lost. Paulette Childress White offers a moving account of how it feels to learn about the pain and embarrassment of going on welfare.

The August morning was ripening into a day that promised to be a burner. By the time we'd walked three blocks, dark patches were showing beneath Momma's arms, and inside tennis shoes thick with white polish, my feet were wet against the cushions. I was beginning to regret how quickly I'd volunteered to go.

"Dog. My feet are getting mushy," I complained.

"You should've wore socks," Momma said, without looking my way or slowing down.

I frowned. In 1961, nobody wore socks with tennis shoes. It was bare legs, Bermuda shorts and a sleeveless blouse. Period.

Momma was chubby but she could really walk. She walked the same way she washed clothes — up-and-down, up-and-down until she was done. She didn't believe in taking breaks.

This was my first time going to the welfare office with Momma. After breakfast, before we'd had time to scatter, she

Paulette Childress White is currently teaching at Henry Ford Community College and completing her Ph.D. in English at Wayne State College, Detroit, Michigan. Her works have appeared in several publications, including *Redbook, The Harbor Review,* and *The Michigan Quarterly.* She continues to write fiction when possible.

corralled everyone old enough to consider and announced in her serious-business voice that someone was going to the welfare office with her this morning. Cries went up.

Junior had his papers to do. Stella was going swimming at the high school. Dennis was already pulling the *Free Press* wagon across town every first Wednesday to get the surplus food — like that.

"You want clothes for school, don't you?" That landed. School opened in two weeks.

"I'll go," I said.

"Who's going to baby-sit if Minerva goes?" Momma asked.

Stella smiled and lifted her small golden nose. "I will," she said. "I'd rather baby-sit than do *that*."

That should have warned me. Anything that would make Stella offer to baby-sit had to be bad.

A small cheer probably went up among my younger brothers in the back rooms where I was not too secretly known as "The Witch" because of the criminal licks I'd learned to give on my rise to power. I was twelve, third oldest under Junior and Stella, but I had long established myself as first in command among the kids. I was chief baby-sitter, biscuit-maker and broom-wielder. Unlike Stella, who'd begun her development at ten, I still had my girl's body and wasn't anxious to have that changed. What would it mean but a loss of power? I liked things just the way they were. My interest in bras was even less than my interest in boys, and that was limited to keeping my brothers — who seemed destined for wildness — from taking over completely.

Even before we left, Stella had Little Stevie Wonder turned up on the radio in the living room, and suspicious jumping-bumping sounds were beginning in the back. They'll tear the house down, I thought, following Momma out the door.

We turned at Salliotte, the street that would take us straight up to Jefferson Avenue where the welfare office was. Momma's face was pinking in the heat, and I was huffing to keep up. From here, it was seven more blocks on the colored side, the railroad tracks, five blocks on the white side and there you were. We'd be cooked.

Summary

According to a 1994 *New York Times* poll, almost 40 percent of workers worry that during the next two years they might be laid off, have to work reduced hours, or take a cut in pay.

Job Insecurity

Percentage of workers who worry

Total
39%

Blue-collar workers
48%

Professional or managerial workers
36%

Experienced layoffs, etc., in the last two years
24%

Northeast
45%

Midwest
38%

South
38%

West
31%

Source: *New York Times*, March 11, 1994.

"Is the welfare office near the Harbor Show?" I asked. I knew the answer, I just wanted some talk.

"Across the street."

"Umm. Glad it's not way down Jefferson somewhere."

Nothing. Momma didn't talk much when she was outside. I knew that the reason she wanted one of us along when she had far to go was not for company but so she wouldn't have to walk by herself. I could understand that. To me, walking alone was like being naked or deformed — everyone seemed to look at you harder and longer. With Momma, the feeling was probably worse because you knew people were wondering if she were white, Indian maybe or really colored. Having one of us along, brown and clearly hers, probably helped define that. Still, it was like being a little parade, with Momma's pale skin and straight brown hair turning heads like the clang of cymbals. Especially on the colored side.

"Well," I said, "here we come to the bad part."

Momma gave a tiny laugh.

Most of Salliotte was a business street, with Old West-looking storefronts and some office places that never seemed to open. Ecorse, hinged onto southwest Detroit like a clothes closet, didn't seem to take itself seriously. There were lots of empty fields, some of which folks down the residential streets turned into vegetable gardens every summer. And there was this block where the Moonflower Hotel raised itself to three stories over the poolroom and Beaman's drugstore. Here, bad boys and drunks made their noise and did an occasional stabbing. Except for the cars that lined both sides of the block, only one side was busy — the other bordered a field of weeds. We walked on the safe side.

If you were a woman or a girl over twelve, walking this block — even on the safe side — could be painful. They usually hollered at you and never mind what they said. Today, because it was hot and early, we made it by with only one weak *Hey baby* from a drunk sitting in the poolroom door.

"Hey baby yourself," I said but not too loudly, pushing my flat chest out and stabbing my eyes in his direction.

"Minerva girl, you better watch your mouth with grown men like that," Momma said, her eyes catching me up in real warning though I could see that she was holding down a smile.

"Well, he can't do nothing to me when I'm with you, can he?" I asked, striving to match the rise and fall of her black pumps.

She said nothing. She just walked on, churning away under a sun that clearly meant to melt us. From here to the tracks it was mostly gardens. It felt like the Dixie Peach I'd used to help water-wave my hair was sliding down with the sweat on my face, and my throat was tight with thirst. Boy, did I want a pop. I looked at the last little store before we crossed the tracks without bothering to ask.

Across the tracks, there were no stores and no gardens. It was shady, and the grass was June green. Perfect-looking houses sat in unfenced spaces far back from the street. We walked these five blocks without a word. We just looked and hurried to get through it. I was beginning to worry about the welfare office in earnest. A fool could see that in this part of Ecorse, things got serious.

We had been on welfare for almost a year. I didn't have any strong feelings about it — my life went on pretty much the same. It just meant watching the mail for a check instead of Daddy getting paid, and occasional visits from a social worker that I'd always managed to miss. For Momma and whoever went with her, it meant this walk to the office and whatever went on there that made everyone hate to go. For Daddy, it seemed to bring the most change. For him, it meant staying away from home more than when he was working and a reason not to answer the phone.

At Jefferson, we turned left and there it was, halfway down the block. The Department of Social Services. I discovered some strong feelings. That fine name meant nothing. This was the welfare. The place for poor people. People who couldn't or wouldn't take care of themselves. Now I was going to face it, and suddenly I thought what I knew the others had thought, *What if I see someone I know?* I wanted to run back all those blocks to home.

FACT

The federal and state spending on AFDC is about $22 billion a year — $128 billion less than the government spent on the bail-out resulting from the Savings and Loans crisis. That means the money lost for the S & L crisis could have paid for AFDC in all 50 states for nearly seven years.

(Source: *Boston Globe*, May 17, 1994.)

I looked at Momma for comfort, but her face was closed and her mouth looked locked.

Inside, the place was gray. There were rows of long benches like church pews facing each other across a middle aisle that led to a central desk. Beyond the benches and the desk, four hallways led off to a maze of partitioned offices. In opposite corners, huge fans hung from the ceiling, humming from side to side, blowing the heavy air for a breeze.

Momma walked to the desk, answered some questions, was given a number and told to take a seat. I followed her through, trying not to see the waiting people — as though that would keep them from seeing me.

Gradually, as we waited, I took them all in. There was no one there that I knew, but somehow they all looked familiar. Or maybe I only thought they did, because when your eyes connected with someone's, they didn't quickly look away and they usually smiled. They were mostly women and children, and a few low-looking men. Some of them were white, which surprised me. I hadn't expected to see them in there.

Directly in front of the bench where we sat, a little girl with blond curls was trying to handle a bottle of Coke. Now and then, she'd manage to turn herself and the bottle around and watch me with big gray eyes that seemed to know quite well how badly I wanted a pop. I thought of asking Momma for fifteen cents so I could get one from the machine in the back but I was afraid she'd still say no so I just kept planning more and more convincing ways to ask. Besides, there was a water fountain near the door if I could make myself rise and walk to it.

We waited three hours. White ladies dressed like secretaries kept coming out to call numbers, and people on the benches would get up and follow down a hall. Then more people came in to replace them. I drank water from the fountain three times and was ready to put my feet up on the bench before us — the little girl with the Coke and her momma got called — by the time we heard Momma's number.

"You wait here," Momma said as I rose with her.

I sat down with a plop.

The lady with the number looked at me. Her face reminded me of the librarian's at Bunch school. Looked like she never cracked a smile. "Let her come." she said.

"She can wait here," Momma repeated, weakly.

"It's OK. She can come in. Come on," the lady insisted at me.

I hesitated, knowing that Momma's face was telling me to sit.

"Come on," the woman said.

Momma said nothing.

I got up and followed them into the maze. We came to a small room where there was a desk and three chairs. The woman sat behind the desk and we before it.

For a while, no one spoke. The woman studied a folder open before her, brows drawn together. On the wall behind her there was a calendar with one heavy black line drawn slantwise through each day of August, up to the twenty-first. That was today.

"Mrs. Blue, I have a notation here that Mr. Blue has not reported to the department on his efforts to obtain employment since the sixteenth of June. Before that, it was the tenth of April. You understand that department regulations require that he report monthly to this office, do you not?" Eyes brown as a wren's belly came up at Momma.

"Yes," Momma answered, sounding as small as I felt.

"Can you explain his failure to do so?"

Pause. "He's been looking. He says he's been looking."

"That may be. However, his failure to report those efforts here is my only concern."

Silence.

"We cannot continue with your case as it now stands if Mr. Blue refuses to comply with departmental regulations. He is still residing with the family, is he not?"

"Yes, he is. I've been reminding him to come in … he said he would."

"Well, he hasn't. Regulations are that any able-bodied man, head-of-household and receiving assistance who neglects to report to this office any effort to obtain work for a period of sixty days or more is to be cut off for a minimum of three months,

> *Poverty is no disgrace,*
> *but no honor either.*
>
> YIDDISH PROVERB

93

at which time he may reapply. As of this date, Mr. Blue is over sixty days delinquent, and officially, I am obliged to close the case and direct you to other sources of aid."

"What is that?"

"Aid to Dependent Children would be the only source available to you. Then, of course, you would not be eligible unless it was verified that Mr. Blue was no longer residing with the family."

Another silence. I stared into the gray steel front of the desk, everything stopped but my heart.

"Well, can you keep the case open until Monday? If he comes in by Monday?"

"According to my records, Mr. Blue failed to come in May and such an agreement was made then. In all, we allowed him a period of seventy days. You must understand that what happens in such cases as this is not wholly my decision." She sighed and watched Momma with hopeless eyes, tapping the soft end of her pencil on the papers before her. "Mrs. Blue, I will speak to my superiors on your behalf. I can allow you until Monday next…that's the" — she swung around to the calendar — "twenty-sixth of August, to get him in here."

"Thank you. He'll be in," Momma breathed. "Will I be able to get the clothing order today?"

Hands and eyes searched in the folder for an answer before she cleared her throat and tilted her face at Momma. "We'll see what we can do," she said, finally.

My back touched the chair. Without turning my head, I moved my eyes down to Momma's dusty feet and wondered if she could still feel them; my own were numb. I felt bodyless — there was only my face, which wouldn't disappear, and behind it, one word pinging against another in a buzz that made no sense. At home, we'd have the house cleaned by now, and I'd be waiting for the daily appearance of my best friend, Bernadine, so we could comb each other's hair or talk about stuck-up Evelyn and Brenda. Maybe Bernadine was already there, and Stella was teaching her to dance the bop.

Then I heard our names and ages — all eight of them — being called off like items in a grocery list.

"Clifford, Junior, age fourteen." She waited.

"Yes."

"Born? Give me the month and year."

"October 1946," Momma answered, and I could hear in her voice that she'd been through these questions before.

"Stella, age thirteen."

"Yes."

"Born?"

"November 1947."

"Minerva, age twelve." She looked at me. "This is Minerva?"

"Yes."

No. I thought, no, this is not Minerva. You can write it down if you want to, but Minerva is not here.

"Born?"

"December 1948."

The woman went on down the list, sounding more and more like Momma should be sorry or ashamed, and Momma's answers grew fainter and fainter. So this was welfare. I wondered how many times Momma had had to do this. Once before? Three times? Every time?

More questions. How many in school? Six. Who needs shoes? Everybody.

"Everybody needs shoes? The youngest two?"

"Well, they don't go to school … but they walk."

My head came up to look at Momma and the woman. The woman's mouth was left open. Momma didn't blink.

The brown eyes went down. "Our allowances are based on the median costs for moderately priced clothing at Sears, Roebuck." She figured on paper as she spoke. "That will mean thirty-four dollars for children over ten … thirty dollars for children under ten. It comes to one hundred ninety-eight dollars. I can allow eight dollars for two additional pairs of shoes."

"Thank you."

"You will present your clothing order to a salesperson at the store, who will be happy to assist you in your selections. Please be practical as further clothing requests will not be considered for a period of six months. In cases of necessity, however, requests for winter outerwear will be considered beginning November first."

Momma said nothing.

The woman rose and left the room.

For the first time, I shifted in the chair. Momma was looking into the calendar as though she could see through the pages to November first. Everybody needed a coat.

I'm never coming here again, I thought. If I do, I'll stay out front. Not coming back in here. Ever again.

She came back and sat behind her desk. "Mrs. Blue, I must make it clear that, regardless of my feelings, I will be forced to close your case if your husband does not report to this office by Monday, the twenty-sixth. Do you understand?"

"Yes. Thank you. He'll come. I'll see to it."

"Very well." She held a paper out to Momma.

We stood. Momma reached over and took the slip of paper. I moved toward the door.

"Excuse me, Mrs. Blue, but are you pregnant?"

"What?"

"I asked if you were expecting another child."

"Oh. No, I'm not," Momma answered, biting down on her lips.

"Well, I'm sure you'll want to be careful about a thing like that in your present situation."

"Yes."

I looked quickly to Momma's loose white blouse. We'd never known when another baby was coming until it was almost there.

"I suppose that eight children are enough for anyone," the woman said, and for the first time her face broke into a smile.

Momma didn't answer that. Somehow, we left the room and found our way out onto the street. We stood for a moment as though lost. My eyes followed Momma's up to where the sun was burning high. It was still there, blazing white against a cloudless blue. Slowly, Momma put the clothing order into her purse and snapped it shut. She looked around as if uncertain which way to go. I led the way to the corner. We turned. We walked the first five blocks.

I was thinking about how stupid I'd been a year ago, when Daddy lost his job. I'd been happy.

"You-all better be thinking about moving to Indianapolis," he announced one day after work, looking like he didn't think much of it himself. He was a welder with the railroad compa-

96

ny. He'd worked there for eleven years. But now, "Company's moving to Indianapolis," he said. "Gonna be gone by November. If I want to keep my job, we've got to move with it."

We didn't. Nobody wanted to move to Indianapolis — not even Daddy. Here, we had uncles, aunts and cousins on both sides. Friends. Everybody and everything we knew. Daddy could get another job. First came unemployment compensation. Then came welfare. Thank goodness for welfare, we said, while we waited and waited for the job that hadn't yet come.

The problem was that Daddy couldn't take it. If something got repossessed or somebody took sick or something was broken or another kid was coming, he'd carry on terribly until things got better — by which time things were always worse. He'd always been that way. So when the railroad left, he began to do everything wrong. Stayed out all hours. Drank and drank some more. When he was home, he was so grouchy we were afraid to squeak. Now when we saw him coming, we got lost. Even our friends ran for cover.

At the railroad tracks, we sped up. The tracks were as far across as a block was long. Silently, I counted the rails by the heat of the steel bars through my thin soles. On the other side, I felt something heavy rise up in my chest and I knew that I wanted to cry. I wanted to cry or run or kiss the dusty ground. The little houses with their sun-scorched lawns and backyard gardens were mansions in my eyes. "Ohh, Ma …look at those collards!"

"Umm-humm," she agreed, and I knew that she saw it too.

"Wonder how they grew so big?"

"Cow dung, probably. Big Poppa used to put cow dung out to fertilize the vegetable plots, and everything just grew like crazy. We used to get tomatoes this big" — she circled with her hands — "and don't talk about squash or melons."

"I bet y'all ate like rich people. Bet y'all had everything you could want."

"We sure did," she said. "We never wanted for anything when it came to food. And when the cash crops were sold, we could get whatever else that was needed. We never wanted for a thing."

FACT

Only 3 in 100 households now conform to the traditional family headed by a working husband with a non-working wife and two children at home.

(Source: Census Bureau, 1990.)

Summary

After registering almost no growth during the 1970s and 1980s, the median family income fell in the early 1990s.

Going Down

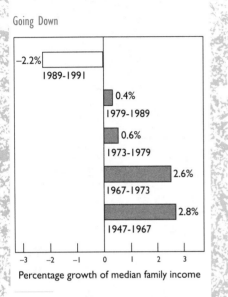

Percentage growth of median family income

Source: Economic Policy Institute (1993).

"What about the time you and cousin Emma threw out the supper peas?"

"Oh! Did I tell you about that?" she asked. Then she told it all over again. I didn't listen. I watched her face and guarded her smile with a smile of my own.

We walked together, step for step. The sun was still burning, but we forgot to mind it. We talked about an Alabama girlhood in a time and place I'd never know. We talked about the wringer washer and how it could be fixed, because washing every day on a scrub-board was something Alabama could keep. We talked about how to get Daddy to the Department of Social Services.

Then we talked about having babies. She began to tell me things I'd never known, and the idea of womanhood blossomed in my mind like some kind of suffocating rose.

"Momma," I said, "I don't think I can be a woman."

"You can," she laughed, "and if you live, you will be. You gotta be some kind of woman."

"But it's hard," I said, "sometimes it must be hard."

"Umm-humm," she said, "sometimes it is hard."

When we got to the bad block, we crossed to Beaman's drugstore for two orange crushes. Then we walked right through the groups of men standing in the shadows of the poolroom and the Moonflower Hotel. Not one of them said a word to us. I supposed they could see in the way we walked that we weren't afraid. We'd been to the welfare office and back again. And the facts of life, fixed in our minds like the sun in the sky, were no burning mysteries.

FROM: *Memory of Kin*, edited by Mary Helen Washington, 1991.

On and then off welfare

AN INTERVIEW WITH JACQUELINE POPE

Dr. Jacqueline Pope is associate professor of political science at Richard Stockton College of New Jersey, with a Ph.D. in Urban Planning from Columbia University. During the War on Poverty, in the late 1960s, she was a welfare rights activist and a mother receiving public assistance. What follows are excerpts from an interview with Dr. Pope conducted in 1994 by the producers of Blackside, Inc.'s documentary series, America's War on Poverty.

I went on welfare because of a divorce and, as I tell women, all of us are one divorce away from public assistance.

When I first went on welfare, I was very ashamed and also extremely angry with my husband for putting me in such a position that I had to ask for assistance....

[Going into the welfare office] was very difficult and the workers were so terrible to the people coming in. It was like they were literally opening their own pockets and taking out the money to give it to you. It was just awful. And you felt so degraded by the whole process.

....You had to bring your children with you because they didn't take your word that you had x number of children. So you had to bring them so they would be there and usually we

Photo: Dr. Ralph Bean, 1994

were there all day. You had to bring rent receipts, you had to bring doctor receipts if there were any. If someone loaned you some money, you had to bring a note from that person saying that that person had loaned you $10 last week. I mean, everything you can think of. And usually all of us would bring our receipts in a brown paper bag. It was like that was our attaché case. We would have everything.

[When the case worker came to your home] that was the worst of all. They would come to your house. Look around your house. Some of them, not all of them, but some of them would actually look in your closets and just take total liberty with the place where you were living, and I think the worst thing was they questioned your children. "Was anyone here? What has been going on since the last time I was here?" Which totally undermined the family unit because the kids being kids will say after the case worker goes, "Well, if you do this or if I can't go outside, I am going to tell the case worker when the case worker returns."

USDA

Food Stamp Program

During the Great Depression, the federal government distributed farm crops in a double effort to feed Americans who could not afford to eat and to relieve farmers whose goods were stockpiling with a shrinking market. In 1961, the Food Stamp program was revived to meet the same ends: to feed hungry Americans and to support the domestic agriculture economy.

To receive federal vouchers for groceries, administered through state welfare agencies, families must meet income and employment criteria and may use the stamps only to purchase food. In 1993, the U.S. Department of Agriculture (USDA) counted nearly 27 million people receiving food stamps, more than half of them children, with an average recipient getting coupons for $69 worth of food each month.

"We have a tremendous opportunity through the Food Stamp Program to educate recipients, to help them to make food purchases based on sound nutrition," said Ellen Haas, Assistant Secretary, Food & Consumer Services, USDA. "If we seize the opportunity, the program is transformed into 27 million opportunities each month to change lives."

In recent years, congressional acts have aimed to reduce the chances for fraudulent use of food stamps, while making a concurrent effort to expand the program to serve homeless people. Restaurants can now be authorized to accept food stamps in exchange for some low-cost meals for elderly or disabled people.

For more information, contact USDA Food and Nutrition Service, Office of Consumer Affairs, 3101 Park Center Drive, Room 813-B, Alexandria, VA 22302; (703) 305-2286.

Douglas, Wyoming: An Oral History

CONNIE ARTHUR

Connie Arthur's oral history is an account of a "blended" family — one in which a married couple brings children from a previous relationship into their household. Currently, nearly 50 percent of all U.S. marriages end in divorce (the highest rate in the world). Alcohol abuse and sudden unemployment have caused Ms. Arthur's family a great deal of trouble, though she is holding on. It is worth noting that in 1990 our funding for prisons was 99 percent higher than it was in 1979. The number of people serving time in prison increased from 329,000 in 1980 to 948,000 in 1993. (The United States has the highest per capita incarceration rate in the world.)

I get my schedule from Safeway on Fridays, and you might say my life goes according to that schedule. I plan my other jobs around it.

So if on a Tuesday I have to be at Safeway at 4:00 in the morning, I get up at 2:00 A.M. — earlier when the roads freeze and it's twenty, thirty below — do the paper route for the *Casper Tribune*, which is about eighty-five papers, then go to the store, stock shelves. Take off at 6:00 A.M. on my lunch-hour break and do the *USA Today* papers. Then clock back in at Safeway and work until 10:00. Take a fifteen-minute coffee break and then work 'til 1:00 P.M. Then go to the Country Inn to clean until 2:00. It's mostly do the kitchen floor, the bathrooms, vacuum, wash the windows. All in all, that makes about a twelve-hour workday.

I make about $91 a month on the *Casper* papers, and on *USA Today* I clear $22 to $36. At my Country Inn job, I get $5 an hour, and I usually work about thirteen to sixteen hours a week.

We have been unable to locate Connie Arthur. This interview appeared in *Below the Line: Living Poor in America* by Eugene Richards, 1987.

Summary

There are now 10 times more people living in mobile homes than there were in 1950.

Mobile Homes

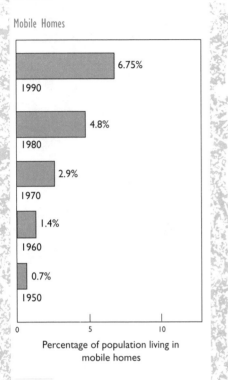

6.75%
1990

4.8%
1980

2.9%
1970

1.4%
1960

0.7%
1950

0   5   10

Percentage of population living in mobile homes

Source: U.S. Census Bureau (1990); American Housing Survey; American Red Cross.

Then at Safeway, I get $8.83 an hour, and since the first of the year I'd say I've averaged about twenty-six hours a week.

So that makes a yearly salary of about $13,000 — that's barely enough for a family in Wyoming. We have a mobile home. It's too small for us really, but then it's ours. I'm making payments on it. I'll have it paid off in one year. I pay $216 a month plus the trailer space, which is $135, plus utilities.

Originally, you know, I'm not from Wyoming. I was born in Yakima, Washington, and raised in Sacramento, California. I lived in Oregon ten years and I've been here in Wyoming about six now.

I'm six nationalities. Heinz variety. I'm German, Irish, Scotch, Spanish *and* Mexican, and Aztec. 'Cause my dad's father came from Spain and my dad's mom is an Aztec Indian out of Mexico City.

In our family, there was four of us children, two boys and two girls. I was the oldest, so I always had a lot of responsibilities. When they did something wrong, I was punished for it.

But the bigger problem that I faced was a nationality one, my dad being dark and Latin and my mom white and of Anglo people. We just experienced things. Like when we went to Yakima to visit my mother's family. I was pushing my cousin in the stroller and she was very white with a red head and some ladies came out of a department store and called me a dirty Mexican and spit at me. And then when I went down to visit my dad's people, I was sort of shut out because I didn't speak the nationality.

We were raised on farms and we had chores to do, and on the weekends we cut wood and got nightcrawlers and helped my dad. Everything was kept immaculate. He had white glove inspections in the house and if things got broke, you would be punished. He had a big two-inch belt. I have a scar here to this day from the buckle.

He beat my mom, too. Just for stupid little things. Like when she was ten minutes late coming home from work. He was a very mean person. He was a very unhappy man himself, an unhappy child himself. I can see that now.

I finished high school. I wanted to be a policewoman, but I was too short. I'm five even. See, in our society when I graduated in 1961, we had a lot of discriminations because of your height and your weight. In fact, I just barely made it into the service. You had to be five even and weigh over 110.

I went into the navy. I was a secretary/receptionist. And the service did a lot for me. It really helped me learn how to talk to people and to have self-confidence. See, my dad raised us the old Mexican way where the man's the boss, the women don't say nothing.

I was three years in the navy. I didn't go overseas, but I got to go places in the United States I never had been before. So for me it was a lot. I was on my own and it was different. Very different.

I met my first husband when I was in the navy. He was Hispanic and in the marines. We both got discharged the same day. I would have spent more time there, but I found out I was gonna have a baby, and then you couldn't have babies in the service.

So we got married and moved to New Mexico where my husband's mama and daddy lived. But I picked the wrong one. My husband just didn't have no spine. When we had a problem, instead of talking it out with me, he went home to his mother.

Maybe I was too young, too, I don't know. I was nineteen, twenty, and I wasn't really happy to be having a baby.

After we got divorced, I suddenly had all this freedom. It was hard for me to adjust. I had been so much under the thumb before and there were all these things I had never done.

I got into drinking. And it totally messed up my life, I'd say from twenty-one on up until twenty-five. I wasn't happy married, but I wasn't happy divorced and then I remarried again and then I had one affair and then I had my baby boy and then I ended up stuck in New Mexico and then I got back to California. Then I had another boy and I had to give him up for adoption 'cause at that time I was about ready to go to the nuthouse.

Finally, I moved up to Placerville, California, and that's how I met Jack. And I met him in a bar and he liked to drink, I liked to drink, and I guess we lived together for a year and then we got married.

We used to fight a lot. Really bad battles. We'd try to outthink each other and smash each other's cars and I'd catch him with

FACT

One in every 16 Americans lives in a mobile home; the percentage is as high as 1 in 5 residents in Montana and 1 in 6 in Wyoming and South Carolina.

(Source: Census Bureau, 1990.)

FACT

The median income for mobile-home households is $18,758, compared to $27,735 in all other households.

(Source: Census Bureau, 1990.)

the girls and try to shoot him with a gun or wait up at night with a bow and arrow for him. Just crazy things.

Still, I stuck with him, married and stuck with him. I don't know why. Probably because I'm not perfect and he's not perfect. We lived a hard life for about five or six years there, and I'm very ashamed of how I treated my life and my kids during those years. I just really screwed up to tell you the truth.

Then one day I came home and we'd been out drinking and the kids were crying and the baby-sitter was asleep and I looked at myself and I looked around and seen what I was doing and I stopped. Just like that. I can't explain it. Maybe the Virgin Mary talked to me, I don't know.

I became like a workhorse. I made sure we had things, whether Jack made money or not. I'd always find work, even when I was pregnant. There's always work. Whether cleaning a barn out, cleaning bathrooms. Some piddling little job. I had a lot of pride. I might have screwed up, but I still had a lot of pride. I'd only go to the welfare when there was no other way to have medical treatment.

Jack kept on drinking. He's a very big man, and he can drink whiskey, wine for two, three days straight. He's tried to stop. He has. He used to go to the AA meeting. But when there's no work and it's wintertime and maybe I complain too much that he's sitting on his butt … Jack's a half-breed, half Shoshone. He was raised in a very lonely life. His mother died when he was three years old, and after his dad died he was raised in foster homes. So he has a story too behind him.

After Placerville, we moved on to Oregon, God's country. We had a little farm up there, and we worked in the sawmills. We were doing really good. But then the work for Jack went down, and he came here. He talked me into coming too. Now I could kick myself in the bottom.

But see, back then, five years ago, the oil boom was on. The population of Douglas was up to ten thousand people. Oh, my God, it was unbelievable. People were making money like crazy. They were paying, what, fourteen bucks an hour plus travel pay, good benefits, the whole works. So Jack got a job in the oil fields, on the pipeline. And then what happened? The oil boom went down, the pipeline closed up. Jack was one of the last to go.

He started to drink. He got disgusted with our society, our government, and himself. He blew paychecks and unemployment checks and lied to me about money. And it always ended up on the same old junk, you know, fightin', and fightin', and fightin'.

Finally, Jack got in real bad trouble and got put away. That was two years, six months ago. He got into a four-day drunk and then supposedly done this certain thing which I don't believe is true. They charged him with third-degree sexual assault. No physical evidence. The jury was out twelve hours, but they gave him four to five years. It hurt me terrible. Because I knew he didn't do this one. I know him. If anyone knows Jack, I do. But because he's had a bad record and he's been in prison before, they just socked it to him.

The prison's 152 miles from here. I have to drive down there and I have to be there by eight o'clock in the morning. It's hard to even get a day off because I have to pay people to do my paper routes and things. But it's important for me to keep the family functioning.

While Jack's been in prison, my boy's got in trouble three times and my daughter's got in a little trouble, too. My son's a good boy, an honest boy, but he had a problem with marijuana and he got arrested, and he got drunk one day and burglarized one of his friend's house. Stupid stuff. Then with Marcie, she fights in school. They had to put her on probation.

I've been on my own supporting the family for nearly three years now. Sometimes I get terribly depressed. I have considered taking my life. Because it comes to the point where it seems no matter what I did, everything was going wrong. I felt that nobody cared. One time, oh, I desperately needed someone to talk to. They have a crisis line here you can contact, and I went down there and the first thing the lady did was hand me a paper to fill out what my income was, what my insurance would cover. Now, if you're in a mental state where you're about to commit suicide, do you think you're gonna have time to fill out papers? I crumpled them up and told the woman, "I'm here to get some help, not to fill out forms. Do you want me to go

> *Poverty is the parent of revolution and crime.*
>
> ARISTOTLE
> Greek Philosopher

FACT

During the 1980s, the fastest growing category of housing was prisons. More than 1 in 250 Americans were housed in a correctional facility — the highest incarceration rate in the world. The second fastest growing category during the decade was mobile homes. The number of mobile homes grew by 60 percent to comprise more than one in seven of the nation's residences.

(Source: Census Bureau, 1990.)

FACT

In 1980, the census counted 315,974 inmates of correctional institutions. Ten years later, the prison population had almost tripled to 1.1 million, or more than the entire population of Detroit.

(Source: Census Bureau, 1990.)

outside and run in front of a car or something?" She just sort of looked at me, you know, like what's wrong with her.

I only have one kid left at home now. Marcie, who's spirited like me. She's fourteen, smokes like a fiend. My oldest daughter's married and living in Oregon. And my boy — who's turned eighteen — he decided to get married this year.

So with my son gone and Jack still away, I get lonely sometimes. Especially on holidays. Christmastime especially. And it's not just physically being alone. It's mentally. You don't have no one to communicate with.

But I do have my jobs and my daughter and my dogs and cats. And Jack'll be up for parole soon. He goes up for parole the eleventh of September, next week.

If they don't let him out, I try to tell myself that I can make it through another winter here. But I don't know. Sometimes I feel I can't handle it no more. I just can't physically and mentally. Because there's just so much you can do and winters are so hard. It gets so cold.

FROM: *Below the Line: Living Poor in America*, 1987.

Options for Recovery

Helping mothers recover from drug abuse

The bilingual counselors at Options for Recovery focus on helping mothers of young children or pregnant women recover from drug or alcohol abuse and improve their parenting skills. The programs are offered at nine sites in southern California.

Through a regular program of individual and group counseling, mothers of children under three or pregnant women work on strategies and techniques that will allow them to face the stresses of parenting without yielding to the pull of narcotics.

Women make a weekly commitment to attend sessions five hours a day, Monday through Friday. Options for Recovery offers child care, transportation assistance, two meals each day, and intensive individual and group counseling.

The staff at Options for Recovery also assist women whose children have been removed from them due to drug and alcohol abuse. Through a series of supervised visits and assistance specific to each family situation, the counselors help women meet the requirements to regain custody of their children.

For more information, contact Options for Recovery, 251 Palomar Street, Suite A, Chula Vista, CA 91911; (619) 498-0908.

OPTIONS FOR
RECOVERY

Families First

A family support and preservation program

"Nancy" had five children and lived in a dangerous housing project in Atlanta. For years, she had used heroin, cocaine, crack — just about any drug she could get her hands on. She neglected her children to the point where the county department of children and families had to intervene.

The agency, cautioning Nancy that she was on the verge of losing her children, referred her to the Family Preservation Program of Families First. Nancy began receiving the around-the-clock assistance of a social worker and parent aide in getting her life back together. Thus, she began the slow process of recovery, sometimes slipping, but always finding her way back.

Today she's married, involved in group drug counseling, living in a safer neighborhood, and working in a hospital. "If it weren't for help from Families First, either I or one of my children would probably be dead now," she said.

The Family Preservation Program is one of a wide range of social and mental health services provided by Families First in metropolitan Atlanta. Its professional counselors and support staff help families cope with such issues as teenage pregnancy, abused children, domestic violence, drug addiction, and child adoption, regardless of ability to pay.

For more information, write Families First, 1105 West Peachtree Street, NW, P.O. Box 7948, Station C, Atlanta, GA 30357-0948; (404) 853-2800.

families first®
Help for Generations

Parents Anonymous

A self-help program for parents

Parents Anonymous (PA) is a national treatment and prevention program for child abuse and neglect, a self-help program for parents. Parents who join PA are looking for a way out of the cycle of abuse. Members meet weekly in small group sessions, where they can vent their frustrations, share ideas, and find a shoulder to lean on. Co-led by a volunteer human-services professional and a parent member, the meetings are free of charge, and confidentiality is protected.

The majority of PA parents were themselves victims of abuse or neglect as children. Such was the case with Jolly K., a California mother who co-founded the group in 1970. Even with therapy, Jolly K. had been unable to stop battering the younger of her two daughters. She told her social worker, Leonard Lieber, "If I could sit down with someone who had problems like mine, maybe we could sort things out together and come up with a better way."

Joining forces with another mother who was struggling to overcome her abusive behavior, Jolly K. and Lieber started what became the original chapter of Parents Anonymous. Both mothers stopped abusing their children, and PA soon grew into a national support network, with 55 offices now active in 48 states.

Evaluation studies have shown that PA is truly effective in reducing abusive behavior and helping parents cope. With the emotional support of their peers, parents feel less socially isolated and can begin to develop more constructive parenting skills.

For more information, check the white pages of your local telephone directory under "Parents Anonymous," or call the national organization at (909) 621-6184.

Confronting Slaughter in the Streets

BRENT STAPLES

Pervasive poverty is clearly linked to violent crime for many reasons. One to which writer Brent Staples calls urgent attention is the phenomenon of violence caused by the high density of poor people living in public housing. He calls for an "evacuation plan" for American cities. Not many nonpoor neighborhoods have shown an openness toward receiving the "evacuated" poor. And few, if any, poor communities are eager to admit defeat and send their young men away. The program profiles that follow Mr. Staples's essay provide evidence that there is much experimenting going on with remedies that seek to save individuals and families by moving them out as well as remedies that attempt to rebuild and improve communities so there is less need for people to leave.

My cousin Paul was shot to death at the age of 16. My brother Blake, a dealer of cocaine, was murdered at 22. My boyhood friend Stephen, number 14 on our football team, was shot four times in the head while conducting his heroin business. A second Stephen, in what sounded like a crack-induced frenzy, murdered three people, one of whom I also knew, then hanged himself in jail. I'd list more, except that space forbids it.

Most people who write for a living don't have lists like this. That's because most people who write for a living are white, and white people tend to die of natural causes. Black people, especially black men, are murdered in inordinately high numbers. Thus, those of us who make up the new and tenuous black middle class live with a grisly backdrop. The prematurely dead number so many that we sort them by category: the violently

Brent Staples is the author of *Parallel Times* and is currently a member of the editorial board of *The New York Times*. He has also served as an editor of the *Book Review*.

dead; the drug-addicted, dead of overdoses; the nearly dead, whose departures we expect at any moment.

In the language of the streets, a person shot to death is sometimes said to have been "smoked," as in incinerated. The metaphor fits conveniently with the notion of a holocaust. From the Greek *holokauston*, the word refers to a sacrifice consumed by fire. What else to call it when black men between the ages of 15 and 24 are murdered at *10 times* the national average?

The slaughter is omnipresent but gets little direct attention until events bring it into focus. One such event was Mayor Sharon Pratt Kelly's attempt to call out the National Guard in Washington, D.C., murder capital of the universe. Another was Senator Daniel Patrick Moynihan's suggestion of an ammunition tax to slow the killing and help finance the Clinton health care program. Still another was Jesse Jackson's national campaign to stem urban violence.

Speaking to high school students in New York, Mr. Jackson invoked images of the civil rights struggle, and compared young people who carry weapons and drugs to the Klansmen who once roamed the night in sheets. The analogy was stirring but simplistic.

The Klan of old was flesh and blood, and relatively easy to isolate. The violence that stalks the cities today is a ghostly presence, made of self-loathing and rage. It haunts the souls of teenage boys who are fatherless and lost, so much so that guns and gangs are the only solace. By fourth grade, those boys are finished at school and have jumped some mental track. By 16, they are so angry that they "smoke" you for staring at them.

Mr. Jackson's campaign is symbolically important but no substitute for legislative initiatives. Better policing and gun control are vital. So is the policy for cities that Bill Clinton might never get around to.

If ever he does, he should first sit down with Dr. David Satcher, the new director of the Centers for Disease Control. Dr. Satcher understands that urban violence is a public health issue and that the methods of prevention need to extend well beyond law enforcement.

During the time he was president of Meharry Medical College in Nashville, Dr. Satcher backed two support groups that

Summary

As of 1990, two-parent families were almost twice as likely to break up during a two-year period if they were living in poverty. The percentage for poor African-American families was 21, compared to 12 for white and 11 for Hispanic.

Poverty and Family Breakup

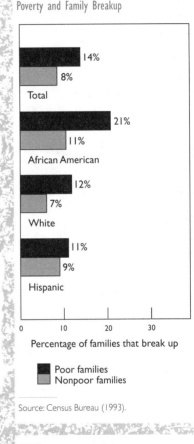

Percentage of families that break up

■ Poor families
▨ Nonpoor families

Source: Census Bureau (1993).

FACT

The marriage rate among African-Americans dropped 20 percentage points between 1970 and 1991 (64 percent to 44 percent), a decrease twice as marked as that of whites (from 73 percent to 64 percent). The rate for Hispanics remained stable at 61 percent to 62 percent.

(Source: *Los Angeles Times*, March 28, 1993.)

Summary

The number of deaths from drug overdoses and other related causes increased by 60 percent between 1980 and 1988. Male deaths almost doubled in that time period.

Drug Abuse

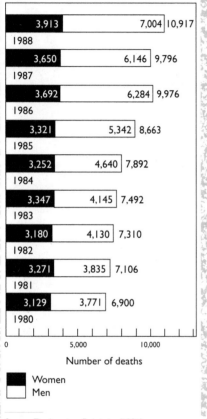

3,913	7,004	10,917
1988		
3,650	6,146	9,796
1987		
3,692	6,284	9,976
1986		
3,321	5,342	8,663
1985		
3,252	4,640	7,892
1984		
3,347	4,145	7,492
1983		
3,180	4,130	7,310
1982		
3,271	3,835	7,106
1981		
3,129	3,771	6,900
1980		

0   5,000   10,000

Number of deaths

■ Women
□ Men

Source: *The American Enterprise* (1991).

> *Your own property is at stake when your neighbor's house is on fire.*
>
> HORACE
> Roman Poet and Satirist

worked in public housing projects. One reclaimed junkies. The other encouraged teenagers to stay clear of trouble.

High-density public housing represents disastrous public policy; it magnifies pathology. Level the projects; disperse the poor into scattered-site housing, among neighbors who work and study and keep up their houses. It's wise policy. It's also light years away.

Meanwhile in the Bedford-Stuyvesant section of Brooklyn, Frances Davis has lost all her sons — three in six years — to butchery in the streets. The last, 18-year-old Frankie, was shot to death last summer near a public housing project. Surely Ms. Davis and thousands of other parents would rather their sons were alive and living in Wyoming, let's say, than dead at home. Remember how Britons shipped their children out of London during the bombing raids?

What American cities need are evacuation plans to spirit at least some black boys out of harm's way before it's too late. Inner-city parents who have the option ship their children to safety in the homes of relatives. Those who are without that resource deserve the aid extended to parents in London during World War II. One way to elude the slaughter is to outrun it.

FROM: *The New York Times*, November 5, 1993.

Gautreaux Program

Moving families out of public housing

The Gautreaux Assisted Housing Program is a Chicago-based initiative that helps low-income families move from the city to middle-class, white suburbs that offer better schools, safer environments, and greater job opportunities.

Created in the late 1970s, the program has since enabled nearly 5,700 families, most of them female-headed, to move out of public housing and into privately owned apartments. The program provides the families with rental subsidies and assistance in locating housing.

Named after Dorothy Gautreaux, a 1960s fair-housing activist, the program grew out of a class-action lawsuit that charged racial discrimination in Chicago public housing. The U.S. Supreme Court upheld the charges and the Gautreaux Program was devised as part of the court-ordered remedy.

The program is administered by the Leadership Council for Metropolitan Open Communities, a private, nonprofit fair-housing agency spawned by the civil rights movement. In 1994, the U.S. Department of Housing and Urban Development launched a five-city pilot project, modelled on the Gautreaux Program, to help low-income public housing families move into more affluent communities.

Some African-American leaders have criticized the Gautreaux program, accusing it of "skimming the cream" from inner-city neighborhoods by encouraging people to leave. Supporters point to the benefits experienced by Gautreaux participants. Most of the relocating families have been

pleased with their new environments, and some evidence suggests they have achieved gains in employment and education. One study, for example, found that 54 percent of the Gautreaux children went on to college, while only 21 percent of their city counterparts did.

For more information, contact Gautreaux Assisted Housing Program, 410 South State Street, Suite 860, Chicago, IL 60605; (312) 341-5640.

Operation Exodus Inner City

Moving children out of troubled neighborhoods

Operation Exodus Inner City (OEIC) is a small Christian ministry that tries to give poor Latino children in New York City a chance at a better life. The agency moves children from the mean streets of Washington Heights to the stable environment of schools across the country.

OEIC was started in 1988 by Luis Iza, Jr., a Sunday school teacher and businessman who grew up in the upper Manhattan neighborhood and witnessed the destructive effect of drugs, crime, and violence on families. "My kids are in a sense trapped in a situation where the cycle could not be broken," he said.

Working with the Fort Washington Heights Presbyterian Church and the Fort George Presbyterian Church, Iza has helped more than 100 children attend 31 different private and religious schools in New York City and across the country. The program accepts students from nursery school to 12th grade — many working below grade level — and includes a summer mentoring component. It should be noted that OEIC, in the belief that spiritual growth is the foundation of personal development, requires families to take part in its Christian ministry for a year before children are eligible for schooling.

Critics of Operation Exodus say that removing the students from their community is a mistake. They stress the importance of children learning pride of place and serving as role models.

Regardless, OEIC reports that within its entire history, only two students have ever left school. This is no small feat in a neighborhood where some high schools see more than half of their students drop out before graduation. All participating children of high school age have taken college preparatory classes, with all ten high school graduates currently in college.

For more information, contact Operation Exodus Inner City, 27 West 47th Street, Room 203, New York, NY 10036; (212) 391-8059.

Three Chicago Strategies

Critics of high-density public housing charge that, far from alleviating poverty, such programs often perpetuate it by concentrating the poor in high-rise buildings plagued by gangs and drugs, isolated from the rest of the city. In Chicago, several alternative public-housing strategies are the crux of that city's controversial program designed not to warehouse the poor but to integrate them into the working class.

Lake Parc Place

The first of these strategies is mixed-income housing, as demonstrated by Lake Parc Place, a high-rise apartment complex overlooking Lake Michigan. Reopened in 1991 by the Chicago Housing Authority (CHA) after extensive remodeling, Lake Parc Place now houses tenants drawn about equally from the ranks of welfare recipients and working families earning 50 percent to 80 percent of the Chicago-area median income. To make the housing attractive to working families, the apartments have been handsomely refurbished. The security is tight, the rules strict, and the buildings scrupulously maintained. Hailed by *Newsweek* magazine as "a housing program that actually works," Lake Parc Place is also seen as a success by most of its tenants.

High Rise to Townhouse

The CHA is now involved in a 10-year, $350-million plan to resurrect Cabrini-Green, one of the most notorious of the "vertical ghettoes." In the first phase, several high-rise buildings will be demolished and replaced by low-rise townhouses built by private developers and occupied by a mix of 75 percent middle-income people and 25 percent low-income. Only half of the new units will be constructed in and around Cabrini-Green; others will be built elsewhere in the city and suburbs — so-called scattered housing.

Housing Vouchers

Another tactic makes use of the federal Section 8 program, which provides low-income people with housing vouchers that they are free to use in the private rental market. Some Cabrini-Green residents may select this option as well.

CHA Chairman Vincent Lane acknowledges that each of these strategies has its limitations, but he argues in a *Chicago Tribune* article: "Central to each of these programs is the creation of neighborhoods with a socio-economic mix that will fundamentally change the nature of the community."

For more information, contact the Office of External Affairs, Chicago Housing Authority, 22 West Madison Street, Chicago, IL 60602; (312) 791-8513.

New Settlement Apartments

NSA
NEW SETTLEMENT APARTMENTS
ASHTON MANAGEMENT CORP., AGENT

At the New Settlement Apartments in Bronx, New York, formerly homeless families live side by side with low to middle income residents in a housing experiment designed to give homeless people a leg up into mainstream society.

Opened in 1990 after extensive rehabilitation, the 14-building complex is now home to more than 260 once-homeless families whose rents are paid by the city of New York. The rest of the 893 apartments are rented to working people with annual incomes up to $53,000, who pay rent on a sliding scale. These tenants find the complex attractive because of its clean, safe environment. Homeless families who have moved into the mixed-income development appreciate not only their new homes but their new neighbors, who they say are friendly and supportive.

Public policymakers advocate mixed-income housing because, they say, the working tenants provide positive role models for the formerly homeless residents. With that motivating influence, plus a stable home and the proper social services, indigent families can begin to pull themselves up from poverty.

The housing project is run by Settlement Housing Fund, a private agency. Project residents and others in the neighborhood have access to a variety of social services, including counseling, literacy classes, and after-school programs, which are funded by rent revenues and donations to the community groups that supply the services.

Although such housing developments are expensive to run, the success of New Settlement has led the city to build five similar projects in the Bronx and Harlem, with plans to create additional mixed-income housing throughout the city.

For more information, contact the Settlement Housing Fund, 1512 Townsend Ave., Bronx, NY 10452; (718) 716-8000.

Community Building in Partnership

Total community revitalization in Baltimore

Bringing about the complete turnaround of an impoverished Baltimore neighborhood is the mission of Community Building in Partnership (CBP), a multifaceted initiative that is supplying resources and tapping into the community's human energy in the troubled Sandtown-Winchester area of that city.

A 72-square-block neighborhood on Baltimore's west side, Sandtown, an African-American community, is home to 10,300 people, more than half of whom live in households with annual incomes under $10,000. It is also home to a host of urban ills, from abandoned housing to violent crime, high infant mortality and school dropout rates, unemployment, and teen pregnancy. CBP's plan for transforming the blighted Sandtown neighborhood targets the entire spectrum of community life—education, health and human services, employment, housing, recreation, commercial development, public safety, and community-building.

A partnership among Sandtown residents, the city of Baltimore, and the Enterprise Foundation, CBP began in 1990 and has since —often in cooperation with existing local groups — initiated nearly 90 projects and services. CBP renovated over 1,000 units of housing; instituted a health outreach program that links pregnant women to prenatal care and reduces infant mortality; and developed a community center offering after-school programs, parent education workshops, and childcare.

 Residents now plant and tend community gardens, volunteer for neighborhood crime watches, and publish their own neighborhood newspaper, the *Sandtown-Winchester Viewpoint*. Though there is still a long way to go, an overarching goal of the project is to empower and enable the community's residents to become self-sufficient. Residents are active in all of the renewal projects as well as in the planning of CBP's blueprint for change.

Funding for this laboratory of urban renewal, which has cost some $76 million already, comes from a variety of public and private sources. Many see CBP as a model for other cities.

"I don't think there's a community in the country that isn't moving in that direction," Christopher Walker of the Urban Institute told the *Detroit News and Free Press*. "What distinguishes Sandtown is [that] they paid an extraordinary amount of attention to citizen participation."

For more information, contact Community Building in Partnership, 1137 North Gilmor Street, Baltimore, MD 21217; (410) 728-8607.

On the Meaning of Plumbing and Poverty

MELANIE SCHELLER

Melanie Scheller's essay is a story about the complex psychological legacy of growing up poor. It is also a story about the simple conveniences and amenities that most of us take for granted — conveniences that, in fact, are not available to many people in the United States. According to the 1990 census, over a million homes lack complete plumbing facilities — more homes are equipped with television sets than with indoor toilets. Other basic amenities of modern life, such as the telephone, are not as universal as one might think. In five of six large cities surveyed by the Federal Communications Commission, the percentage of households without telephones almost doubled between 1988 and 1992.

If any one thing proves what bad shape this country is in, it is the growing number of children who live in poverty. In 1969, following the Kennedy and Johnson administrations, 9.7 million children, or 14 percent of all persons under age 18, were living in poverty. Twenty years later, at the end of the Reagan era, that figure had jumped to 12.6 million. A fifth of all U.S. children are now living in poverty. We're all aware of the physical problems poverty creates — hunger, cold, and illness, to name just a few — but only those who have experienced it can tell us about an insidious long-lasting psychological consequence: shame.

Several years ago I spent some time as a volunteer on the geriatric ward of a psychiatric hospital. I was fascinated by the behavior of one of the patients, an elderly woman who shuffled at regular intervals to the bathroom, where she methodically flushed the toilet. Again and again she carried out her sacred mission as if summoned by some supernatural force, until the flush of the toilet became a rhythmic counterpoint for the ward's activity. If someone blocked her path or if, God forbid,

Melanie Scheller won the North Carolina Writer's Network Creative Journalism Contest in 1990. She is the author of the children's book *My Grandfather's Hat*. Her writing has also appeared in *The Utne Reader*. She is currently working on an essay on the emergence of an artist through the experience of poverty.

the bathroom was in use when she reached it, she became agitated and confused.

Obviously, that elderly patient was a sick woman. And yet I felt a certain kinship with her, for I too have suffered from an obsession with toilets. I spent much of my childhood living in houses without indoor plumbing and, while I don't feel compelled to flush a toilet at regular intervals, I sometimes feel that toilets, or the lack thereof, have shaped my identity in ways that are painful to admit.

I'm not a child of the Depression, but I grew up in an area of the South that had changed little since the days of the New Deal. My mother was a widow with six children to support, not an easy task under any circumstances, but especially difficult in rural North Carolina during the 1960s. To her credit, we were never seriously in danger of going hungry. Our vegetable garden kept us stocked with tomatoes and string beans. We kept a few chickens and sometimes a cow. Blackberries were free for the picking in the fields nearby. Neighbors did their good Christian duty by bringing us donations of fresh fruit and candy at Christmastime. But a roof over our heads — that wasn't so easily improvised.

Like rural Southern gypsies, we moved from one dilapidated Southern farmhouse to another in a constant search for a decent place to live. Sometimes we moved when the rent increased beyond the 30 or 40 dollars my mother could afford. Or the house burned down, not an unusual occurrence in substandard housing. One year, when we were gathered together for Thanksgiving dinner, a stranger walked in without knocking and announced that we were being evicted. The house had been sold without our knowledge and the new owner wanted to start remodeling immediately. We tried to finish our meal with an attitude of thanksgiving while he worked around us with his tape measure.

Usually, we rented from farm families who'd moved from the old home place to one of the brick boxes that are now the standard in rural Southern architecture. The old farmhouse wasn't worth fixing up with a septic tank and flush toilet, but it was good enough to rent for a few dollars a month to families like mine. The idea of tenants' rights hadn't trickled down yet from

Summary

As of 1989, almost one-fifth of all poor households were living in deficient housing (with moderate to severe physical or structural problems). The situation was especially critical for poor black families, 29 percent of whom lived in such housing. As many as 26 percent of all poor Hispanic households lived in overcrowded housing.

Poor Housing

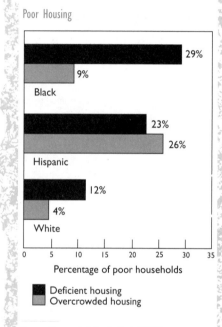

Percentage of poor households

- ■ Deficient housing
- ▨ Overcrowded housing

Source: Economic Policy Institute (1993).

the far reaches of the liberal North. It never occurred to us to demand improvements in the facilities. The ethic of the land said we should take what we could get and be grateful for it.

Without indoor plumbing, getting clean is a tiring and time-consuming ritual. At one point, I lived in a five-room house with six or more people, all of whom congregated in the one heated room to eat, do homework, watch television, dress and undress, argue, wash dishes. During cold weather we dragged mattresses from the unheated rooms and slept huddled together on the floor by the woodstove. For my bathing routine, I first pinned a sheet to a piece of twine strung across the kitchen. That gave me some degree of privacy from the six other people in the room. At that time, our house had an indoor cold-water faucet, from which I filled a pot of water to heat on the kitchen stove. It took several pots of hot water to fill the metal washtub we used.

Since I was a teenager and prone to sulkiness if I didn't get special treatment, I got to take the first bath while the water was still clean. The others used the water I left behind, freshened up with hot water from the pot on the stove. Then the tub had to be dragged to the door and the bath water dumped outside. I longed to be like the woman in the Calgon bath oil commercials, luxuriating in a marble tub full of scented water with bubbles piled high and stacks of thick, clean towels nearby.

People raised in the land of the bath-and-a-half may wonder why I make such a fuss about plumbing. Maybe they spent a year in the Peace Corps, or they backpacked across India, or they worked at a summer camp and, gosh, using a latrine isn't all that bad. And of course it's *not* that bad. Not when you can catch the next plane out of the country, or pick up your duffel bag and head for home, or call mom and dad to come and get you when things get too tedious. A sojourn in a Third World country, where everyone shares the same primitive facilities may cause some temporary discomfort, but the experience is soon converted into amusing anecdotes for cocktail-party conversation. It doesn't corrode your self-esteem with a sense of shame the way a childhood spent in chronic, unrelenting poverty can.

In the South of my childhood, not having indoor plumbing was the indelible mark of poor white trash. The phrase "so poor they didn't have a pot to piss in" said it all. Poor white trash were viciously stereotyped, and never more viciously than on the playground. White-trash children had cooties — everybody knew that. They had ringworm and pinkeye — don't get near them or you might catch it. They picked their noses. They messed in their pants. If a white-trash child made the mistake of catching a softball during recess, the other children made an elaborate show of wiping it clean before they would touch it.

Once a story circulated at school about a family whose infant daughter had fallen into the "slop jar" and drowned. When I saw the smirks and heard the laughter with which the story was told, I felt sick and afraid in the pit of my stomach. A little girl had died, but people were laughing. What had she done to deserve that laughter? I could only assume that using a chamber pot was something so disgusting, so shameful, that it made a person less than human.

My family was visibly and undeniably poor. My clothes were obviously hand-me-downs. I got free lunches at school. I went to the health department for immunizations. Surely it was equally obvious that we didn't have a flush toilet. But, like an alcoholic who believes no one will know he has a problem as long as he doesn't drink in public, I convinced myself that no one knew my family's little secret. It was a form of denial that would color my relationships with the outside world for years to come.

Having a friend from school spend the night at my house was out of the question. Better to be friendless than to have my classmates know my shameful secret. Home visits from teachers or ministers left me in a dither of anticipatory anxiety. As they chattered on and on with Southern small talk about tomato plants and relish recipes, I sat on the edge of my seat, tensed against the dreaded words, "May I use your bathroom, please?" When I began dating in high school, I'd lie in wait behind the front door, ready to dash out as soon as my date pulled in the driveway, never giving him a chance to hear the call of nature while on our property.

With the help of a scholarship I was able to go away to college, where I could choose from dozens of dormitory toilets and take as many hot showers as I wanted, but I could never openly express my joy in using the facilities. My roommates, each a pampered only child from a well-to-do family, whined and complained about having to share a bathroom. I knew that if I expressed delight in simply having a bathroom, I would immediately be labeled as a hick. The need to conceal my real self by stifling my emotions created a barrier around me and I spent my college years in a vacuum of isolation.

Almost 20 years have passed since I first tried to leave my family's chamber pot behind. For many of those years, it followed behind me — the ghost of chamber pots past — clanging and banging and threatening to spill its humiliating contents at any moment. I was convinced that everyone could see it, could smell it even. No college degree or job title seemed capable of banishing it.

If finances had permitted, I might have become an Elvis Presley or a Tammy Faye Bakker, easing the pain of remembered poverty with gold-plated bathtub fixtures and leopard-skinned toilet seats. I feel blessed that gradually, ever so gradually, the shame of poverty has begun to fade. The pleasures of the present now take priority over where a long-ago bowel movement did or did not take place. But, for many Southerners, chamber pots and outhouses are more than just memories.

In North Carolina alone, 200,000 people still live without indoor plumbing. People who haul their drinking water home from a neighbor's house or catch rainwater in barrels. People who can't wash their hands before handling food, the way restaurant employees are required by state law to do. People who sneak into public restrooms every day to wash, shave, and brush their teeth before going to work or to school. People who sacrifice their dignity and self-respect when forced to choose between going homeless and going to an outhouse. People whose children think they deserve the conditions in which they live and hold their heads low to hide the shame. But they're not the ones who should feel ashamed. No, they're not the ones who should feel ashamed.

FROM: *North Carolina Independent Weekly*, January 4, 1990.

PrairieFire Rural Action

Training, organizing, and advocating for family farmers

Through research and education, this rural non-profit organization helps family farmers respond to the many social and economic challenges facing them.

PrairieFire's program directors train and organize rural communities in the impact of corporate agriculture trends, the rights of immigrant and migrant workers, flood and other weather disaster recovery techniques, ecumenical initiatives in struggling rural congregations, the unique challenges of farm women, and land policy development.

The changing role of women, for example, is demonstrated by the high number of women now either working off the farm to supplement the family income or working on the farm, but doing manufacturing piecework instead of more traditional farm chores. As Kim Ode, writing in the *Minnesota Monthly* magazine, reflects, "The farm woman I hark back to doesn't exist anymore."

PrairieFire publishes information in journals such as *Prairie Journal* and *The Agribusiness Examiner* about changes affecting the workings of the family farm and offers organizing and training services to help local communities adjust and thrive. In addition to working with local communities, PrairieFire also collaborates with a wide variety of organizations to influence regional and national policies.

Founded in 1981, PrairieFire promotes social, environmental, and economic justice in farm policies and rural community economic issues. In response

to the growing pressures on agriculture from the international economy, PrairieFire publicly advocates for policies that will sustain family farms and keep rural communities economically sound.

For more information, contact PrairieFire, 550 11th Street, Des Moines, IA 50309; (515) 244-5671.

The Death of a Farm

AMY JO KEIFER

In the last 50 years, the number of farms in the United States has dropped by 66 percent. According to economists who describe such things, we were to have transitioned from an agricultural economy to an industrial economy years ago; our current transition ought to be from an industrial to an information or service economy. But people don't always change with changing economies. As Amy Jo Keifer points out in this brief essay, the call of family, tradition, and culture is often at odds with the evolving efficiency of the marketplace.

Bangor, PA — I am a farmer's daughter. I am also a 4-H member, breeder and showman of sheep, and showman of cattle. My family's farm is dying and I have watched it, and my family, suffer.

Our eastern Pennsylvania farm is a mere 60 acres. The green rolling hills and forested land are worth a minimum of $300,000 to developers, but no longer provide my family with the means to survive. It's a condition called asset rich and cash poor, and it's a hard way of life.

My grandfather bought our farm when he and my grandmother were first married. He raised dairy cattle and harvested the land full time for more than 20 years. When he died, my father took over and changed the farm to beef cattle, horses, and pigs, and kept the crops. But it wasn't enough to provide for a young family, so he took on a full-time job, too.

I can remember, when I was young, sitting on the fence with my sister and picking out a name for each calf. My sister's favorite cow was named Flower, and so we named her calves Buttercup, Daisy, Rose, and Violet. Flower was the leader of a herd of more than 20. The only cattle left on our farm now are my younger sister's and brother's 4-H projects.

Amy Jo Keifer graduated in 1994 from American University with a B.A. in International Relations. She teaches social studies at Paint Branch High School in Montgomery, Maryland.

124

I can remember a huge tractor-trailer backed into the loading chute of our barn on days when more than 200 pigs had to be taken to market. That was before the prices went down and my father let the barn go empty rather than take on more debt.

I can remember my father riding on the tractor, larger than life, bailing hay or planting corn. When prices started dropping, we began to rent some land to other farmers, so they could harvest from it. But prices have dropped so low this year there are no takers. The land will go unused; the tractor and the equipment have long since been sold off.

I don't remember the horses. I've seen a few pictures in which my father, slim and dark, is holding his newborn daughter on horseback amid a small herd. And I've heard stories of his delivering hay to farms all over the state, but I can't ever remember his loading up a truck to do it.

Piece by piece, our farm has deteriorated. We started breeding sheep and now have about 25 head, but they yield little revenue. My mother, who works as a registered nurse, once said something that will remain with me forever: "Your father works full time to support the farm. I work full time to support the family."

I've seen movies like "The River" and "Places in the Heart." They tell the real struggle. But people can leave a movie theater, and there's a happy ending for them. There aren't many happy endings in a real farmer's life. I was reared hearing that hard work paid off, while seeing that it didn't. My younger brother would like to take over the farm some day, but I'm not sure it will hold on much longer. Its final breath is near.

FROM: *The New York Times*, June 30, 1991.

Summary

Since 1980, the number of farmers under the age of 25 has dropped by half, while the number of those over 65 has held steady.

Vanishing Farmers

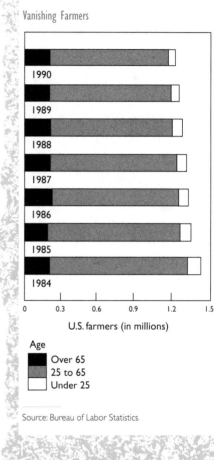

U.S. farmers (in millions)

Age
- ■ Over 65
- ▨ 25 to 65
- □ Under 25

Source: Bureau of Labor Statistics.

FACT

Between 1980 and 1990, farm employment in the United States declined 22 percent.

(Source: U.S. Department of Agriculture; U.S. Bureau of Economic Analysis.)

National Family Farm Coalition

A local and national advocacy group

National Family Farm Coalition

In a commitment to support the family farm system of agriculture, a rural way of life that many fear is nearing oblivion, the National Family Farm Coalition combines the efforts of farm advocacy and resource conservation groups from across the United States.

According to a U.S. Department of Agriculture (USDA) report (*The Economic Well-Being of Farm Operator Households 1988-1990*, USDA Economic Research Service analysis), "only $5,742 of the total income for farm operator households in 1990 was income from their farms." Of the 1.7 million farm operator households in the country in 1990, the USDA counts 21.9 percent of those below the poverty threshold.

"The economic situation in the countryside is bleak," testified Katherine Ozer, National Family Farm Coalition Director, at the USDA Public Forum on July 20, 1994. "Economic projections for moderate-sized farms are on the sharp downturn while over 40,000 farmers are on the brink of economic collapse due to drops in farm income in the last year alone."

Founded in 1986, the National Family Farm Coalition unites 39 member organizations from 30 states — grassroots farm alliances, produce associations, local activist groups, conservationists, and voters leagues. They testify at state and national hearings; advise government offices; and publicly advocate for such family farm issues as increased federal grants and loans to family farmers, minority farmer support, comprehensive health care reform, environmentally sound farming practices, and farm and food price policies that protect the future of the family farm.

"The rural economy needs to be revitalized from the farm up," said Denise O'Brien, Vice President of the National Family Farm Coalition at a USDA forum in August 1993. "Federal farm policy plays a critical role in helping to make this happen."

For more information, contact National Family Farm Coalition, 110 Maryland Avenue, NE, Suite 307, Washington, DC 20002; (202) 543-5675.

Circling Raven

JANET CAMPBELL HALE

Janet Campbell Hale, a Coeur d'Alene Indian, writes about growing up in a dysfunctional family that is rent by poverty, alcoholism, and abuse. Her allegiance to her family and to her community puts into focus the complex compromises that all of us — but especially people living in poverty — must make when we seek independence from such a family. There are over 1.9 million Native Americans in the United States today; 31 percent of them live at or below the poverty line.

When I was ten years old, in 1956, my parents and I left our home reservation for the last time. None of us would ever live there again though my parents maintained strong ties. My father was active in tribal politics all of his life and never failed to vote in an election though he had to make a trip to Coeur d'Alene to do so since the tribe never permitted absentee ballots. Two of my sisters and their families returned after many years to live once more as part of the tribal community.

Thirty-six years after I left the reservation, in December of 1992, the Coeur d'Alene Tribal School (grades one through eight) invited me to visit. The school has been in existence for about twenty years.

I just visited the younger ones, saw their writing, heard them read, admired their artwork and the Christmas trees they had selected and cut and brought back to their classrooms to decorate.

I spoke to the oldest group, aged eleven through thirteen, which, as it turned out, included two great-nephews of mine. One I'd never met before. The other I'd not seen since he was about six years old.

The (white) teacher (all but one of the teachers were white) asked me if I were able to maintain my "ethnic identity" where

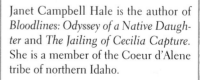

Janet Campbell Hale is the author of *Bloodlines: Odyssey of a Native Daughter* and *The Jailing of Cecilia Capture*. She is a member of the Coeur d'Alene tribe of northern Idaho.

Summary

Native Americans are three to five times more likely to suffer from unemployment, alcoholism, and tuberculosis than non-Native Americans.

Chronic Problems

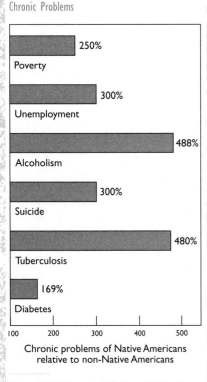

Chronic problems of Native Americans relative to non-Native Americans

Source: FDCH Congressional Testimony (October 5, 1993).

I lived in New York. Or, he asked, was that important to me anymore. I answered that I am as Coeur d'Alene in New York as I am in Idaho, that it is something that is an integral part of me. I told the class to learn all they could about our history and culture because being a tribal person is something special, something non-Indian Americans don't have, and it can be a source of strength. It can provide a sense of continuity, of being connected to the land and to each other. Just think about it, I told them, how long our tribe has existed right here in this very place. Thousands of years. Many, many generations. We have survived as a tribal people for a long, long while. And, we're becoming stronger. When I was your age, I told them, there was no tribal school. There was no Tribal Enterprises or Tribal Farms. There were no privately owned Indian businesses back in those days as there are now. Today, our tribe is waging a battle for the return of the illegally taken lakes. I didn't say anything about the poverty, the lack of employment opportunities, the high crime rate, the many social problems that plague modern reservations. Things are better now than when I was their age. I told them I spoke to a group of non-Indian high school students the week before and one of them told me she thought it "unfair" that Indians had to live on reservations. It had taken me a few minutes to figure out that the student thought Indians were forced to live on reservations the same way that people in South Africa had been. The native people of South Africa were allowed out during the day to go into the white cities and towns to work at low-level jobs but had to go back to their guarded, wretched reservations at night and that is the way some non-Indian people in America believe we have to live too. And that is sort of the way it was in the beginning. Indians had to give up buffalo hunting and root gathering and all the rest and stay put. But the government's intention all along was to get us to assimilate into the mainstream of America and to a large extent we have. We all speak English today and we go to school and we work and pay taxes. We drive cars and watch television and see all the big movies (if we want to). The government would like nothing better, at this point, than to abolish the reservations and get all our tribes to disband, to get rid of us. Only the reservation is our landbase, our home, and we don't want to let go of it.

I told them how I'd often heard non-Indians say they didn't know why Indians make such a big deal out of cultural retention. Why not be like other Americans? Like the Irish or Italian communities, for instance, who have big Saint Patrick's Day or Columbus Day celebrations once a year and then, for the most part, forget about their ethnic identities. The most important difference is this: If Irish or Italian culture dies in America it really isn't that big a deal. They still exist in Italy and Ireland. Not so with us. There is no other place. North America *is* our old country. And you kids, you are the future of our people.

Their teacher said something about my being a good role model. I don't know whether or not they bought it. I hope they didn't. I'm not a role model. At least not in the conventional sense.

If this were not a school visit, if I were with these children in a different context, I might say a few things more. I would say that yes, tribal identity and commitment to the community and family ties are important. But some of you kids, like me and like many other people from all kinds of racial and ethnic backgrounds, don't come from families that can and will encourage and support you. Some families will, if they can, tear you down, reject you, tell you you are a defective person. You could end up brokenhearted and brokenspirited.

If you come from such a family and you have no one else to turn to, then you must, for the sake of your own sanity and self-respect, break free, venture out on your own and go far away. Then you will have to rely on yourself and what you've managed to internalize regarding strength, stamina, identity and belonging.

Sometimes it will take a lot of courage to want to live and do well in spite of it all. But being courageous is part of our heritage. The most admired quality among the old Coeur d'Alene was courage. Courage has been bred into you. It's in your blood....

When I was twenty-three and writing my first novel, *The Owl's Song*, I told my mother I was stuck. I was afraid of writ-

129

ing something that would offend people. The protagonist's family was poor and the father and the sister drank a lot. Things like that. I was torn between writing a novel that was true to my own vision and one that presented a positive image of Indian people.

My mother, who only went to grade three and almost never read novels, told me, "Maybe I'm just ignorant, but I thought it was a writer's business to write the truth as she sees it. Isn't it? What is the point of writing, why would anyone even want to do it if she's going to just write some nonsense to please someone else?"…

I think my parents started out loving each other. I think they had miserable times as the years passed (most, but not all, related to his drinking). And, I think maybe their love survived in spite of all of it, though in a crippled form. Nothing ever happened to set things straight. (Maybe nothing could.) Their family, the one I was born into, was a troubled one.

I used to have an old black-and-white photograph of my family: my parents, my three sisters, and myself, the only one ever taken of us together before any of us married or had children, when we were all still living with our parents.

This photograph was taken in 1946 in Tijuana, Mexico, just before we left California and went back to Idaho. We went there to buy nylon stockings for my mother, as nylons were very scarce in the United States during and just after the war.

When we got there, though, my father announced his intention to win free drinks at "The Longest Bar in the World." If anyone could sit on every barstool and have one drink, and still be able to stand when the last one was finished, all of his drinks would be on the house. It was impossible for anyone to have that many drinks and still be alive, let alone standing. Many had tried. No one had ever made it to the last barstool. My father said he would be the first and he went into The Longest Bar in the World.

But he came out a few minutes later, having had just one *cerveza*. He didn't feel like it, he said. Maybe another day. That day there were other things to do. We found a vendor and my mother bought four pairs of nylons. We did touristy things. A good time was had by all.

We had our picture taken on a set that looked like a covered wagon with a little burro hitched to it. My mother, father and two older sisters, then thirteen and fourteen, sit together side by side on the board seat of the wagon. My father holds me, a bright-eyed little baby, on his knee. My youngest sister, a beaming, apple-cheeked ten-year-old, sits on the burro.

My two older sisters, who have just recently passed from childhood into young womanhood, seem to be posing just a bit, trying to affect a little glamour. Both are wearing lipstick so dark it appears black in the photo. My middle sister is on the far left. She is the one I loved so much as a young child, the one who drew paper dolls for me, which we would color and cut out together, the one who would read Little Lulu comic books to me over and over again until I memorized all the dialogue verbatim and could fake people into thinking I could read. She bought me a beautiful Raggedy Ann doll with her first paycheck from her first job, which was, I think, at a Five and Dime, and got in trouble with Mom over it, for "throwing money around." (I was five years old when my middle sister married and left home. I wept and would not kiss her or even tell her good-bye. It hurt that she would leave me. We would never be close again, I thought. And I was right.) She is very thin in this photo. She had already been through a long, severe bout of TB and would be sick again in another few years and have to return to the sanitarium. But she doesn't look sick here. She looks fine.

My oldest sister is seated between my father and my middle sister. She is the family beauty (she would actually be, for a brief time, a small-time beauty queen and ride on floats and wear tiaras and wave to people on the sidelines). She never looked beautiful in photographs, though, and this one is no exception. But, like my other sisters, she looks young and innocent, fresh and pretty.

My youngest sister, according to my middle sister, had had a sweet, easygoing personality. She never did in my memory. But looking at the smiling ten-year-old on the burro in Mexico, it isn't hard to believe.

My mother is still pretty here. Her hair, mostly hidden by a sombrero with "Tijuana" written on the front, isn't grey yet. Her

Summary

The Asian and Pacific Islander population is expected to grow five times larger by the year 2050, while the Hispanic population will triple and the black population will double.

The New Melting Pot

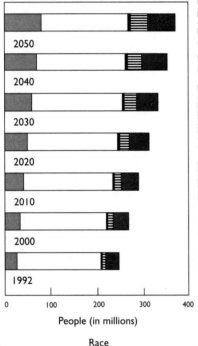

People (in millions)

Race
(percentage of projected growth 1992–2050)

All (50.2%)
Black (93.8%)
Asian and Pacific Islander (412.5%)
American Indian, Eskimo, & Aleut (109.1%)
White (29.4%)
Hispanic (237.5%)
May be of any race

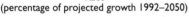

Source: Census Bureau 1992 projections.

eyes are large (and you can tell they aren't dark because all of us, in the photo, have black, black eyes) and her lashes are thick and dark. She has a pretty mouth, a happy smile. She is Irish-pretty, not at all what anyone would call "exotic." She does not look nonwhite. She isn't yet overweight, as she would be all of the years I was growing up, but she has lost the slimness of her youth. She is "full-bodied" and she does look her age.

My father, surrounded by his family, looks silly in a sombrero that says "Just Married" on it. He is handsome in a rugged sort of way. He looks strong and vigorous. He is in his mid fifties but looks ten years younger. His shirt sleeves are rolled up to his elbows and his forearms are muscular and smooth. I look very small sitting there on his knee, his big hand holding me, and I look like I feel very secure. My eyes are almond-shaped. My hair is very thick for a small baby's, a wild mop.

We are smiling in Tijuana, having a good time. A happy, handsome family. No one here is sick or old. The sun is shining on us that spring day in Mexico in 1946. What I wouldn't give to be able to set everything right for us from that moment on.

What if Dad had walked out of the Longest Bar in the World that day a changed man, what if he had experienced an epiphany in there as he downed his Mexican beer ... realized exactly what he was doing and had been doing and what he had to do in order to stop and told our mother, when they were alone that night, that he would never take another drink. And what if he hadn't.

And what if Mom, in time, had truly forgiven him and trusted him and finally allowed herself to love him again just like she had when the two of them first laid eyes on one another and knew right away?

Or, what if Dad hadn't stopped drinking, but Mom had been able to support herself in some other way than she did when she left him (as a scrubwoman, a fruit-picker, a hotel maid)? Say, as a teacher, a nurse, a photographer? She could have had more than brief respites. She could have made a life for herself. What if she hadn't suffered from rheumatoid arthritis? What if her own family had been happier and stronger and more supportive? What if. What if things had been different.

They weren't. *What if* does not exist. There is nothing but what was and is and we're all stuck with that and have to struggle to do our best with the hand we've been dealt. It has to do. It's all we have....

EXCERPTED FROM: *Bloodlines*, 1993.

It is almost impossible to help poor children without helping their families.

LISBETH SCHORR
Author, *Within Our Reach: Breaking the Cycle of Disadvantage*

Dineh

A successful Navaho community development corporation

Dineh Cooperatives, Inc. (DCI) is the community development corporation of the Navaho Nation. Since 1971, DCI has created and managed a wide range of Navaho ventures, employed 775 persons, and brought an estimated $55.7 million in outside investments to the Nation, located in northern Arizona and New Mexico.

DCI is proudest of owning and operating the Tseyl Shopping Center and Tooh Dineh Industries, both of which have been recognized for excellence by the U.S. Department of Housing and Urban Development. The shopping center employs 178 full-time workers, serves more than 33,000 customers, and has attracted numerous businesses including four owned by Navahos. DCI has received $2 million in grants and loans to expand the shopping center.

Tooh Dineh Industries has 375 full-time employees and has annual sales of about $45 million. It produces precision tools, electronic goods, and computer system boards.

In addition to economic development, DCI has played a role in developing a hospital/housing complex and a community fire department. The $32 million Chinle Comprehensive Health Care Facility was opened in 1982 and is said to be one of the finest hospitals on Indian lands in the United States.

Finally, DCI provides a wide range of services on a contractual basis, including business accounting and management assistance.

For more information, write Dineh Cooperatives, Inc., P.O. Box 2060, Chinle, Navaho Nation 86503; (602) 674-3411.

Teach for America

A teacher corps for recent college graduates

Attracting some of the nation's most promising college graduates to teach in some of its toughest, most disadvantaged schools is the purpose of Teach for America, a national teacher corps launched in 1990.

Teach for America recruits graduating seniors, mostly noneducation majors, at 150 colleges and universities and places them in public schools in 17 urban and rural areas where attracting qualified staff is difficult. The fledgling teachers commit themselves to a two-year assignment working as regular salaried employees of the school district. TFA's underlying mission is to promote equal access to excellent education for all children.

The program was founded by Wendy Kopp, who first proposed the idea in her senior thesis at Princeton in 1989. After the Mobil Corporation stepped in with a $26,000 seed grant, Kopp raised an additional $1.5 million in a year. Since its inception, TFA has placed nearly 2,800 teachers in 400 schools. More than half of those completing their two-year stints have chosen to remain in the profession afterwards.

TFA members train for their assignments during two consecutive summers, and the program's critics charge that it sends young teachers into the classroom without proper preparation. But those working with TFA's teachers have high praise for them. "I'm amazed at the energy these [corps members] have," said Gerald Works, a school principal in Gould, Arkansas. "I'd like to have a hundred of them. They are outstanding teachers and

TEACH FOR AMERICA

they have outstanding rapport with the community, students, and other teachers."

For more information, contact Teach for America, 20 Exchange Place, 8th floor, New York, NY 10005; (800) 832-1230.

Daniel

LARS EIGHNER

In this excerpt from his autobiographical account of three years of being homeless on the road with his dog Lizbeth, Lars Eighner offers us a remarkable picture of the makeshift friendships and families that sometimes must serve as a substitute for the traditional family. Mr. Eighner gives us a glimpse of social service as seen from the perspectives of provider and recipient and explores what it means to accept responsibility for other people.

One evening at dusk a young man approached the pew and called Lizbeth by name. I did not recognize him and I did not know how he came to know my dog's name.

He explained that he had roomed with Jerry. Lizbeth was supposed to have been Jerry's dog. He adopted her when he lived with me at the shack on Avenue B, and when he moved out he woke me from a nap to say that he could not afford a pet deposit at his new apartment, but he would take Lizbeth to be destroyed if that was what I wanted.

Jerry now lived somewhere that Lizbeth and I passed often. He had pointed us out to this young man. In fact, the young man said, he had just come from Jerry's place. He had hoped to spend the night there, but Jerry had not come to the door. Whether Jerry was avoiding him or was sleeping, the young man did not know. Jerry is a sound sleeper.

The young man told me his name was Daniel. Lately he had been staying at an apartment he had supposedly vacated. The manager had not changed the lock and Daniel had been letting himself in with a duplicate key. But at last Daniel had been discovered and he did not dare return.

Daniel said he was on the waiting list for admission to an AIDS hospice in Houston. He expected to be admitted within a matter of days. In the meantime he had no place to go.

Lars Eighner is the author of *Travels with Lizbeth*. His work has been published in *The Threepenny Review, The New York Times Book Review, Harper's, The Advocate, The Utne Reader,* and *The Pushcart Anthology*. He no longer lives on the streets, but lives in Austin, Texas, with Lizbeth.

I nodded. Daniel looked as if he had AIDS. I never knew it if I had met anyone before with full-blown AIDS. Daniel had the hollow cheeks and the emaciated look about the neck that I had seen in photographs of people with AIDS and otherwise only in photographs of concentration-camp survivors. I asked Daniel what the local AIDS agency had done for him. He said they were mostly burned-out on him.

Although I had donated what I could to the AIDS agency, I did not have much confidence in them. I could see, however, that Daniel was a hard case, a prickly pear.

Most agencies, and especially their volunteers who do so much of the real work, want cuddly, warm clients. In the case of AIDS, that means the volunteers are best prepared for people who will lie down and die quietly. Many people who apply to work with persons with AIDS envision themselves as ministering martyrs among the lepers. They imagine the work will involve many tender and touching moments as their patients struggle to express eternal gratitude before expiring gently. Such scenes are filmed through gauze and Vaseline.

But what if the client was not a model citizen before he became ill? What if having AIDS really pisses him off? What if suffering silently is not his cup of tea? What if he resents the hell out of having to have things done for him? What if he feels entitled to steal five dollars from Florence Nightingale's purse?

And even when the client is a saint, there is a great deal more to being of real service than fluffing pillows and holding hands.

I asked Daniel whether it really had come to the point that the agency would do no more for him. He said he was afraid that it was so.

They had discovered he had been trading his hard-won food stamps for marijuana. That was, I gathered, only the last straw. In the present crisis, the agency had given Daniel the name of a man who supposedly had a standing offer to put up people with AIDS. But the agency had made a point of saying they did not recommend Daniel call the man, but passed the name along for Daniel to do with as he wished.

Other than to make this rather peculiar referral, the agency would do no more. Having no better plan, Daniel called the number in spite of the agency's disclaimer. The man invited

> *It is not so much that people being "helped" resent what is being done for them; needing assistance they are glad to get it from any quarter. But they are simply unwilling to accept the kind of condescension that goes with the postures their benefactors take up. Especially the posture that turns pain and suffering into some heroic form of salvation.*
>
> ROBERT COLES
> Child Psychiatrist,
> Educator, Author

Summary

As of 1987, almost two-thirds of the homeless people living in cities of 100,000 or more were alone, while one-fifth were families with children.

Homeless and Alone

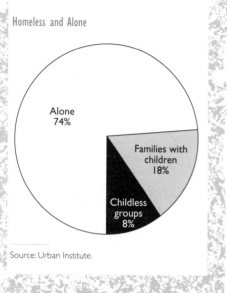

Alone
74%

Families with
children
18%

Childless
groups
8%

Source: Urban Institute.

FACT

Only 27 percent of the families with incomes below $14,000 have Medicaid, while 35 percent have private insurance and 37 percent have no coverage at all.

(Source: National Center for Health Statistics.)

Daniel to stay with him and gave Daniel directions to a house in Hyde Park.

When Daniel got to the address, the man offered him a sofa bed, and Daniel, being by then very tired, lay down. He said he had almost fallen asleep when the man began to massage him. Daniel did not want this attention, but he was too weary to make an issue of it until the massage reached his crotch, whither it arrived with uncommon haste.

Daniel asked the man to stop, but the man had not. And thus Daniel left.

I recognized Daniel as a manipulative sort of person. That someone would open his home to people with AIDS in order to make passes at them seemed incredible.

But Daniel mentioned the man's profession — which was an uncommon one for men — and the neighborhood of the man's home. These rang a bell with me. Daniel had not written down the man's name and had forgotten it. But he had the slip of paper on which he had recorded the man's telephone number. I wanted to take the number to the telephone book at the convenience store across Twenty-ninth Street to see if I could confirm my suspicions. But as I questioned Daniel, he remembered the man's name in a flash. I knew the man.

I cannot say that Daniel's story was true, but only that, whether fiction or fact, it captured the salient features of the man's character better than any other single anecdote might. I believed Daniel then and all the more because he could see I could not give him any money.

What Daniel did want was to sleep on the pew as Lizbeth and I watched over him. He proposed to take a number of Valium and he perceived that the bench was not the safest place in the world. I sat on the curb beneath the pew. As the evening was growing cooler, I offered Daniel my sleeping bag. He threw it over himself and, after being reassured I would not leave him until morning, took some pills and promptly fell asleep.

Lizbeth was upset to lose her place on the pew. She paced for a while and then curled up under the pew, where she was hidden by the drape of the sleeping bag.

Daniel left his pill bottle standing on the pew near his head. Without disturbing the bottle I could read its label. The

138

patient's name matched the one Daniel had given me. The doctor was one of two in town I knew to have a large AIDS practice, and even before the AIDS crisis he was known for prescribing drugs like Valium with a free hand. I saw Daniel had exceeded his prescribed dose, but not to an alarming degree. Eventually I nodded off to sleep, my back braced against the pew.

Lizbeth roused me three or four times when men approached the pew. The adult arcade, which was in the storefront next to Ramblin' Red's, stayed open all night, and any of its patrons might have inquired of us, since late at night the pew is usually occupied by hustlers or other available men who cannot or will not pay the two-dollar admission.

Occasionally when I worked late into the night, the staff of the arcade came out to investigate complaints of a possibly dangerous vagrant. But I enjoyed the favor of the clerks on the night shift at the arcade, for I had once seen a number of magazines fall from the pants leg of an inebriated shoplifter as he stumbled away from the arcade. I knew inventory of the display items was taken every shift and the clerks must make up any deficit as much as if the cash drawer were short, so I had returned the magazines.

We had nothing to fear from the staff of the arcade or its regular customers, but perhaps one of the men who approached us in the night had meant us harm. All of them were surprised when Lizbeth leapt from concealment to announce them.

Daniel woke shortly after dawn. He was to go to some agency that would give him a voucher for a bus ticket if the hospice was ready for him. I told him I would leave the sleeping bag under the steps at Sleazy Sue's in case he had no better place to stay that evening and I was, for some reason, elsewhere.

When Lizbeth and I returned to the pew that afternoon, Daniel was wrapped in the sleeping bag although it was an hour before sunset and still very warm. He had taken a chill and what is more he had not got anything to eat all day. Lizbeth and I had eaten as we came to things. Our reserves were exhausted.

I left Lizbeth with Daniel and my gear and went around to the Dumpsters to find what I could while there was light remaining.

FACT

Almost 10 percent of San Francisco's homeless are HIV-positive.

(Source: Stanford University; University of California at San Francisco, 1994.)

FACT

Compared with the average adult, the poor and the homeless each experience poor health at a rate about three times that of people at large (32 percent of the poor and 44 percent of the homeless, as opposed to 12 percent of the general population).

(Source: *Washington Post*, July 28, 1992.)

Summary

According to a number of local surveys, one in three homeless people have mental or physical health problems.

Street Health

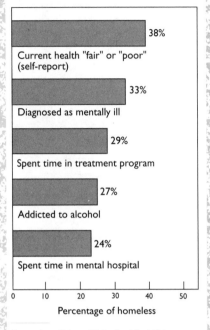

Source: Anne Shlay and Peter Rossi, *Social Science Research and Contemporary Studies of Homelessness* (1992).

These were bleak days at the Dumpsters. We ate orts from the dormitories. I did not think I could give anything of the sort to a person with AIDS. I stirred through the Dumpsters with little hope of finding canned goods or other sealed items such as I had taken in better times to the AIDS food bank. I found a few open things that I would have eaten myself. But I had a recollection that one of the more perilous opportunistic infections to which PWAs are subject is transmitted by cat shit, and few Dumpsters are entirely free of used cat litter. I found nothing I could give Daniel.

At the end of the line of the best Dumpsters I turned and retraced my steps. I sifted through the Dumpsters again, determined to make them yield something.

When I reached, save by one Dumpster, my starting point, a college woman came down the back stairs of one of the apartment buildings. She carried a paper bag that I believed she was going to discard. I returned to business, taking as little notice of her as I could for fear of alarming her. "Do you want something to eat?" she asked, startling me slightly. I had not realized she had approached me. She handed me the crisp brown bag. "I made some sandwiches," she said.

I was not speechless but nearly enough that I said nothing intelligible. I do not appear much in need of food. The woman meant to do a little good by feeding me, but had done much more than she meant by feeding Daniel. Unfortunately I tried to tell her so all at once and she understood not a word.

The sandwiches were freshly made and not her leftover lunch and she had put a nice apple in the bag. Daniel made quick work of the food and I could believe he had not eaten all day.

We spent the night at the pew as we had the night before. But the next night Daniel did not return and I assume he went to Houston.

EXCERPTED FROM: *Travels with Lizbeth*, 1993.

AIDS Action Council

The AIDS Action Council is a Washington advocacy group that speaks for organizations serving people with Acquired Immune Deficiency Syndrome and seeks to shape AIDS-related public policy.

Founded in 1984, AAC has successfully lobbied for increases in the federal AIDS budget every year since then, winning record levels of funding for AIDS programs in fiscal year 1994.

Persons living with AIDS sometimes find themselves thrust into sudden poverty when they lose their jobs either because of discriminatory firing or because they become too debilitated to work. AAC advocates for antidiscrimination measures and was instrumental in the passage of the AIDS Housing Opportunities Act, a $156 million federal program to provide housing to people with AIDS or HIV and their families.

To date, AIDS has struck more than a quarter of a million people in the United States. There is no cure, and the disease has claimed some 170,000 lives in this country alone. AAC supports nationwide AIDS prevention counseling; the implementation of a nationally coordinated plan to fight the disease; health care reform; and, in the absence of a cure, expeditious development of AIDS treatments.

With an annual budget of $2 million raised from private sources, AAC represents more than a thousand community-based AIDS programs nationwide. It counts among its successes the 1990 enactment of the Ryan White Comprehen-

sive AIDS Resource Emergency (CARE) Act, a federal law that provides special relief to areas hard hit by the disease.

For more information, contact the AIDS Action Council, 1875 Connecticut Avenue, NW, Suite 700, Washington, DC 20009; (202) 986-1300.

Rachel and Her Children

JONATHAN KOZOL

It is often said that millions of Americans are but one disaster away from poverty. A single catastrophe — a divorce, an arrest, a disabling accident, or, as in Rachel Andrews's case, illness — can effectively destroy a family's financial resources. Such an event can be particularly devastating in today's society, with extended families scattered and other support networks simply not available to many people. Furthermore, with more than 37 million Americans not covered by health insurance, a single medical crisis can quickly sap the finances of even those who consider themselves middle class.

A woman living on the tenth floor of the Martinique is told that she has cancer. She calls me late at night in Boston. It is, of course, the kind of news that terrifies all people, even in the best of economic situations. Most of us at least have systems of support. We live near neighbors. Some of us have family members near at hand; sometimes they are close enough to drive to our homes, sit up and talk with us, pack our clothes, our children's clothes, and take us back with them into their safer world. They can bring us to the hospital. If the information is unclear, they can bring us to another doctor to confirm the diagnosis, to be sure.

When you are homeless there are no supports.

Mrs. Andrews is forty-two. The first time that we met, before Thanksgiving, she told me she had worked for seventeen years as a secretary and bookkeeper — nine of those years for one firm. She'd lived in the same house for seven years.

How did she end up in the Martinique?

Jonathan Kozol is the author of *Rachel and Her Children*, and the award-winning *Death at an Early Age* and *Illiterate America*. For the last 30 years, as a writer and teacher, he has brought attention to the education and care of children as seen in his books, *Free Schools, On Being a Teacher, The Night Is Dark and I Am Far from Home* and *Children of the Revolution*.

Like many people in this situation, she had been hit with two catastrophes in sequence. First, she had learned that she had cancer in her large intestine. Hospitalized for removal of a part of her intestine, she had to have a hysterectomy as well. Three successive operations coincided with a time in which the man to whom she had been married thirteen years fell into depression, caused by difficulties of his own. He had had a prior drinking problem and it now became much worse. Debilitated by her medical concerns, she had no strength to offer him support. He, in turn, became destructive and disorganized. She had to leave their home.

She had three children: two daughters and one son. With the breakup of her household and her inability to work for several months, she found her economic status dropping very fast. She turned to welfare. One night, six months after her third and final operation, she was sitting with her children in the office of the Church Street EAU.

For several nights the city is unable to assign her to a shelter. When a place is found, it is the Hotel Carter. Bad as it is, she never gets beyond the door. When she arrives at 1:00 A.M., the manager says he can't accommodate a family of four. Why was she sent here? She is too dazed to ask. At 2:00 A.M., she gets back on the subway and returns to the same EAU she has just left. On her return, a social worker seems annoyed. He asks: "Then you refuse this placement?" Although she explains what has transpired, she is forced to sign a paper formally refusing placement at the hotel which has just refused her.

I have asked her about this several times. "I had to *sign* the paper."

Mrs. Andrews is articulate, well organized, and neatly dressed. If this woman could be savaged with so little hesitation, how much more savage is the treatment meted out to women who don't have her middle-class appearance and do not display the style and articulation with which social workers might identify?

"We spent another seven days sitting in the welfare center, 9:00 to 5:00, and every evening 6:00 to 8:00 A.M., trying to sleep there at the EAU. All we had to eat that week was peanut butter, jelly, and cheese sandwiches." Not wanting to exaggerate,

Summary

More than one in three (36 percent) Americans with annual incomes below $10,000 have no health coverage at all. The percentages for people earning more than $35,000 a year is 10 times smaller.

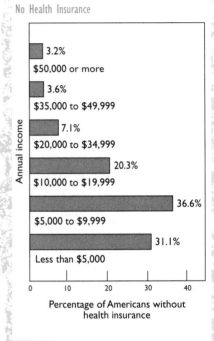

No Health Insurance

- $50,000 or more — 3.2%
- $35,000 to $49,999 — 3.6%
- $20,000 to $34,999 — 7.1%
- $10,000 to $19,999 — 20.3%
- $5,000 to $9,999 — 36.6%
- Less than $5,000 — 31.1%

(Annual income) / Percentage of Americans without health insurance

Source: National Center for Health Statistics (1992).

FACT

In 1991, uninsured patients had death rates 44 percent to 124 percent higher than privately insured patients.

(Source: Georgetown University; Johns Hopkins University, 1992.)

Summary

For more than two decades, an increasing number of low-income renters (the poorest 25 percent of households) has been competing for a shrinking pool of low-cost housing (that which rents for 30 percent or less of their income).

Housing Squeeze

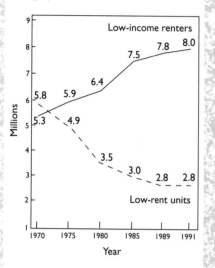

Source: Low Income Housing Information Service; Children's Defense Bureau.

FACT

Poor people go to the hospital more often, and stay longer. For families with incomes under $14,000, the hospitalization rate in 1989 was 131 per 1,000, compared to 72 per 1,000 for families with incomes over $50,000. The poorest group spent more than twice as many days in the hospital as the affluent group.

(Source: National Center for Health Statistics.)

she adds: "They gave my children juice and little packages of milk."

After seven days she's given a week's placement at the Holland Hotel on West Forty-second Street, a few blocks from the Carter. This hotel, which has been likened by the *New York Times* to "a kiddie park designed by Hogarth and the Marquis de Sade," was cited in 1985 for nearly 1,000 health and building violations. The owner was later found to have been taking in $6 million yearly, half of which was profit.

At the time that Mrs. Andrews was sent by the city to the Holland, part of the building housed nonhomeless tenants. Only certain deteriorated floors were used to house the homeless. The fourteenth floor, to which the Andrews were assigned for their first night of sleep in thirteen days, had no running water. "Even the toilet had no water," Mrs. Andrews says. "We had to carry buckets to a bar across the street. There was a line of homeless families waiting to bring water back to the hotel. Only one elevator worked. You had to wait an hour."

Two days later, unable to face this any longer, she goes with her children to the EAU. There she is asked to sign another form refusing placement. "We gave you a room. You turned it down,' they said." She's given a referral slip and told that she must bring this to her welfare center. At the welfare center she presents the paper to her welfare worker, sits in a chair, and waits until the office closes, then is sent back to the EAU to sit up in another chair until the morning. In this way, she and her children pass the next twenty-seven days.

During this time, Mrs. Andrews' fourteen-year-old daughter, Carol, becomes ill. She develops pain and swelling in her abdomen. Examination leads to the discovery of a tumor on her kidney. The kidney has to be removed. Also removed in the same operation are the ovary and fallopian tube on her right side. Carol's doctor tells her mother that she must not be allowed to sit up in a welfare office. Armed with a letter to this effect signed by the physician, the family goes back to the welfare center, then — after another day of waiting — to the EAU, only to repeat this ritual for three more days.

After forty-five days of homelessness, the Andrews are sent at 6:00 A.M., on a day in late September 1984, to a small room

144

without a closet but with four beds in the Martinique Hotel. Seven months later they are moved into a slightly larger room two floors below. It is in this room that we first meet in 1986.

The room has the smell of fresh paint on the day I visit. Also, a new door has been installed. These changes, she believes, were made throughout the building and were prompted by some pressure from the Office of the Mayor. Unfortunately, the keys distributed to residents to match the locks on the new doors were incorrectly made. They are interchangeable in many cases. Mrs. Andrews has been robbed four times.

When we meet, she talks for hours of her fears. Fear is plainly written in her eyes. Forty-five days of destitution, sickness, subway travel, waiting lines, followed by two years of residence in the Martinique, have worn away much of her confidence.

"My mother and father are deceased. Except for the children I have only my grandparents. My grandmother is in a wheelchair. My grandfather is ninety-four years old. I pray for them. When they are gone I have nobody but the kids. I was not religious when I came here. People become religious here," she says, "because each day that you survive seems like a miracle."

Mrs. Andrews' husband has been in and out of psychiatric wards throughout the past two years. Her former boss has told her that he wants her back. She's reluctant to accept the job until she saves some money. If she returns to work she loses welfare and can't stay in the hotel. But welfare rules forbid her to save money. Any significant savings pose the risk of being cut from all support. So she cannot start a bank account in order to prepare for the unlikely chance of moving into an apartment. Even if she had her old job back, she couldn't pay a month's rent and deposit and security, buy furniture, or pay for health insurance. The city is said to have a program that sometimes assists with some of these expenses; few families have been given this assistance. Mrs. Andrews has not heard of such a program.

"I don't eat. I'd stopped smoking back in 1983. Now I smoke three packs a day."

Only in state prisons have I seen so many people craving cigarettes. She lights one cigarette after another, presses it out, looks for a match, hunts for another pack.

People who are homeless are not social inadequates. They are people without homes.

SHEILA MCKECHNIE

FACT

Children now make up an estimated 30 percent of all homeless persons seeking shelter.

(Source: United States Conference of Mayors, *A Status Report on Hunger and Homelessness in America's Cities: 1993: A 26-City Survey*).

FACT

One in five poor children had no health insurance at all during 1992.

(Source: Census Bureau, *Poverty in the United States: 1992*).

FACT

Young families with children — those
headed by someone younger than 30
— are nearly six times more likely to
be poor than childless families overall.
More than two in five children (42
percent) in these families lived in
poverty in 1992.

(Source: Children's Defense Fund, 1994).

FACT

An estimated 100,000 American
children are homeless each day.

(Source: National Academy of Sciences, Institute of
Medicine, 1988).

"Food is very scarce right now, worse than any time since I've
been here." She had received $185 a month in food stamps on
June 1. That was cut to $63 in August. It will be cut again to $44
in January. "I have trouble sleeping when we're short of food.
I cannot sleep if I don't know that I can feed them breakfast."

Food-stamp cuts have forced her for the first time to accept
free bags of food from local charities. "On Saturdays I go to St.
Francis Church on Thirty-first Street. Tuesdays, I go to St.
John's." In compensation for her loss of food stamps — a net
loss of $122 each month — she receives an increase of $8.75 in
restaurant allowance every two weeks from the city. Her room
rent at the Martinique is about $2,000. Her rent allowance for
a permanent apartment, if she were to find one, is $270.

She forces herself to eat one meal a day. Her children, knowing of her cancer history, have tried to get her to stop smoking.
She wants to know: "How will I get them out of this?" I want
to know: Why do we do this to her?

Her phone call brings me back to talk with her when cancer is again suspected, this time on her skin, just under her left
eye. At the hospital, the spot in question has been tested. The
results are positive. The doctor, she says, is also concerned about
a lump that has developed on her throat. She has to go into the
hospital but puts it off two weeks.

On New Year's Eve she phones again. She's going to go into
the hospital. She'll have to leave her kids alone. She needs some
cash so they can buy necessities until she's home. I send a postal
money order for $250. The post office tells me: "It's as good as
cash. Any postal clerk will honor it."

The money order is not honored. Even with identification,
she is told that she needs someone else to "vouch" for her.

A friend in Manhattan helps me. He calls someone he knows
at the post office and she finally gets the cash. She is embarrassed by the trouble she believes she's caused me. On the telephone she tells me that conditions in the building have grown
worse. "There's been no light in the elevator for a month. People use cigarette lighters. Or you ride up in the dark. I can't face
it. I walk up ten floors."

When she gets out of the hospital, she has good news. The
spot on her face and lump on her throat turned out to be

benign. By now, however, sleeplessness and fear have left her drained. She's also feeling the results of the last round of food-stamp cuts. Everyone in the hotel, she says, is short of food. The president this month requests a billion-dollar cut in food stamps and in child-nutrition funds for 1987.

Coalition for the Homeless

A social service and housing program

COALITION
FOR THE
HOMELESS

The Coalition for the Homeless is a Washington, DC, organization that pairs emergency and transitional housing with supportive social services to help homeless people attain self-sufficiency and permanently emerge from homelessness.

Serving more than 3,000 homeless individuals and families each year, CFH enlists the involvement of a variety of social-service agencies in steering clients toward the road to independent living. For men, CFH operates two emergency shelters as well as several transitional housing facilities where residents work toward gaining the skills and resources they need to find employment and move into permanent homes. Clients pledge to work on recovery from drugs and alcohol, while staff members help them find employment and housing and re-establish family ties. Once they find work, the men are required to open an interest-bearing savings account.

CFH also offers emergency and transitional housing for families, a service designed not just to meet immediate needs but to target some of the root causes of poverty, family dysfunction, and homelessness. The Spring Road Family Shelter, located in an attractive residential neighborhood, provides families with two- or three-bedroom apartments and an interdisciplinary team that includes substance abuse specialists, an employment development expert, and a housing counselor. The DC public schools operate an after-school tutorial program for the children on the premises, and there is a reading corner where parents and volunteers can spend time with the little ones. Other groups pitching in to meet the children's developmental and educational needs include local churches and the Jewish Community Center.

For more information, contact the Coalition for the Homeless, 1234 Massachusetts Avenue, NW, Washington, DC 20005; (202) 347-8870.

Service for Shelter

Service for Shelter is a multifaceted project that seeks to address a spectrum of housing needs among North Carolina's low-income residents. Subtitled "Building Hope, Building Homes, Building Communities," the three-year initiative attempts to do just that.

As a pilot program of AmeriCorps, the Clinton Administration's national service initiative (see page 219), Service for Shelter employs 22 corps volunteers at sites throughout the state. The North Carolina Low Income Housing Coalition (NCLIHC), a statewide advocacy group working for affordable housing for poor people, is coordinating the project in partnership with a dozen social- service agencies.

As elsewhere in America, the housing crisis affects a wide diversity of North Carolinians — 8,000 homeless people in need of emergency shelter; low-income tenants living in crumbling dwellings; and thousands of homeowners who greet each day with a trip to the outhouse. Through Service for Shelter, NCLIHC strives to match these diverse needs with diverse strategies.

For instance, while two AmeriCorps volunteers are working directly with clients of a homeless shelter in Raleigh, helping them with basic tasks and coordinating literacy classes and legal assistance, another is at work in Hendersonville coordinating a volunteer home repair program for low-income homeowners. Still other project volunteers perform duties ranging from counseling prospective home buyers on credit and budgeting, to educating low-income tenants about their

housing rights, to negotiating with private landlords to get them to accept Section 8 certificates from prospective tenants.

In the simultaneous "Building Communities" component of the project, six AmeriCorps volunteers will serve in five agencies to teach low-income people about community organizing. Residents will learn about such matters as fundraising, forming tenants' groups and coalitions, and leadership skills, so they can continue to address their own needs through grassroots action when the AmeriCorps project ends.

For more information, contact the NCLIHC, 3901 Barrett Drive, Suite 200, Raleigh, NC 27609; (919) 881-0707.

PART THREE

Communities in Poverty

Rain does not fall on one roof alone.

African proverb

What we do for ourselves dies with us. What we do for our community lives long after we are gone.

Theodore Roosevelt

Communities are more than geographic enclaves where people live. Communities are made up of institutions, associations, traditions, businesses, families, and social interactions. They are made through meetings, campaigns and elections, entertainments, classroom visits, guest speakers, boycotts, food pantries, and religious services. Communities have histories: where they were built, by whom, and for what gain; who left; who stayed behind — these are historical forces that shape our communities' lives today. This is as true for people living in wealthy neighborhoods as it is for those living in poor neighborhoods. A community is made up of all the things that connect us to life outside our front door. When we observe people living in poverty, we tend to dwell on the deficits of their community: crime, drugs, teenage pregnancy, and more. However, if our goal is to help people to leave poverty, focusing on the deficits may not be as productive as finding the strengths in the community and bolstering and working with those strengths.

Ours is a mobile society, particularly for corporations and for the nonpoor. It is difficult to build temporary communities. A neighborhood that is held together only by a common desire for convenience and practicality is more a motel than a community. Problems of individuals are seen as just that, individual problems not requiring a community response.

Many are the American communities built around a steel plant, computer hardware company, coal mine, or textile mill, which now find themselves struggling to survive, to adapt, and not to lose most active citizens after the major employer closes up or moves away. In his book, *Broken Heartland*, author Osha Gray Davidson points out the pattern facing rural communities (though most of his observations are relevant to other communities as well) hit by an economic crisis:

> a severe economic jolt sets in motion three interconnected processes: (1) it begins a pattern of intergenerational poverty that families have profound difficulty breaking; (2) it touches off a class-selective migration, in which more prosperous residents move, leaving behind a community in which poverty is even more concentrated; and (3) the social and economic structure of the rural community adapts to economic shock in ways that accelerate and ultimately lock into place the downward cycle of ghettoization. Poorer communities are more likely to attract low-wage, labor-intensive industries looking for inexpensive land and a cheap labor pool.

As the following stories and essays show, vibrant communities, even without financial resources, are finding ways to adapt. What has become clear is that isolated, individualistic responses to poverty have largely failed. After participating in a series of roundtable discussions with people living in poverty, Charlotte Kahn, director of the Boston Foundation's Boston Persistent Poverty Project, wrote in a 1994 article in the *Boston Review*,

> we need a new broad-based approach to eradicating persistent poverty, one that turns conventional anti-poverty practice on its head. At its heart, this approach seeks to end poverty by building community. It calls for a fundamental shift from servicing low-income communities' deficits — treating the poor as "clients" — to investing in their strengths as colleagues, neighbors, and citizens. It builds on the cultural traditions, family networks, and institutions of low-income communities as a way to tailor more effective — and more cost-effective — strategies for community development. Finally, it requires a transformation in the way we think about poverty. It replaces the idea that poverty is intrinsic to certain people — the "culture of poverty" — with the conviction that poverty results from specific obstacles to economic self-reliance that can be identified and then reduced, removed, or overcome.

The Milagro Beanfield War

JOHN NICHOLS

Many important elections happen beyond the confines of a voting booth. When community members join together, identify a problem, form an association, and begin to take action, that is as much a part of the democratic process, some would argue more so, as is a political campaign. In this excerpt from John Nichols's novel, The Milagro Beanfield War, *we witness the beginning of a local movement to fight for water rights and to fight against a proposed tourist development that is likely to drive the residents of Milagro away from their community.*

Ruby Archuleta then took the floor. "Listen, friends," she began. "You all know what's been happening in the valley. You remember when this church was the heart of a town that no longer truly exists. You remember the days when we were not rich, but when poverty was different, not a thing to be ashamed of, and we got along okay. You remember when we had a certain freedom, and you know we don't have it anymore, and you remember when our children grew up and stayed home and raised their children in Milagro. Well, look at us now. We're a congregation of old men and old women and where have all our children gone?"

She paused, pacing back and forth in front of them.

"Listen, my friends, my cousins," Ruby continued quietly. "My little grandmothers and my little grandfathers. I love you. But when I wake up in the morning sometimes I want to cry. I think of recent history, and then I think of this Indian Creek Dam and the Indian Creek Conservancy District, and I know that if they come about it will be the end for most of us. And I cannot bear to let this happen without a fight. We are old, and many of us are tired, we have been on welfare too long, and

John Treadwell Nichols is the author of nine novels, among them *Conjugal Bliss* and the New Mexico Trilogy: *The Milagro Beanfield War, The Magic Journey,* and *The Nirvana Blues.*

food stamps have sapped our pride and dulled our fighting spirit. I know the conservancy district and the dam are difficult to understand, but our response to complexity can no longer be, 'Well, that's just the way things are, what can we do about it?' I have spent too much of my life watching bad things happen to us, to my people. I know our problems. And at this point I think we have become a little like land that has been overgrazed, or like land that hasn't been planted correctly or fertilized for many years, and so it has lost its richness, becoming thin and weak and played out; there are no more vitamins in the soil, and all the crops growing out of it are poorer each year — "

Ruby stopped, losing the thread, confused in her own metaphor, aware of saying incorrectly what needed to be said. She was scared, too, because she had never really spoken to a group before, and because she was worried that a woman should not be saying these things, and that maybe because she was a woman with a mysterious history who lived outside the town proper they would refuse to listen.

Suddenly she changed her tack.

"Look, I'm not saying it right, I know that I'm not our leader. I want to do what's good and I want to fight in whatever way the people want to fight, that's all. I'm speaking now because we haven't chosen a leader. But maybe there's somebody who can speak better than me, who would like to talk now about these things?"

They stared at her impassively, in absolute silence, for a good thirty seconds.

"Alright," she said gently. "I had an idea before I came to the meeting. I was hoping maybe we could form ourselves into a group, and I thought we might call our group something like the Milagro Land and Water Protection Association, I don't know. We'll think about that, and maybe we can have an election at the end of the meeting or sometime soon. Maybe, too, we can elect the officers of our association, if we choose to make ourselves that, and we can discuss future meetings. But right now I asked somebody to talk to us, because he has written articles about this dam and he understands the conservancy district better than me, and perhaps he can help us all understand

Summary

Nonpoor people are more likely to participate in community or citizen groups than poor people. However, a similar percentage of poor and nonpoor people have actually taken the initiative to solve their problems.

Doing Something About It

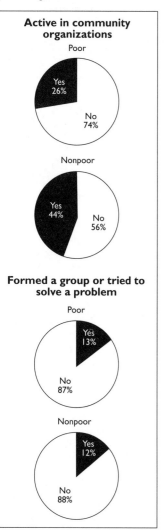

Active in community organizations

Poor

Yes 26%
No 74%

Nonpoor

Yes 44%
No 56%

Formed a group or tried to solve a problem

Poor

Yes 13%
No 87%

Nonpoor

Yes 12%
No 88%

Source: Jeffrey M. Berry, Kent E. Portney, and Ken Thomson, *The Political Behavior of Poor People* (1991).

the technicalities, so we'll know what we're up against. As you know, he lives with us here in Milagro, and I consider that he is on our side — "

Charley Bloom went to the front; Ruby smiled and shook his hand and sat down — he faced the people. Their familiar faces were neither hard nor soft. Searching for glints of humor, for smiles, for compassion, he could not find any. Their faces seemed so old, so dark, calling forth overworked clichés about the earth and the sky and the wind. Old, wrinkled, simple, profound. Bloom was afraid of these neighbors, feeling simultaneously superior and less of a man. God help him not to sound either patronizing or defensive! He knew they were weary and frightened, too, but on no one face did this seem evident, and he was afraid that he broadcast it from his body as if someone had painted him a Day-Glo chickenshit yellow that shone in the dark. Although he knew many of them must lead confused and desperate lives (wasn't his own wife Linda an example?), he still could not help but feel they were confident men and women who believed in themselves, holding in their lives to truths that were self-evident and irrefutable. He sensed, too, that they were unafraid of danger and of dying, and this they held over him more than anything. A part of him knew he was wrong, knew that he did no credit to these friends and neighbors (as he had done no credit to his wife) by romanticizing them just as they probably romanticized him, but he couldn't help it. He envied them because they were different from him, and because, despite their poverty, their language and their culture seemed to offer a viable and dignified alternative. Looking at them, he translated their faces into a strength he had once hoped somehow to marry into.

But then, too, there was this thing in Bloom: at heart, and especially today after that tête-à-tête with Bruno Martínez, the lawyer did not want to commit himself to these hostile, impervious old people; he had no desire to carve some kind of niche for himself on the state police shit list because of their dead houses and their pathetic abandoned beanfields.

But he was willing to do it anyway, and he really did not understand why. He was simply caught, trapped, wishy-washy, doomed.

Apologizing for his bad grammar, Bloom began to speak in Spanish, knowing even as he did so that his Spanish was much more formal and correct and classical than their own; knowing also that he could read books and newspapers in Spanish, and write letters in that language, whereas most of them could not; they were illiterate in Spanish as well as in English; very few had progressed as far as the fifth or sixth grade.

Ruby Archuleta and her son Eliu, Ricardo Córdova, and Tranquilino Jeantete held up the maps while he spoke. Tracing the conservancy district boundaries, the lawyer showed where the dam would be constructed, and then ran down who owned each piece of land within the district. He repeated himself, talking slowly, trying to make a very confusing thing simple and clear. He tried to make them understand technically what they all knew instinctively, that they were going to be taxed heavily for water which would be used mostly by a very few people, and those people would by and large be connected with the Devine empire.

Leaving the maps, then, Bloom talked about the history of the north, about land grants and how they had been lost, strayed, or stolen, divvied up. He named thieves and quoted statistics, working hard to relate what he knew of the far past and the near past to the present. He spoke of sociological trends in Chamisa County, in the entire United States. He ran down for them a history of other conservancy districts in the state which had effectively destroyed subsistence farmers by forcing them into cash economies where they could not compete. He did everything possible to probe and expose the hypocritical rhetoric surrounding the Indian Creek Dam — the state engineer's pronouncement, for example, that it was "the only way to save a dying culture." He tried to demonstrate how the conservancy district and the dam was just one more component of the economic and sociological machinery which for a long time had been driving local small farmers off their land and out of Chamisa County. He quoted figures about per capita income and median incomes; he outlined what the real costs of the dam could balloon into, and broke those costs down to an amount per acre, per year, per person, regardless of that person's wealth. He explained how the proposed Ladd Devine Miracle Valley project would drive their land values sky high, and what that would do to their taxes. He told them that when middle-class or wealthy people from other states bought expensive vacation homes up in the canyon or around the golf course on the subdivided west side, they would want a school for their children, sewage systems, a cleaner water supply, and for that *all* the people of Milagro would have to pay. And once the ski valley was completed there would be pressure to raise taxes for a better road up to it. And Bloom did his best to question the myth that this development would bring wealth to every inhabitant, and jobs and security for all. For forty years, in Chamisa County, there had been a tourist boom: and yet most of the profits went into a few pockets at the top. Skilled construction workers and technicians were always brought in from outside. For the poor and the rural people little had changed, except that in taking service jobs for low wages they no longer had the time to work their land, and so had often wound up selling it, only to discover themselves poorer than before, with not even the security of their own land and a home on it to take the sting out of a poverty as bitter as Chamisa tea.

"In 1950 this county was 85 percent Spanish-surnamed people," Bloom said quietly. "Now it's only 60 percent Spanish-surnamed and declining fast. In 1950 the per capita income was eight hundred and seventy dollars a year; now it's one thousand two hundred and eight dollars, but that increase isn't because people are making more money, it's largely because of inflation. Actually, everyone, all the rural people, are a little poorer than before in spite of the tourist boom these past fifteen or twenty years…"

In the end he petered out. Their faces, perhaps paying close attention, perhaps not, never seemed to change. He couldn't tell if he was making a point, helping to explain the specific workings of what they already understood all too well in general, or if he was talking to seventy-five or a hundred walls. Judging from their expressions it occasionally seemed as if they heartily mistrusted him and hardly believed a word he was saying. Then he picked up on hostility: they were thinking, he thought, What right does this smart aleck have to come in and tell us what is happening, and what is going to happen, to our lives?

He stopped.

"Hay preguntas? Yo puedo tratar a explicarles qualquiera cosa que tal vez no entienden."

There were no questions. Incredibly, after an hour of talking, there were no questions. People shifted, coughed, did not take their eyes off him, but still seemed not to respond. He hadn't even made a dent. Embarrassed, hating them, and hating himself for getting into this thing, for butting into their affairs, for daring to think he had any answers (let alone the courage of his convictions) after only a few years in their town, Bloom sat down, thoroughly ashamed.

After thanking him, Ruby Archuleta asked, "Who wants to speak?"

Tobías Arguello creaked erect. "We are a peaceful people," he said, his voice trembling. "We don't play the Anglos in their own game because they are possessed by the devil. I have a gun, but I use it only to hunt for food. I detest violence. I don't want no more Smokey the Bear santo riots. I'm also a good American. I fought for my country in the First World War. I love being an American, and I am proud. I think maybe if we are violent, we are un-American. I am a man of peace. So we should be peaceful. If we don't watch out, Snuffy Ledoux will come back and start another riot. Thank you."

Sparky Pacheco stood up and, hat in hand, nervously croaked, "These goddamn Anglo bastards like the Zopilote will steal our land and everything else, our babies, and our tractors, and even — please excuse me — our testicles if we don't say 'Stop!' I for one hope Snuffy Ledoux comes back to start another Smokey the Bear santo riot!"

A smattering of voices croaked feebly: "*Que viva Snuffy!*"

Another old man said, "The gabachos, and especially their lawyers, are always deceiving us. They are full of lies."

And, a little stronger this time: "*Que viva Snuffy!*"

Panky Mondragón growled ferociously: "We deceive ourselves. We're full of our own hypocrisy and lies. For years we have stolen our land from each other and from the Indians.

Men are men and women are women, to hell with the colors and languages. Charity begins at home."

A woman, Lilian Chávez, said shyly: "I am ashamed of Nick Rael and Eusebio Lavadie, and all the others who work with the Zopilote. They have betrayed my race. All the same, though. God forbid we should have another Smokey the Bear santo riot in this town."

"*Que viva Snuffy!*"

"Wait a minute!" Onofre Martínez stammered excitedly, emotionally placing his only hand on Ray Gusdorf's shoulder. "This is my neighbor, and he is a gringo, not even a little bit coyote. But he's been in the valley as long as I remember, and I consider him to be of my people. And that white man over there who told us these things about the dam and the conservancy and showed us the maps, I consider him to be of my people, too, even though he is a lawyer, and even though he speaks a funny Anglo Spanish you can hardly understand. But I believe he at least tries to speak the truth, and a lawyer who does that should get a big gold medal to hang around his neck. I don't consider Nick Rael to be of my people, because he works against my interests, I think. He's too busy counting money to care about the people. So I don't believe this is a brown against white question. This is only one kind of people against another kind of people with different ideas. There are brown and white people on both sides. Remember, too, there are brown chotas as well as white chotas and brown políticos as well as white políticos. People are people. My own son will roast in hell, I hope, for becoming a chota. The brown and white people on our side are better people because they are on the correct side, that's all. And if I am ashamed of Nick Rael it's only in the same way I am ashamed of Jimmy Hirsshorn and the Zopilote. If there was no Zopilote or Jimmy Hirsshorn, in their places would be a Mr. González and a Jimmy Pacheco, I think. And if I love my brother Tobías, it's only in the same manner I love my brother Ray, here, who is a good neighbor and a good human being, even if he isn't even part coyote. Let that be understood by everybody, please. And another thing: if Snuffy Ledoux comes back to start another Smokey the Bear statue riot, I'm gonna be the first to shake his hand. Que viva Snuffy!"

"*Que viva Snuffy!*"

And when he sat down, Onofre stared fixedly ahead, lips trembling — for he had spoken.

"Who else wants to speak?" Ruby asked.

"I wanna speak," Joe's brother Cristóbal said. "I nominate my brother José to be president of the Milagro Land and Water Protection Association."

Joe leaped up. "Oh no you don't, not me! I ain't no president!"

"You're the one with the beanfield!" Cristóbal shouted. "You started all this! If the state chotas stick a bullet in my ear, it's because of your pinche beanfield!"

"Bullshit! I didn't start nothing! *I* didn't call for this meeting! *I* didn't ask for nobody's help with my beanfield! What am I, crazy to ask for help from mental retards like you?"

"It's because he won't ask nobody to help him that he endangers us all!" Fred Quintana said.

Joe spluttered: "Oh Jesus Christ. If that's the way it's gonna be, as soon as this meeting is over I'm going to start up my tractor and drive it to the west side and plow up that beanfield and get all you people off my back!"

"You do, José," his wife Nancy threatened, "and I'll shoot you! I'll put ant poison in your enchiladas!"

"Wait a minute!" Ruby cried. "Wait just a minute, *please—*"

"We should tie José up and throw him in a closet before he wrecks everything!" Seferino Pacheco bawled.

"That's *my* beanfield!" Joe howled. "That's my private *property!* Nobody here's got a right to tell me what to do with my property!"

"*Well, we'll kill you if you plow under those beans!*" Sparky Pacheco fairly screamed.

There ensued a sudden silence as these words echoed in the church. By now, half the congregation was standing.

"Well…" Joe pouted, "I still ain't gonna be no president."

"There wasn't even a motion on the floor to make ourselves an association," Ruby soothed. "This is no time to vote for a president when there's nothing to be president of."

"Why are we shouting at each other?" Tobías Arguello asked softly. "We should be peaceful."

Panky Mondragón explained, "We're not shouting at each other anymore, so siddown."

Tobías held his ground. "I got a right to speak. This is an open meeting — "

"But we're not shouting anymore," Panky snarled. "So you can siddown. And besides, you're blocking my view.

"When I'm ready to sit down, I'll sit down—"

"You siddown!" Panky shouted, waving a fist. *"We're not shouting anymore, dammit."*

Lilian Chávez asked, "How can we steal eggs from the Zopilote's nest when you idiots are fighting about who's shouting or not?"

And Onofre Martínez stood up again. "Outside, my evil son, the state chota, is having a good laugh because we're all growing donkey ears in here. Now you take me personally, I get sick to my stomach whenever that chota son of mine has a chuckle at my expense. So I'm sorry to say that if everybody doesn't shut up pretty soon and sit down, I'm gonna barf."

For some reason, Onofre's attitude, tone of voice, words, or all three taken together did the trick. Muttering unhappily, everyone sat down, folded their hands in their laps, and returned their quiet, sullen (though pious) attention to the front.

"Alright," Ruby Archuleta said calmly. "Does anyone wish to talk quietly and in turn, first about this Milagro Land and Water Protection Association, and second about electing leaders?"

Tranquilino Jeantete arose, taking forever to adjust his hearing aid and clear his throat. "These are probably good ideas but we should think about them and talk among ourselves for a while before deciding."

The rest of the gathering nodded, murmured, stirred about, ready for fresh air.

"Alright," Ruby said quietly, frowning warily. "Then I guess this meeting is over."

"Que viva Snuffy!" Sparky Pacheco cried, as everyone else got up to go.

Avance

A program for family intervention and support

The Avance Family Support and Education Program has over 43 comprehensive social service centers in Texas and Puerto Rico dedicated to strengthening hard-hit families. Avance specializes in serving Latino families.

Since 1973, Avance's community-based centers have supported poor families in the belief that "the strength of the community lies in the strength of the family." Its programs include parenting education, adult literacy, employment training, bilingual education, child abuse and neglect intervention, and child development classes.

Avance's family intervention program has been nationally recognized as a model for preventing child abuse beginning with infancy. During a nine-month period, adults take parenting classes and learn about relevant resources in the community while social workers observe the family in the home.

"What we need throughout the country are family centers directly in the neighborhood, or the housing projects, where families can get the help they need before Head Start," said Gloria Rodriguez, president and chief executive officer of Avance.

An estimated 5,000 adults and children participate in Avance annually. A 17-year study of children who had been in the program found that most had graduated high school and that about half had attended college.

For more information, contact Avance Family Support and Education Program, 301 S. Frio, Suite 310, San Antonio, TX 78207; (210) 270-4630.

Dudley Street Neighborhood Initiative

Innovative community revitalization

This nonprofit community development organization began in 1984 by cleaning up vacant lots and closing down illegal dumps. The area's residents suffer from unemployment and poverty rates that are twice that of Boston residents as a whole. But as the organizers worked on cleanup campaigns, they conceived an idea that would turn traditional urban redevelopment upside down.

In the heart of the neighborhood, 30 acres were vacant due to disinvestment, arson, and demolition. And nearly all of the privately owned vacant land was in some form of tax default. After a dramatic struggle, the DSNI was granted the right of eminent domain as a way to turn abandoned property into affordable housing, the first group of its kind in the country to be given that power. The city and state gave over $1 million to the effort and the Ford Foundation loaned DSNI $2 million to help build a comprehensive network of 1,000 affordable housing units, plus playgrounds, community centers, a town common, and other amenities. After attending DSNI-sponsored homebuyer classes, the first residents began moving into their new homes in 1993.

DSNI now describes itself as a "holistic community development" organization with a mission to inspire in residents a locally directed process of community renewal. The group coordinates dozens of human service and education outreach efforts, reaching children, parents, families, veterans, and senior citizens. Most important, says DSNI Vice President Clayton Turnbull, is the organization's push to develop neighborhood pride and self-respect. "If someone asked me what I would want to do," Turnbull said, "building pride in urban America should be the number-one thing."

For more information, contact the Dudley Street Neighborhood Initiative, 513 Dudley Street, Roxbury, MA 02119; (617) 442-9670.

Dudley Street Neighborhood Initiative

Ernesto J. Cortes, Jr.: Organizer

AN INTERVIEW BY BILL MOYERS

One of the greatest responsibilities of any community action work, beyond the immediate task at hand, is the development of leaders. Developing leaders from the grassroots is to many at the heart of a vibrant democracy. Ernesto Cortes learned many of his earliest lessons from Saul Alinsky, a community organizer who began his work in the Chicago stockyards of the late 1930s (he also established a school for community organizing in the 1960s). Alinsky's confrontational style is certainly not the only model. Many organizers today practice a more collaborative style of social change, but virtually everyone agrees with the importance of developing leaders among people living in poverty. As he makes clear in this excerpt from an interview with Bill Moyers, organizer Ernesto Cortes takes very seriously the responsibility of nurturing new leadership and empowering communities to speak for themselves.

MOYERS: What kind of people come to you for training in the art of public life? And what is it they want to know?

CORTES: They care deeply about cities. They care about the city as a place where people come together and enter into relationships, where people's families are raised, and children are mentored, and old people are cared for. They see that cities all over the country are having very great difficulties.

The economy of the city is in great disrepair. The infrastructure is crumbling. There's urban violence, drugs, alcohol, and gangs. None of these things are conducive to families developing and growing and nurturing. There are all kinds of pressures on families in the city — economic pressures, cultural pressures. So they need mediating institutions, intermediate

Ernesto J. Cortes is a member of the Industrial Areas Foundation, a nonprofit organization that helps communities organize to make changes. He is the founder of Communities Organized for Public Service (COPS) and was named a MacArthur Fellow in 1984.

Bill Moyers is a television journalist primarily on PBS. He was a correspondent with CBS News and served as press secretary to President Lyndon Johnson. The interview with Ernesto Cortes was a part of his "World of Ideas" series that aired on PBS in the Fall of 1988.

Summary

In all but one of the 15 largest U.S. cities, at least one in every 10 residents was poor as of 1989.

City Poor

Source: Urban Institute.

institutions which enable people to negotiate with those pressures and with the corporate people who sometimes stand behind those pressures — the developers, the utility companies, et cetera.

They're also worried about the educational system, which is in very great difficulty in the United States. But most important, they're deeply concerned about the need for meaningful and nurturing relationships, which are so hard to maintain in the isolation and alienation of our cities today.

MOYERS: Some of your critics say that you are actually too conservative. They say you're bringing more people into a system of existing institutions that are ossified and out of date, when you should be changing that system.

CORTES: Well, I've very seldom been privileged to be called too conservative, but I guess in some ways, we are advocating a culturally conservative strategy. It's important for people to be connected to institutions. We have to make a distinction between tradition, which is the living ideas of the dead, and traditionalism, which is the dead ideas of the living. If you say I'm conservative because I think the family's important, I plead guilty. If you say I'm conservative because I think the church is important, I plead guilty. If you say I'm conservative because I think communities are important, I plead guilty. If you say I'm conservative because I think the public schools could be made to work, then I plead guilty. And if you say I'm conservative because I believe America can work, then I plead guilty as well.

MOYERS: I don't see much evidence over the last 15 years that the poor are a lot better off than they were when you began organizing.

CORTES: There's no question that we've got some serious problems. In San Antonio, my own city, studies have demonstrated that over the last 10 years people are getting poorer. We're dealing with some very powerful global economic forces, but we're also dealing with some very powerful and somewhat mean-spirited political forces in this country, and we haven't been able to overcome them yet. But people still have hope. We've been able to do some things that I think are important.

164

MOYERS: In San Antonio you took some housewives and turned them into experts on zoning, on sewage treatment facilities, on sanitation. What was that all about?

CORTES: First of all, I appreciate the compliment, but I'm not sure it's fair. All I did was point them in the right direction by teaching them how to build the COPS organization — Communities Organized for Public Service. They were very bright, eager, energetic people — housewives, Kelly Air Force Base workers, priests, nuns — just a whole range of people who were really concerned about what was going on. So there was a great deal of commitment and energy and desire to do something: flooding, toxic waste, the city water supply. People wanted to fight the development that was going to degrade that water supply.

But in order to do so they had to learn things. They had to learn about water and how it worked. They had to learn about development strategies and policies. They had to present alternative solutions. Saul Alinsky used to say that the price of a constructive criticism is a creative alternative. You have to not only organize against, but organize for. You have to come up with some alternatives.

MOYERS: What's the key to organizing?

CORTES: A love of politics, in the Greek sense, not in the electoral sense. We have to understand that we are social beings, that our development only takes place to the extent that we engage in public life and public discourse. That there is, in Hannah Arendt's phrase, the joy of public happiness.

MOYERS: But there doesn't seem to be much discourse in politics today.

CORTES: There's not much discourse in the quadrennial electronic plebiscite that we have every four years in this country, but that has very little to do with politics. It has more to do with marketing strategies, marketing segments, direct mailing, polling. That's not what de Tocqueville talked about as America's great strength — the people's love of public discourse and debate and willingness to deal with local issues from an institutional base, working through these mediating institutions. He

> *Being eyeball-to-eyeball is a hundred times more effective than writing a letter.*
>
> CLAUDINE SCHNEIDER
> Former U.S. Representative,
> Rhode Island

> *The problem of drugs is a national failure. We do not grow cocoa leaves in Albany.*
>
> GOVERNOR MARIO CUOMO
> Governor, New York State

FACT

53.9% of Americans state they have not had a conversation with a poor person (other than a panhandler) in the prior three months.

(Source: A Report on Americans' Attitudes Toward Poverty—poll conducted in late 1994.)

was enormously impressed by the potential these institutions offered. Of course he also saw some serious problems, like slavery. People were left out.

One of the things in fact that we're most interested in now is making sure that people who are normally considered the have-nots don't get left out. The IAF [Industrial Areas Foundation] wants to organize people who are not part of decision making in communities to be part of the decision-making process. To be involved in politics. For them to see that there is a way in which they can qualitatively improve their lives.

MOYERS: Not just to turn out and vote?

CORTES: Voting is important, but it's the least important aspect of any democratic decision making. It's the affirmation of a decision that was made through a process of discussion and debate. They have voting in totalitarian countries, too.

MOYERS: Gorbachev was just elected president with virtually no opposition.

CORTES: Yes. Augusto Pinochet used to have plebiscites in Chile, which was not a very democratic society under Pinochet. There was no discussion. There was no debate. There was no free press. There was no opportunity for people to engage.

Timothy Garton Ash says that in Central Europe an internal immigration takes place where people withdraw into their own cocoons. It takes place when there's no public space, when there's no opportunity for debate. I see some of that occurring in the United States. Not because of some totalitarian dictator, but because of the role that the media play in politics. People feel alienated and disconnected from it.

We can't rely on people by themselves to be good. They have to participate through institutions. We need institutions and a political culture that hold people accountable and teach them certain values. We're bombarded by all kinds of information, but there's no framework for developing political judgments. The institutions that used to teach people — whether they were political parties, labor unions, churches, voluntary associations — those institutions have been weakened, or they've been rendered incompetent. That's why the IAF seeks to build some sort of institutional framework to enable people to acquire the requisite skills and information so they can make political judgments. In a real sense, organizations like COPS or United Neighborhood Organizations in East Los Angeles are mini-universities for these skills.

MOYERS: What kinds of skills?

CORTES: Our leaders need to understand power. How it operates, who wields it. You have to know not only what a politician says, but who gives him money and how those people influence his decisions. You have to know his record. You have to understand how to negotiate with people. You have to know how to present your issue carefully. You have to understand how to do the research behind a particular issue. Secondly, our leaders have to know how to build what we call public relationships. An organization like Valley Interfaith or COPS is not going to work unless ordinary people can build relationships with other people they don't know very well. The IAF organizers must teach people how to develop sustaining mechanisms for maintaining a collective leadership....The job of an organizer is to agitate. Now, people have the stereotype of what agitation is. But in the sense the IAF teaches it, the agitator raises questions, gets people to look at their choices, to look at their options, to understand that power depends upon consent. The ethics of power really hovers around the question of how you go about obtaining consent. You can obtain consent by force or violence. You can obtain consent by deceit, by lying to people. You can obtain consent by manipulating people, withholding information, rendering them incompetent. But finally you can learn to obtain consent through informed judgment.

There is a tradition in south Texas I call "learned helplessness." People have been taught to be incompetent by all the institutions: family, the church, the school. There was a tradition among the *quinieros*, the workers of the King Ranch. They didn't have to worry about their retirement, they didn't have to worry about their kids' education, they didn't have to worry about anything because the boss would take care of them. Well, the King Ranch is no longer owned by a family; it's now owned by anonymous corporations. The *quinieros* who are now out of work have no skills, no education, nowhere to go because

Summary

The poor and the nonpoor share a similar perception of the community, but within the poor population, more blacks than whites have a strong sense of community.

A Sense of Community

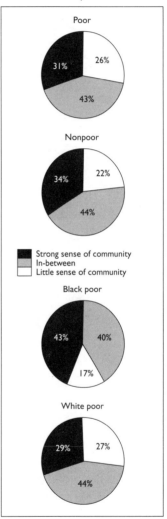

Source: Jeffrey M. Berry, Kent E. Portney, and Ken Thomson, *The Political Behavior of Poor People* (1991).

they've been raised in this almost feudal system where they were taken care of. They were taught to be dependent upon the patrón.

MOYERS: They never questioned his authority?

CORTES: Why should they? He always took care of them. If he told them how to vote, what did it matter? In those days, those things weren't important. What was important was the integrity of that relationship between you and the land, and between you and your work, you and your family. I'm oversimplifying it just a bit, but that tradition holds all across south Texas. Part of what these organizations do is to teach people how to exercise responsibility with power.

MOYERS: Give me an example. How do you teach the consequences of actions?

CORTES: One of the most confrontational actions COPS ever organized in San Antonio involved window shopping. My mother and my aunts used to love to browse in the department stores. We didn't have any money so they'd go downtown and window shop, just look at things. The sales clerks would call them "pills" because they never bought anything.

We were having trouble getting the City Council in San Antonio to pay attention to our counterbudget, which included provisions to fight flooding and all kinds of public improvements in the city. So we decided that we had to take it outside the conventional political establishment and get the corporate community involved. I said, why can't we get a whole lot of people to go window shop at Josky's of Texas, the biggest department store of San Antonio? COPS took 500 folks and we went window shopping. They went in and they looked at furs and sables and so forth. More than 500 of them went up to the most exclusive department store in town, just trying things on. They didn't hurt anything. They didn't do anything illegal. Window shopping is legal. But they did it at one time and one place.

MOYERS: And the owner got the message?

CORTES: Yes.

MOYERS: What was it Saul Alinsky said? Make the enemy live by his own book of rules. That's what you were doing there?

168

CORTES: COPS had made this commitment to justice and equality and fair play, and we were trying to get the corporate community, the political community, in San Antonio to be responsive. Sometimes you've got to get people's attention first. You've got to get recognition. And sometimes you've got to deal with the most disenfranchised force to get everybody else to deal with what's not going right in the culture. In religious tradition, the poor have got to evangelize the rich. It's a responsibility of poor people to teach rich people how to be human.

MOYERS: What do you think we are when we are most human?

CORTES: We're rational. We're caring. We are reciprocal. We give and take. We share. Bernard Loomer wrote an essay called "Two Kinds of Power." He says that most of our institutions practice what he calls unilateral power, the power of domination, what Lord Acton would call unaccountable power. Power which is inaccessible and therefore unaccountable. I think that people can learn a different kind of power. Power which includes sharing and collaboration. Power which involves people learning how to work together. I'm not trying to preach pie in the sky, but I'm saying that people have got to recognize other people's interests. Sometimes there has to be hard bargaining, hard negotiating. Sometimes arguing, sometimes confrontation. Alinsky used to say that if you had to define democracy in one word, it would be compromise. There has to be a deal. A political philosopher said once that in politics, it's not enough just to be right. You also have to be reasonable. You have to give and take. You have to compromise.

MOYERS: It's easy to say that to the poor, though. How do you say that to the rich who have been winning in this country all along?

CORTES: That's true. But the rich have got to understand that they've got a stake in this too, unless they want to live in a Third World country. I'm not sure that America can make it without a decent public school system. I'm not sure America can make it without cities.

> *If there is no struggle, there is no progress. Those who profess to favor freedom, and yet deprecate agitation, are men who want crops without plowing up the ground, they want rain without thunder and lightning. They want ocean without the awful roar of its many waters.*
>
> FREDERICK DOUGLASS
> *Writer, Abolitionist*

Summary

Between 1984 and 1994, the United States spent 3 times more on defense than on its combined human needs, and approximately 15 times more on defense than it did on education.

Defense or Social Spending?

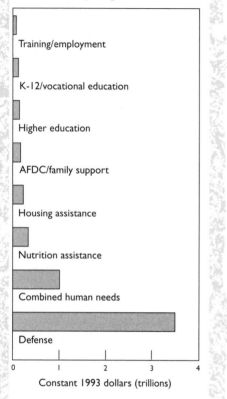

Training/employment

K-12/vocational education

Higher education

AFDC/family support

Housing assistance

Nutrition assistance

Combined human needs

Defense

0   1   2   3   4

Constant 1993 dollars (trillions)

Source: Campaign for New Priorities.

MOYERS: I agree with you. But parts of our culture, parts of San Antonio, are already a Third World country. All the border of Texas-Mexico is a Third World country. You're not talking about something that could be, you're talking about something that is.

CORTES: That's correct. And that's why I think Texas has a real role to play. We could be a model, or we could be an example of the future that doesn't work.

MOYERS: The Nigeria of America?

CORTES: That's right. That concerns me. I know there are people in the corporate community and the political community who understand that. Ross Perot, for instance, is deeply involved in the education issue. He tells his friends, "I know you don't like black. And I know you don't like brown. But I know you love green."

MOYERS: It comes down to that, doesn't it?

CORTES: Sometimes. One of the things that IAF teaches is that people sometimes do the right thing for the wrong reasons. Some of my friends who are idealists expect people to do the right thing for the right reason. They want people's motives to be pure. But with the world as it is, people operate on the basis of their own interests. We have got to find out what is the interest of people.

MOYERS: What's going to happen in Texas and in California when the people who are now in the minority become, in another 15 years, the majority?

CORTES: Well, that's a good question. I would ask it of people who think that it's not in their interest to be concerned about those people. Just ask them how their Social Security checks will be paid when the ratio of workers to retired people is two to one, and one of those workers is uneducated, can't read, can't function in a working environment. Now where is that Social Security check going to come from? Where is his pension going to come from?

MOYERS: You're asking us — rich and poor — to think of self-interest as something more than just our own aggrandizement, our own reward.

CORTES: That's correct. Properly understood, self-interest leads people to be their brothers' and sisters' keepers. You recognize you need people. I can't get what I want unless you get what you want. We're in this together.

MOYERS: That's not the way the world seems to have been working.

CORTES: No question about it. But that's why we need to build broad-based organizations. That's why the IAF is recruiting organizers. That's why no matter how hard I work myself out of a job, I'll always have one, because people need these organizations that teach them how their self-interest is connected to other people's interest. How they're not going to get what they want unless other people get what they want. How compromise is not a dirty word. Half a loaf is still bread, you can still eat it. But then there's the compromise of Solomon, which is half a baby, a corpse. The question is, which compromises do you take? Which compromises are appropriate?

MOYERS: What does it mean when you say you want to empower the poor?

CORTES: In a word, I want to teach people. I want to teach people how they can take their private pain, their private hopes, their private aspirations, and translate that into public issues that are going to qualitatively improve their lives and those of their children. But that's going to require work on their part. It's going to require responsibility, because the flip side of power is responsibility. It means they have to be owners of their own destiny. That means everything from raising the money to build an organization so that the organizers work for them and aren't being paid by some outside sources. It means understanding the issues. They have to be their own spokespersons. They have to speak for themselves. They have to understand the arguments, because they have to engage in the discourse with the mayor of San Antonio, or the mayor of Houston, or the bank president. It means they have to be willing to teach others.

MOYERS: How do you do that, though? Because in Texas, as you said, the Hispanics have been taught for so long to conform that it must be very difficult now for them to learn to challenge authority or to believe that authority will deal with them.

CORTES: You take institutions — the family, the church — and you use them as a source of power, of confidence, of authority. If you get people to talk about what's in the interest of their families, what are the threats to their families, what are the threats to the churches and community, then they're willing to look at things like zoning, and they're willing to look at things like the school.

The most important lesson IAF has to teach is the iron rule. The iron rule is never, ever do for people what they can do for themselves. It's the opposite of learned helplessness. The iron rule respects people's dignity. It says, "You have to challenge people." It's the opposite of what Alinsky called "Welfare Colonialism," where you treat people as if they were children. John Stuart Mill wrote an essay on representative government which said that the act of participation teaches people confidence in their own competence. That's central to understanding the iron rule. People have got to have the opportunity to learn. It's what we teach our kids! We enable them to grow and develop through victories. And we teach them how to manage their own lives, their own destinies. We do a horrible thing to them when we take away that responsibility.

MOYERS: The organizer is not more important than the organized.

CORTES: Well he is and he isn't. She is and she isn't. That's part of the contradiction, if you will, the dialectic involved in this business. It won't happen without you, but it can't be dependent upon you.... And it's important to have a vision of where you're going. It's important to have a vision. Without a vision, people perish. The Scripture tells us. People have to be challenged to develop their own vision and their own values about what's important. Otherwise it's not their thing, it's your thing.

MOYERS: What have you learned — in almost a generation of organizing — about power in America?

CORTES: You don't see enough examples of it, but you see when it can work. You can teach people. You can teach people to be effective. I've learned that.

MOYERS: Have you had it confirmed for you that absolute power is corrupt?

CORTES: Lord Acton was on the money! Unaccountable, inaccessible power is corrupting. Not only corrupt, it's corrupting.

MOYERS: But absolute powerlessness corrupts, too, doesn't it?

CORTES: Yes. If the flip side of power is responsibility, then people who have no power are irresponsible. They become wards of the state. And you see it all the time. The worst example, of course, is a 14-year-old girl who's on cocaine who has a child. Children having children. Now to me that's a product of absolute powerlessness. The degradations of people who have no choices; who don't see any options, who are victims.

MOYERS: Do you believe God is just?

CORTES: Yes.

MOYERS: Then why so much suffering? Why so many poor?

CORTES: I don't know! I'm not an expert on all this business.

MOYERS: Are you still a practicing Catholic?

CORTES: Yes. I see a great deal of beauty and joy in my own children. They're wonderful people. My son, my daughters, my wife. I've been gifted with a good relationship; I've been gifted with what the Hebrews would call *"Shalom"*: family, health, friends, meaningful work...

MOYERS: In this case, God is just.

CORTES: He's been good to me! I feel that we're responsible, though, for creation. I believe Genesis is the most important book in the Bible sometimes, and that we've been given lordship over creation. We're responsible for what happens, and I think we can make choices. We can make choices whether or not we blow up the planet. We can make choices about whether or not we degrade it. Or we can make choices to leave our future generations a legacy, a heritage.

MOYERS: The future is not something abstract to you.

CORTES: No, my future is in my son. He's my future. My future is in my daughters. My future is in the children they're going to have. A political scientist once wrote that political decisions revolve around a relevant time period. The relevant time period for a politician is two years or four years; for a general it's five years; for a corporate executive, it's every quarter. He said, "But the relevant time period for a grandmother is a generation, because she's concerned about her grandchildren." Well, I'd like to appropriate that time period into our IAF organizations, into our culture, into our psyche, into our political leadership, too.

COPS

Communities Organized for Public Service

It seems like a simple idea: Employment training programs should prepare workers for good jobs that actually exist in their city. Yet, in San Antonio, this wasn't the case — not until a coalition of employees, workers, and community leaders came together to form San Antonio Communities Organized for Public Service (COPS).

Under COPS, city leaders created an employment skills program that trains workers for jobs that will be available upon completion of the program. It's called Project Quest (Quality Employment through Skills Training).

Project Quest was developed in response to San Antonio's changing economy. Throughout the 1980s, the city lost 14,000 blue collar manufacturing jobs while gaining 19,000 high-tech jobs. This change was brought home to city leaders in 1990 when the city was caught off guard by the sudden closing of a popular clothing factory. At the same time that blue collar workers were being laid off, the city's high-tech industries were begging for workers.

COPS created a new type of job training. About 650 persons a year are trained for guaranteed jobs that pay at least $7.50 an hour and include benefits and opportunities for advancement. COPS also helps city and school officials develop programs for inner-city neighborhood improvement, public school enhancement, and affordable housing rehabilitation and mortgage financing.

For more information contact COPS, P.O. Box 830355, San Antonio, TX 78283; (210) 222-2367.

Travels

ALICE WALKER

Voting, particularly in local elections, is as much a social act as a political act. Registering, listening, discussing, weighing arguments and then ultimately deciding how you want to allocate funds, override tax limits, or elect a new person to office, are some of the key ways we are connected to our communities. It is a connection that we seem to be losing. Over the last 30 years, participation in presidential elections has decreased by 20 percent. "What good is the vote, if we don't own nothing?" asks the character in this excerpt from Alice Walker's novel Meridian.

"Mama," a half-naked little boy called as they walked up to the porch, "it's some people out here, and one of 'em is that woman in the cap."

The wooden steps were broken and the porch sagged. In the front room a thin young man worked silently in a corner. In front of him was a giant pile of newspapers that looked as though they'd been salvaged from the hands of children who ate dinner over the funnies. Meridian and Truman watched the man carefully smooth out the paper, gather ten sheets, then twenty, and roll them into a log around which he placed a red rubber band. When he finished the "log" he stacked it, like a piece of wood, on top of the log pile of such "logs" that ran across one side of the poorly furnished, rather damp and smelly room.

Through the inner door he had a view of his wife — when he turned around to put the paper on the pile — lying on the bed. He nodded to them that they should enter his wife's room.

"How're you?" asked Meridian, as she and Truman looked about for chairs.

Alice Walker is the author of several books, including the Pulitzer prize-winning bestseller *The Color Purple*. In addition, she has written five volumes of poetry, two collections of short stories, and two collections of essays.

"Don't sit there," the woman said to Truman, who sat in a straight chair the young son brought. "You blocks my view of my husband."

"I'm sorry," said Truman, quickly moving.

"I'm feelin' a little better today," said the woman, "a little better." Her small black face was childlike, all bony points and big brown eyes that never left her husband's back.

"My husband Johnny went out and got me some venison and made me up a little stew. I think that's helping me to git my strength up some." She laughed, for no reason that her visitors could fathom. It was a soft, intimate chuckle, weak but as if she wanted them to understand she could endure whatever was wrong.

"Where did he get deer this time of year?" asked Truman.

"Don't tell anybody," the sick woman chuckled again, slyly, "but he went hunting out at one of those places where the sign says 'Deer Crossin'.' If we had a refrigerator we wouldn't need any more meat for the rest of the year. Johnny — " she began, showing all her teeth as one hand clutched the bedspread with the same intensity as her rather ghastly smile.

"Did you say somethin', Agnes?" asked Johnny, getting up from his chore with the newspapers and coming to stand at the foot of the bed. "You hongry again?"

"I gets full just lookin' at you, sugah," said the sick woman coquettishly. "That's about the only reason I hate to die," she said, looking at her visitors for a split second, "I won't be able to see my ol' good-lookin' man."

"Shoot," said Johnny, going back to the other room.

"He used to be a worker at the copper plant, used to make wire. They fired him 'cause he wouldn't let the glass in front of his table stay covered up. You know in the plant they don't want the working folks to look at nothing but what's right on the table in front of them. But my Johnny said he wasn't no mule to be wearing blinders. He wanted to see a little bit of grass, a little bit of sky. It was bad enough being buried in the basement over there, but they wanted to even keep out the sun." She looked at her husband's back as if she could send her fingers through her eyes.

"What does he do with the newspapers?" asked Truman.

Summary

Voter turnout dwindles steadily as income level declines; only 26.4% of the poorest voters exercised their franchise in 1992.

Why Vote?

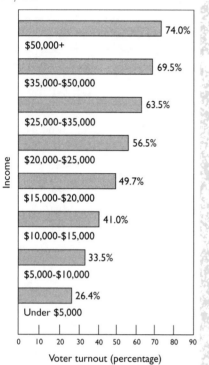

Source: Committee for the Study of the American Electorate.

"Did you see how many he has? asked the woman. "You should see the room behind this one. Rolled newspapers up to the ceiling. Half the kitchen is rolled newspapers." She chuckled hoarsely. "So much industry in him. Why, in the wintertime he and little Johnny will take them logs around to folks with fireplaces and sell'em for a nickel apiece and to colored for only three pennies."

"Hummm — " said Meridian. "Maybe we could help him roll a few while we're here. We just came by to ask if you all want to register to vote, but I think we could roll a few newspapers while you think about it."

"*Vote?*" asked the woman attempting to raise her voice to send the question to her husband. Then she lay back. "Go on in there and git a few pages," she said.

As soon as she touched the newspapers Meridian realized Johnny must have combed the city's garbage cans, trash heaps, and department store alleys for them. Many were damp and even slimy, as if fish or worse had been wrapped in them. She began slowly pressing the papers flat, then rolling them into logs.

The sick woman was saying, "I have this dream that if the Father blesses me I'll die the week before the second Sunday in May because I want to be buried on Mother's Day. I don't know why I want that, but I do. The pain I have is like my kidneys was wrapped in that straining gauze they use in dairies to strain milk, and something is squeezing and squeezing them. But when I die, the squeezing will stop. Round Mother's Day, if the merciful Father say so."

"Mama's goin' to heaven," said Johnny Jr., who came to roll the papers Meridian had smoothed.

"She's already sweet like an angel," said Meridian impulsively, rubbing his hair and picking away the lint, "like you."

"What good is the vote, if we don't own nothing?" asked the husband as Truman and Meridian were leaving. The wife, her eyes steadily caressing her husband's back, had fallen asleep, Johnny Jr. cuddled next to her on the faded chenille bedspread. In winter the house must be freezing, thought Truman, looking at the cracks in the walls; and now, in spring, it was full of flies.

"Do you want free medicine for your wife? A hospital that'll take black people through the front door? A good school for Johnny Jr. and a job no one can take away?"

"You know I do," said the husband sullenly.

"Well, voting probably won't get it for you, not in your lifetime," Truman said, not knowing whether Meridian intended to lie and claim it would.

"What *will* it get me but a lot of trouble," grumbled the husband.

"I don't know," said Meridian. "It may be useless. Or maybe it can be the beginning of the use of your voice. You have to get used to using your voice, you know. You start on simple things and move on...."

"No," said the husband, "I don't have time for foolishness. My wife is dying. My boy don't have shoes. Go somewhere else and find somebody that ain't got to work all the time for pennies, like I do."

"Okay," said Meridian. Surprised, Truman followed as she calmly walked away.

"What's this here?" asked the husband ten minutes later as they came through his front door with two bags of food.

"To go with the venison," Meridian grinned.

"I ain't changed my mind," said the husband, with a suspicious peek into the bags.

And they did not see him again until the Monday after Mother's Day, when he brought them six rabbits already skinned and ten newspaper logs; and under the words WILL YOU BE BRAVE ENOUGH TO VOTE in Meridian's yellow pad, he wrote his name in large black letters.

FROM: *Meridian,* 1976.

> *Politicians are unlikely to be especially attentive to the needs of "constituents" unwilling to vote, help get out the vote, or contribute to political campaigns. Many in America's lower four-fifths are engaged in a political vicious circle where cynicism about American politics is rewarded by government decisions which confirm their worst suspicions.*
>
> ROBERT B. REICH
> *The Work of Nations*

DSC
Delta Service Corps

The Delta Service Corps (DSC) invites residents from Arkansas, Louisiana, and Mississippi to serve as community workers on critical education, environmental, health care, human service, and public safety needs.

In exchange for a minimal living allowance, people from diverse backgrounds and ages work together on such projects as teaching prison inmates workplace skills, assisting public aid workers with natural disaster relief, bringing together teens to brainstorm ways of reducing youth violence, refurbishing a community park, or delivering care baskets to elderly residents.

In return, corps workers learn community leadership skills of their own and get a partial tuition reimbursement for college or vocational training.

Founded in 1992, the DSC is a demonstration model for AmeriCorps program (see page 219), a national initiative of the Corporation for National and Community Service to offer educational opportunities in exchange for community service. Funding comes from federal and state grants, foundation and corporation support, community organizations, and the general public. The program's mission is to promote civic responsibility, address urgent community needs, and enhance educational opportunities.

Nick Crossley, DSC National Service Representative from Arkansas, describes what the program has meant to him. He writes, "Without their offer of full-time community service, I may not have realized that I could take my knowledge and ambition and devote it to serving my community. DSC has helped me develop a connection and sense of duty to Arkansas that I never felt before."

Membership in the Delta Service Corps is open to any U.S. citizen in Arkansas, Mississippi, or Louisiana; of any age over 17; with a high school diploma or equivalency degree.

For more information, contact Delta Service Corps, P.O. Box 2990, West Memphis, AR 72303; (501) 735-4373.

Cooperative Home Care Associates

Cooperative Home Care Associates dovetails a critically needed service with the employment needs of low-income women in a system that provides specialized training and eventual employee control of the organization.

Although an aging and more medically stable population is fueling the demand for home health care, pay and benefits are generally poor for the aides who bathe, feed, and assist the ill and elderly clients of the service providers.

Rick Surpin founded Cooperative Home Care Associates in South Bronx, New York, in 1985 as a profit-sharing program that gradually turned control of the agency over to the health care workers themselves. Nine years later, close to 300 employees, most of them women of color and former welfare recipients, are employed by the cooperative, earning profits for themselves and their co-workers.

The success of this worker-owned agency has prompted it to duplicate its effort in other cities, with the oversight of its close affiliate, the Home Care Associates Training Institute. Boston Home Care Associates opened its doors in April 1994 and so far 19 home health aides have completed the training program and are working for the cooperative. Seth Evans, President of the Boston cooperative, anticipates employee control in the next three to four years.

"Home health care often suffers because workers are part-time and poorly paid and their jobs aren't treated with the importance that they're

due," Evans said. "We say, quality jobs equals quality care. We hope to be the higher quality provider in our areas by empowering the workers."

Funding for the Institute's replication efforts comes from a number of private foundations and, in Boston, the U.S. Department of Health and Human Services.

For more information, contact the Home Care Associates Training Institute, 349 East 149th Street, Bronx, NY 10451; (718) 993-7140.

Photo: © 1994 Valarie Seabrook

Inside Trey-Nine

BY REPORTERS AT *NEWSWEEK*

Urban poverty is not the same in New York or Chicago as it is in Cleveland or Los Angeles. While some problems are shared among poor people in our cities, we ought to avoid painting with too broad a brush. The differences among cities are due to (among other things) immigration, employment patterns, political history, ethnic and racial composition, and social welfare variations. One question we ought to ask is, Why is urban poverty so often portrayed through Chicago? In part, the stage was set by Chicago's early embrace of public housing. The large, tall, isolated buildings provide modern media with a dramatic setting for examining very real problems. But this can be misleading. Most public housing is not a high-rise nightmare. In fact, the vast majority of public housing works quite successfully in smaller cities and smaller projects across the country. The following article, by reporters from Newsweek *headed by Sylvester Monroe, a former resident of the Robert Taylor Homes project, offers a poignant portrait of a community in distress. "Trey-nine" is what many residents called their building within the project at 3919 South Federal Street. This article is an excerpt from a longer story that was reported by Sylvester Monroe, Vern E. Smith, Monroe Anderson, and Terry E. Johnson, and it was written by Peter Goldman for* Newsweek.*

Monroe Anderson was a correspondent for the Chicago bureau of *Newsweek*. He is currently the Director of Station Services and Community Affairs at WBBM-TV, Chicago.

Peter Goldman, the writer of "Inside Trey-Nine," is a contributing editor for *Newsweek* and co-founder of the Special Projects Unit.

Terry E. Johnson is a political activist in Philadelphia, and publisher of two community newspapers, *Real News* and *Business Review*. Prior to this, he was a national affairs writer in New York.

Sylvester Monroe was at *Newsweek* for more than 15 years and has since become a Los Angeles–based correspondent for *Time*.

Vern Smith is *Newsweek*'s Atlanta bureau chief, a position he has held since 1979. He has served as a key reporter with the Special Projects Unit.

Fresh paint. So much more had seemed possible when their generation first moved in. Trey-nine was new then, and like them, it had a look of innocence and hope. There were no rats or roaches. The gangs hadn't arrived — not yet. Neither had drugs. The paint was fresh. The lawns were green and flowered. The elevators worked. There was heat and hot water and breathing space, at prices poor people could afford.

182

But for too many, it turned out to be a place where hope died. Projects like the Taylors were built by conscious design in those parts of town where black people already lived and were intended to keep them there; rather than break up the ghetto, the planners rebuilt it, straight up, with all its poverty and debilities piled 16 stories high. The Taylors became a city within a city, poor, black, insular, dependent, and dangerous. Its official population today is 19,000, mostly mothers and children. Perhaps 5,000 men are in fact *around* at any given moment, living off the books, but two-parent families are scarce; to be a boy in the Taylor Homes is to apprentice at becoming an invisible man.

Honk Johnson's own father had floated in and out of Honk's boyhood. He was a hardworking man, a tailor and presser by trade. But he was a drinker and a lady-killer as well, and after siring his fourth child he began straying from apartment 410; to stay home would have been to live with the evidence of how little material support he had to give his growing brood.

Their rearing fell mostly to Honk's mother, Ernestine. She was a good woman, raised in the church in Alabama and brought north by her own daddy, a steelworker. She had been 13 then and pretty as a model, but when her path crossed Roy Johnson, Sr.'s at a social club called the Black Spider, she was lost. She married too young, at 17, and had too many children, until there were 11 and she was overwhelmed by their sheer number.

She felt powerless to affect which ones would turn out good and which would not. Her second son, Roy Jr., mystified her most of all; it was as if Trey-nine had taken him away and sent back a stranger called Honk. He was an undersize child through his teens, a runty boy with innocent eyes, but early in his life he got obsessed with wanting to be rich. His sins multiplied as he grew older, and the flat of his father's hand was not enough to stop him.

Neither was the old man's example; little Roy's role models instead were two teenage cousins who ran with the Egyptian Cobras, had been in and out of jail and always had money, guns, and style. They looked like someone you could be, Roy thought, and he tried. His mother, like most who moved to

Trey-nine, imagined that raising children would go better there — that it would get them away from the worst influences of the ghetto. But things didn't work that way with little Roy. Trey-nine became his finishing school instead, a seminar in making crime pay.

As a grade schooler, he developed his skills filching franks at the ballpark. At 12 he first tasted codeine cough syrup, at 13 he was trafficking in it. By 15 he was a skilled B&E man, plundering the shopping center across the street for food and clothing and reselling it at Trey-nine. He was growing up as hard and glittery as a dime-store pinkie ring, and when his new friends renamed him Honkie, for his light skin, his mother barely knew him anymore.

Class change. *His* American dream was wealth and, as he came to understand later, glory — an assertion of size in a world that discouraged it. Nigger has to make a mark, he told himself. He knew *he* wasn't going to be like his daddy, slaving for chumpchange, and he wasn't going to bump along from one minimum-wage job to another like some of his homeboys. He figured he could stand out on the corner looking sharp as a MF in his Stacy-Adams wingtips and a $100 hat and *think* up more money in an hour than they made in a whole sweaty day.

He sometimes thought in later years that he might have done better taking a job and working his way *toward* something besides easy money. But he wasn't gaited for it; he had trouble taking orders from anyone. No teacher had ever reached him; the only heroes he ever had were the studs out in the street holding that paper, the green kind with pictures of dead presidents on it. Honk wanted that quick bankroll and couldn't even imagine a straight-up way to get it; he wasn't no million-dollar basketball player like Billy Harris, out there every day working on his shake-and-bake moves, and he wasn't bringing home straight-A report cards like Brainiac Monroe.

So Honk dropped out of school and the work force and became what the brothers on the block call a player — a trafficker in anything the law disallows. In the years thereafter he would scheme, rob, deal, kill, and make money, a lot of it. He'd hear some stud complaining about how he couldn't get no job, and Honk would answer impatiently, "Nigger, you don't *need*

FACT

The average annual income of public housing residents decreased from 33 percent of the national median in 1981 to 17 percent in 1993.

(Source: Congressional Testimony, March 22, 1994.)

no job." He himself had not had one since his teens, but he had never wanted for anything. All Honk ever hungered for was more.

"One year as a millionaire," his homeboy Little Jimmy was saying at the barbecue at Trey-nine. "That's all I want."

Honk shook his head. The notion that enough was enough was heresy to him.

"You wanta be a ole Howard Hughes," Little Jimmy was saying. "Shoot, if you had a million bucks right now, you still wouldn't be satisfied. If he had 10 million," Jimmy went on, turning to a visitor, "he *still* wouldn't be happy."

Honk grinned. "What I wanta get enough of it for?"

Honk sipped his wine, his smile now masking his feelings, he *had* achieved a kind of royalty on 39th Street, but it was a very small principality, a corner left behind by The Man. He glanced up at Trey-nine. He was still a regular commuter, taking care of business *and* pleasure, and his mama still lived in 410 with his younger brothers and sisters. But the project no longer had the promise he remembered.

From upstairs you could still see the spires of downtown Chicago, but they remained as distant and unreal as the Emerald City of Oz. The old lawns had gone bald, the brick was graffitied and scarred, and the open-air galleries on each floor had long ago been screened in with steel-mesh fencing. It was as if people had been sealed inside — as if, Honk thought, they weren't *supposed* to escape. If you came from Trey-nine, he thought, prison was just a change of address. Prison was where you were *from*.

SONNY SPRUIELL WAS LOUNGING with some of the brothers outside Trey-nine one day in the middle '60s when an apparition came floating up Dearborn Street toward them — a dude in a flowing black cape with a blood-red lining. Some older tenants smelled trouble and began easing inside. The boys did not; they sat tight until the dude was almost in their face.

"My name is Jesus," he said, pronouncing it *Hey-soos* in the Spanish way, "and these are my Disciples."

Summary

More than 50 percent of the families living below the poverty line are headed by African-American single mothers.

Families in Poverty

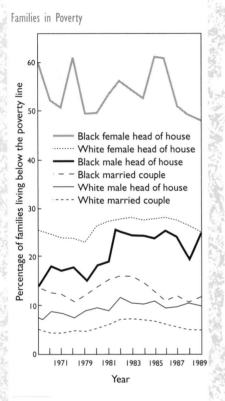

Source: U.S. Census Bureau (1990).

He flung the cape wide, a flare of black and crimson, and the project came alive with armed invaders — members of a gang called the Devil's Disciples from down on 53rd Street. No one had seen them coming, and it wasn't much comfort that they were only passing through on their way to battle at Stateway Gardens, the next project to the north. Sonny thought of himself as a hard guy, a hope-to-die nigger, but he and his partners were trembling at the *crack-crack* of gunfire across 39th Street. He glanced at the grown-ups cowering up on the galleries. They ain't gonna look out for us, he was thinking. We're gonna have to look out for ourselves.

Gangs were pandemic on the South Side, warring tribes who called themselves Disciples or Del Vikings or, rising to primacy, the Blackstone Rangers. Sociologists kept finding things to romanticize about them — the sense of pride and purpose they brought to young lives in the anarchy of the ghetto. But the people who lived there were frightened by the gang-banging — in Chicago, the term meant gang war, not gang rape — and their fear rose as the arms race escalated to real guns.

Trey-nine was in a particularly vulnerable position, standing alone on a block. Its solitude made it easy prey to gang-bangers from Stateway to the north or from the other Taylor high-rises to the south. Just leaving the grounds meant trespassing on some enemy's turf, a crime punishable by a beating or worse. But the Disciples' raid showed how vulnerable they were even on their home territory, and some of the older guys were telling them they had to stand up and fight. James Bonner, for example; he was a stone killer in the eyes of the police, 260 pounds of violence on a 5-foot-8 chassis, but he was the man of the house to the fatherless boys of Trey-nine, and when *he* said fight, they knew he would clean up for them if they got beat.

So they called a council of war next day on the 12th-floor gallery. Sonny was there, more or less in charge, along with Pee Wee Fisher, and Honk, and Half Man Carter, and Moose Harper, and Nate the Albino, and a hard dude called Crazy Horse from south of 40th Street.

"I'm tired of running," Sonny began. "We got to do something."

Zip guns. What they did was organize their own gang, Satan's Saints, though they didn't really think of it as a gang at first. It was all cowboys-and-Indians then, a game, Moose thought, until people started getting killed. Even their early adventures in banditry had a kind of boyishness. Once, they gang-mugged a stray white hitchhiker, discovered that he had no money and, feeling sorry for him, gave him some of their own. But the feudal wars on the South Side were getting serious, and so were the armaments. Zip guns appeared first at Trey-nine, treacherous one-shot contrivances homemade with scraps of wood, metal, and rubber that were at least as much danger to the shooter as to his target. But other gangs were laying up real guns, raising the stakes, and one day Crazy Horse led some of the Saints to his bedroom at home. He turned back the mattress to reveal a sawed-off shotgun. The Saints, like it or not, were armed for war.

Not all of them liked it. Crazy Horse was hard core, and so were Sonny and Ed Hamilton. But Moose hated gang-banging once it turned deadly, and even Pee Wee Fisher, a main man for the Saints, was losing his heart for it. He had been watching guys get *doggish*, moving up that escalator from clubbing to stabbing and now shooting each other, his enthusiasm faded as the slugs hit closer to home.

He saw *how* close the day they put on their black Saints jackets, fueled up on sweet wine and went hunting for a Del Viking who had pulled a gun on a Trey-nine brother. They found him in an alley under the el tracks, leaning against a car with a .38 in his waistband. He had been drinking.

"Mighty Satan's Saints!" Crazy Horse yelled. The code required that you "represent" what gang you were from.

"Mighty Dels!" the dude yelled back. He upped the .38 and started shooting, only one of the Saints beat him with a blast from six feet. It hit the dude in the shoulder. His body fell forward. His shoulder stuck to the car.

The Saints ran home. "Pee Wee, you think he killed him?" Sonny whispered.

"I don't know, man, I don't know," Pee Wee answered.

Balkan Empire. The answer drifted back: yeah, the ole boy died. There had been nothing personal; the dude represented

> *Such poverty as we have today in all our great cities degrades the poor, and infects with its degradation the whole neighborhood in which they live. And whatever can degrade a neighborhood can degrade a country and a continent and finally the whole civilized world, which is only a large neighborhood. Its bad effects cannot be escaped by the rich.*
>
> GEORGE BERNARD SHAW
> English Playwright, Critic,
> Social Reformer

wrong, and what followed was automatic. When you were a gang-banger, things happened.

And got worse. The strength-in-numbers impulse that had moved the Saints to organize in the first place got them entangled in mergers with larger, deadlier gangs — first the I (for Imperial), Supreme Cobras, then the deadliest of them all, the Blackstone Rangers, a Balkan empire spreading by force of numbers and arms across the South Side. Once, their attendance was commanded at a Stones meeting at a South Side church, the white clergy there was persuaded that the Stones were a potential force for good, Junior Achievers with guns. The Trey-nine brothers took seats in the back. Jeff Fort, the reigning Black Prince of the gang, was in the pulpit, presiding over a ritual called Truth Night, and some of his men were policing the aisles with rifles, clubs, and pool cues. If someone nodded off, they would go upside his head.

Someone was introducing a new recruit, a little dude with a large reputation in his own neighborhood branch of the Stones. "And you know what, Jeff?" the guy presenting him said. "He says he F'd you up. He told us that when he was in jail with us."

"*What?*" Fort exclaimed, "Send him up."

The dude slunk up. At a signal, two huge bodyguards materialized.

"Get him!" Fort commanded.

The two of them took turns hitting the dude in the ribs, the punches landing so hard they lifted him off his feet, but he took their best, shot for shot. Someone produced a bullwhip, and they laid on 10 lashes. The dude still wouldn't break.

Someone finally brought out a .38 revolver, dropped in a single round, spun the cylinder and put the muzzle to the dude's head. The choice was his, the Stones said. When they pulled the trigger, he could take his chances like a Stone-to-the-bone Ranger, or he could knock the gun away.

The brothers in the pews figured he would knock it away, toward them, and they began diving for cover.

They heard a *click* down front.

Heads poked up over the pews. The dude had accepted the 1-in-6 chance that his brains would wind up splattered on the altar. He had passed the test, and Fort commissioned him war-lord of his home gang.

But in the back of the church, the newly made Imperial Supreme Rangers sat shaken. Their young lives were surrounded by violence, but Ranger justice was cold. Ed Hamilton was hoping no one could see his heart thumping. Moose Harper broke out in hives and wound up in the hospital. None of them was feeling particularly imperial or supreme, and most of them didn't care about being Rangers anymore.

A Better Chance

Leroy Lovelace sat before his freshman English honors class at Wendell Phillips High School one autumn day in 1965, sweeping the room with a severe gaze and an inward smile. Phillips was a discouraging place most days, a warehouse overstocked with youngsters from the surrounding projects, and not, for the most part, the brightest youngsters; *they* commonly wound up at Dunbar Vocational, on the theory that slower learners couldn't be trusted around the fancy shop machinery there. The leftovers went to Phillips with its crowded classrooms and gang-infested corridors. There was an air of despair about the place, so heavy that Lovelace had almost succumbed to it himself. But he had endured, a lonely voice for excellence, and now he had the means to change — no, save — three young lives.

The magic that had fallen into his hands was a program called *A Better Chance*, ABC for short. It was the byproduct of the civil-rights movement and the aftershocks of conscience it set off in white philanthropy. A consortium of upscale public and private secondary schools in the East and Midwest would integrate, and not just with the sons and daughters of the black bourgeoisie.

Lovelace's eyes roamed over the room. "*Monroe...*" he intoned.

Vest Monroe was the easy choice. He was already reading two or three years ahead of his grade level; some of Lovelace's honor students were a year or two behind.

"... *Steward...*"

Steve Steward was less obvious. He was almost as gifted a student as Vest — when he wanted to be. He had a flair for math in particular. His problem was getting serious, about school or life, he couldn't think of anything he wanted to *do*. He was a coddled, mischievous child — a *joker*, Lovelace thought, yet the talent was there.

"...*Stingley*..."

Charles Ray Stingley, too, was a student of unrealized promise, he needed a kick start to get him going. Ray came from one of those big ghetto families, dysfunctionally big by the conventions of urban sociology; he was the seventh of 12 children crammed into a flat at the Prairie Courts project near Trey-nine. But the family was whole and warm, and Ray's parents, refugees from rural Mississippi, wanted their children to go further than they had. Their insistence made school a chore for Ray, and his lack of enthusiasm showed till Lovelace gave him an F at midterm to get his attention.

"...*I want to see you after class.*"

The three boys stole glances at one another. He's gonna give me another F, Ray was thinking, but what Lovelace had in mind instead was another life. He pushed some papers toward them. They were about going somewhere else to school — somewhere rich, white, and far away. It was a little scary for boys to whom even downtown Chicago was another country, but Lovelace made it sound like a ticket to tomorrow. "We've got to get you away from here," he said.

Home runs. So in the fading summer of 1966, just shy of his 15th birthday, Ray Stingley sat on a bus bound for a distant galaxy called Indiana and wondered if he could breathe the air there. Growing up, all he had wanted to be was a ballplayer; he had spent numberless hours on a vacant lot near home, a solitary boy hitting rocks with a stick, pretending he was belting home runs out of Comiskey Park. He had rarely worked that hard at his lessons, yet here he was, watching the highway slide past, headed for someplace named Culver Military Academy and a future he wasn't sure he could even imagine. He asked himself, not for the last time, what the F he was doing it for. The answer was for *them*.

"Them" meant J.C. and Cora Mae Stingley. He still remembered the day he had come home with the news that he had a chance to go away to school. "Boy, stop lying," his mother told him at first; she thought it was a joke. Ray himself considered it a mixed blessing until he saw what a fuss people made over him. It was nice reading his name in the school paper. It was nicer still seeing his mama looking happy and his daddy puffing his chest out just a little bit.

It was hard to please J.C. Stingley, or so it seemed to his 12 children. He loved them but had no idea how to show it; Ray was a grown-up the first time his daddy ever hugged him, and by then the old man was dying of emphysema. J.C. had spent his manhood at hard labor, as a sharecropper, a millhand, and finally a janitor in the projects. He gave his work so much of himself, his wife thought, that he had neither time nor emotion left for his children.

It was only later, as he sifted his boyhood memories, that Ray came to understand the man inside the granite shell. He remembered being home one day, feeling sorry for himself because everyone but him had a bicycle. He looked out the back window, and there came his daddy, plodding across the grounds, pushing an old red bike in front of him. He had salvaged it from the junk heap at the Dearborn Homes, the project where he worked. It was battered, but the two of them labored over it until they got it working. Ray had his bike. He wished long afterward that he had also had the words to tell his father he loved him.

Cora Mae Stingley worked, too, starting when she married at 17 and continuing through a low-paid lifetime. But it was she who governed the children, steering them away from bad company. A bright child like Ray had an easier time falling in with the right crowd. His inseparable friends from second grade on were Steve, Vest, and Gregory Bronson, all of them good students. They would read, hungrily and competitively, till they were racing one another through a book a night.

And then the ABC program came along, delivering Vest, Steve, and Ray to their separate white worlds. The fact that Culver *was* mostly white did not trouble Ray greatly, his butterflies had more to do with whether he was good enough to handle the work, and once he had survived his first quarter, he concluded that he could. He knew he was different, that he was black and poor in the land of the white well-to-do, and he wondered how he would react the first time some white boy called him nigger. But he resolved not to let those worries dominate his life. Hey, he thought, scanning the opaque white faces around him, you ain't gotta like me and I ain't gotta like you.

There were bad moments. English class was a torment when they were studying *Huckleberry Finn*, and everybody in the room was going "nigger-nigger-nigger," as if Twain's using the word made it OK to say. It wasn't, black people tossed it around freely where he came from, coloring it with their own ironic shadings, but they regarded it as family property. For white boys to speak it in Ray's presence was like touching a match to a short fuse. His belly said fight. His will said no, and there wasn't much he could do by way of protest anyway. He couldn't *afford* to be radical, he was a scholarship student scraping along on B's and C's, and he set himself a survivalist course — hit the books and stay the F out of the way.

He did, and to a degree that surprised him afterward. Charles Ray Stingley, late of Prairie Courts, became a part of Culver. He thought, while he was there, that he hated it. In fact, his discontents were the standard cadet complaints about chow, reveille, and regimentation, and his involvement in the barracks bitching was a measure of his assimilation. It wasn't until he had graduated and gone on to Albion College in Michigan that he realized how much he missed the academy — the people, the uniform, the routines, even the square-cornered military discipline — and how much they had formed him as a man. Ray was going to make it, Leroy Lovelace thought, watching his progress. Ray knew who he was....

FROM: *Newsweek*, March 25, 1987.

In a country well governed, poverty is something to be ashamed of.

CONFUCIUS
Chinese Philosopher

The triple whammy

AN INTERVIEW WITH SYLVESTER MONROE

Sylvester Monroe is currently a Los Angeles-based correspondent for Time. *This interview was conducted by producers of Blackside, Inc.'s documentary series,* America's War on Poverty.

In the Robert Taylor Homes…there were intact two-parent working families. That's who used to be the population of the Robert Taylor Homes in the beginning. And people were screened. You couldn't just get into the Robert Taylor Homes, you had to sit down and go through a screening and fill out all kinds of applications. If you did something or your children did something wrong, you were called down to the office. Then something changed. The people who were able to do [so] moved out. And the people who were left there were the people who did not have those options, who had fewer options. And so what happened is this place became this sort of warehouse for poor people.

So what happens, you get the stigma…from the outside in which people associate the Robert Taylor Homes with a certain kind of activity. Then there is a more subtle burden which is the burden inside…that you grew up here. You know that the Robert Taylor Homes is a low-income public housing project. You know what people think about it and so—if you are not strong, if you are not lucky enough to have the kind of support system that comes from family—all of a sudden you can say "Well, I'm black, I'm poor, I live in the Robert Taylor Homes. I can't make it. I can't do this. I can't do that." You begin to buy into the racism and to think that all those things that have been drummed into you about perhaps being inferior are true…. I think that's what happens, what can happen when you live in social isolation. It's what I call the triple whammy. People say all the time, "These people who live in the Robert Taylor Homes, they're poor, I was poor too. I overcame it." Well, people who live in the Robert Taylor Homes not only have to overcome poverty, they have to overcome race and social isolation. It's a triple whammy….

From the time I was old enough to understand the meaning of the word, my mother, my grandparents, my uncles—who were not very educated people themselves but who understood the value of education—drummed into me that education is the key. Education is the one thing that no one can take away from you. The interesting thing is that back then, being educated in the Chicago public schools, people complained about the quality of education in Chicago public schools. The fact of the matter is, the quality of education in Chicago public schools was actually pretty good. You might even say exceptional compared to what it is today. I'm a product of Chicago public schools from kindergarten through the ninth grade. When I left to go away to boarding school there was not much of a gap. I went from a 99.9 percent black inner-city Chicago public high school to a New England boarding school and did quite well without any kind of remedial help. I think many things have changed.

ABC

A Better Chance

A Better Chance (ABC) is a national talent search program that helps minority youths attend some of the country's distinguished high schools and college preparatory schools.

ABC recruits highly motivated students for enrollment in 180 schools in 26 states. The selection process is competitive: only one in five applicants is accepted. An estimated 1,140 African-American, Latino, Asian, and Native-American students participated in the program in 1994.

"It's one of those quiet programs that makes a difference. It ranks right up there with Head Start," said Walter Clair, an ABC student in the 1970s who went on to become a cardiologist.

ABC was founded in the 1960s by 23 New England prep school headmasters with the intent of nurturing the talents of minority youths from disadvantaged school systems. ABC has had its critics: For some students, the transition from one world to another has been fraught with unforeseen cultural identity problems. The agency has learned from its mistakes and has instituted guidance and counseling resources.

Each year, ABC places more than 300 new students free of charge. Schools provide students with financial aid based on family income. Over the past 30 years, more than 7,800 ABC students have graduated from member schools. Nearly all have gone on to graduate from college and to become contributors in business, government, education, and the professions.

A BETTER CHANCE

FOR THE KIDS, FOR YOU, FOR ALL OF US

For more information, contact A Better Chance, Inc., 419 Boylston Street, Boston, MA 02116; (617) 421-0950.

Teens on Target

Not long ago, Sherman Spears was a 19-year-old "gang enforcer" noted for carrying a gun. Today, he is disabled from the waist down, a victim of a gang shooting, and spends his time trying to convince other youths to avoid his folly. Spears is a spokesman for Oakland's Teens on Target, a unique antiviolence program that trains teenagers to become advocates for violence prevention.

"We've got to stop making guns. We don't talk out problems anymore because so many guns are available," Spears said. "We need to market prevention the way Bud markets beer."

The teenagers have spoken to more than 4,000 youths and provided expert testimony to city and state officials.

The programs operate under the jurisdiction of Youth Alive, a California public health agency. In Oakland, Teens on Target is a collaborative effort of Youth Alive and The Oakland Unified School District. In Los Angeles, it operates from the Pediatric Spinal Injury Service of Rancho Los Amigos Medical Center. Both cities are regarded as having widespread youth violence problems.

For more information, contact Youth Alive, Summit Medical Center, 3012 Summit Avenue, Suite 3670, Oakland, CA 94609; (510) 444-6191.

Since 1989, Teens on Target has trained about 50 teenagers in Oakland and 50 in Los Angeles to speak out against violence. The youths, often at risk of violent injury themselves, talk with students at schools and communicate to the public through community groups, city councils, and the media.

Like a Prison

DAVID GONZALEZ

The Immigration Act of 1965 was a part of Lyndon Johnson's Great Society program. Earlier, the quota system in place had given preferential treatment to immigrants from Europe and Canada; people of color were not given an equal chance to immigrate. Within 15 years of the Act's passage, 40 percent of new immigrants came from Asia and 40 percent from Latin America. The conflict between assimilation and retaining a cultural identity increased as nonwhite immigrants arrived. Asenhat, the subject of New York Times *writer David Gonzalez's report, offers a personal view of how difficult it was for this young woman to leave her close-knit community in the Dominican Republic and to try to fit into a new community in Brooklyn today.*

Asenhat Gomez used to peer out the windows of her childhood home in the Dominican countryside and relish a landscape of willowy palm trees and verdant fields where her extended family would gather for daylong reunions.

In her new home in Brooklyn — a cramped apartment on Williamsburg's South Side — the windows frame a claustrophobic vista of brick walls, and the few relatives she has in this country are so preoccupied with making ends meet that family get-togethers seem as long gone as the father who died a dozen years ago.

It has been nearly a year since Asenhat was reunited with her mother, who six years before had left her children with their aunt and illegally entered the United States in search of the opportunities that had eluded the family in the Dominican Republic.

David Gonzalez joined *The New York Times* as a metro reporter in September 1990. Prior to this, he worked at *Newsweek* as the New York correspondent. His work has appeared in *Pursuits, Arete,* "Our Town," *Hispanic Monitor,* and *Latin NY Magazine.*

Longing for Home

But the immigrant journey of Asenhat Gomez is only beginning. For 18-year-old Asenhat, the joys of reunion are constantly tempered by the struggles of life in a hard new land. Hundreds of miles from all that was familiar, unable to shake her longing for home, she tentatively ventures into a future that beckons with equal measures of promise and fear.

In many ways, hers is the oldest of immigrant stories, played out time and again by wave after wave of newcomers to America's shores. But for today's immigrant children, in places like Williamsburg, that process of adjustment is made all the more difficult by the modern plagues of drugs, guns, and recession.

Asenhat, a shy girl, has become even shyer since arriving last May, the strangeness and the frustrations coalescing in a sometimes overwhelming feeling that she is trapped.

"Sense of Confinement"

"Everybody talked about the sense of confinement," she said recently, recalling her first weeks in New York. "I expected that, but just not so much."

"Lying in bed I would think about what I left behind. There you got accustomed to visiting people, my friends from school, since we were infants. The whole place was different; you could go out to play. I miss my school."

Williamsburg — its bumpy narrow streets lined with age-worn two-family homes and apartment buildings closed in by the shadows of hulking waterfront factories and the Williamsburg Bridge — can seem forbidding to someone used to the easy freedom of the countryside. The family's two small bedrooms are shared by six people who subsist on meager earnings.

Still, even as she bridles at her confinement, it has become her defense mechanism in a city whose ways and language are not her own. She seldom ventures beyond her neighborhood, partly from fear of getting lost on unexplored streets and subway lines and partly from fear of drug dealing and violent crime on nearby blocks.

"It makes you feel insecure," said Asenhat, a short girl whose floppy ponytail and baggy jeans give her the look of someone

Summary

The percentage of immigrant families living below the poverty level increased markedly in the late 1980s.

Poverty Haunts Immigrants

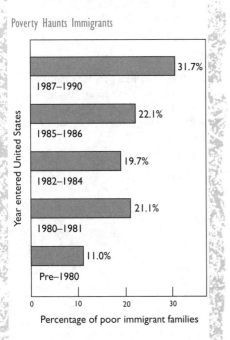

Source: Census Bureau.

just entering her teenage years. "You can be going down the street and not know what can happen."

She has few friends, feeling that she has little in common with American-born teenagers, who she feels are too "liberal" — so preoccupied with boyfriends, clothes, and the latest fads that they squander the opportunities available to them.

She has tried, and failed for lack of English, to find a job. Even her hopes for improving the family's lot through education are in limbo. An honor student who breezed through high school and a year of premedical studies in the Dominican Republic, she plans to continue her studies at Hunter College in Manhattan. But she has been forced to sit out a year while she learns English and qualifies for financial aid.

In her own reticent way, Asenhat (pronounced ah-seh-NET) will admit to a certain disappointment with her new life. "It's been more difficult than I thought," she says. And while she allows that "there are more opportunities here," she is quick to add that "there, people looked out for you."

Still, she resolutely hews to the immigrant dream.

"After a while I'll feel better," she said. "Especially after I learn English. After I begin school. I like to study, and that's the best way to progress."

Death on a Farm

Asenhat Gomez was born in the countryside near Moca — a farming community in the Cibao region of the Dominican Republic — where her family owned a comfortable three-bedroom house, with a big yard filled with fruit trees, on land where her father and uncles grew plantains and cassava.

She still recalls how on weekends, her father, Vicente, would take her and her friends to fairs or for a cool ice cream, or how they would all gather with relatives to spend the day eating, talking, and playing.

But there were hints of darker times ahead, she said; her father suffered from depression that seemed to feed on itself.

"When he got sick with that problem, he would get depressed because he could not work," she said. "He went into a clinic."

"There Was No Other Way"

When Asenhat was nearly 6, he accidentally shot himself to death while cleaning a pistol, the family says. She was in the room when it happened. She talks little about it.

With three children and no husband, Asenhat's mother, Esperanza, tried in vain to keep the family afloat, getting money and food from her in-laws. But seven years ago, she took the children to her sister's house, told them she was going to take a nursing course in a nearby city and slipped off on a nine-day journey through Guatemala, Mexico, and California, and finally to New York.

"There was no other way," she says now. "A mother does it only thinking of her children."

Working as a live-in maid in Brooklyn, she would send money back home, promising to send for the children as soon as she had legal residency, which happened last year.

Esperanza had told them some of what they could expect, but she knew, too, that her advice could go only so far.

"Talking about it," she said, "is very different from living it and seeing it."

Arrival: Disappointment, Four Flights Up

Asenhat had barely arrived in New York last May when the disappointment hit. In her new home four flights up a dimly lighted stairway, she and her 20-year-old brother, Harold, shared a bedroom with their sister, Amalia, 14, who had preceded them to America by several months. Her mother slept in the bedroom off the kitchen with her new husband, Jose Aybar, and their 3-year-old daughter, Josephine.

"This house looked so strange to me," Asenhat said. "It was so confining, such a big building with so many people and such little apartments."

Life inside the apartment, with her new family, was strained. At first, Josephine would jealously cry "Mami mia!" whenever Asenhat approached her mother. Relations with her stepfather have remained cool.

"He is almost illiterate," she said. "We don't have that much in common." They barely speak.

"I would like to talk about my dreams," she said. "Sometimes I miss my father a lot because he was close to us. He was very caring, very sweet with us."

"I Don't Go Out Alone"

For a while, however estranged she felt, fear of what lay outside, of being speechless in an English-speaking city, kept her imprisoned in the apartment. She spent her days reading the Bible or absentmindedly watching television. She lost weight.

"There are no places for people to go around here," she said. "I don't go to the park. I don't go out alone."

While her block is relatively calm, the surrounding streets have seen an increase in drug dealing and violence. There was a shooting at her sister's school. Sometimes she hears gunshots at night.

She remembers how in Moca, gunshots were sometimes heard ringing out in celebration of some holidays. "Here," she said, "it's not because people are happy."

The one solo venture she made early on — to enroll in a summer youth program — ended in tears in Bushwick after she couldn't speak English with the person taking her application, who angrily shouted at her. Her frustration and fear only increased when she wandered outside and quickly got lost.

"I was scared to ask for directions because I didn't think anyone spoke Spanish," she said. Finally, she got up enough courage to ask a Spanish-speaking passer-by.

"He said I was lost," she said. "I knew that."

Even now, her daily schedule is an unwavering routine played out within six blocks of home: a noontime visit to her mother's job, English classes, several hours at a local youth center, and back home to her family.

Asenhat's confinement can be as much emotional as physical, made worse by being sidetracked in her schooling. While her parents were never able to go to college, they wanted to make sure their children would. Asenhat's belief in the bedrock American value of success through education seems absolute. When she talks about becoming a doctor, "a professional," her face brightens and she sits up a little prouder.

Both Asenhat and her brother Harold — who studied civil engineering and worked in a medical laboratory in Santo Domingo but now works six days a week at a bodega — plan to attend the City University of New York [Hunter College]. But they have had to wait a year to qualify as New York City residents for the cheaper tuition and to learn English.

The only studying she does now is in her daily English class at the Brooklyn Public Library, where her afternoons are filled with children's songs and dialogues.

"It's like being little again," she said of the class, though she might have been describing the entire humbling experience of learning English.

Asenhat also realizes that while the constant presence of Spanish in her neighborhood makes it easier to adjust, it makes it harder, too.

"It's more difficult to learn English here because everybody speaks Spanish," she said. "If you hear more English, your ears get used to it faster."

A few nights ago, Asenhat slowed down as she approached her building, where two boys boxed playfully. As she got nearer, one of the boys smoothly pulled out a knife, opened it, and feinted a slash at his friend. She barely blinked as she sweetly asked them if they had a key to the wrought-iron lobby door that always is locked.

After 11 months in Brooklyn, she still finds it hard to decipher the rituals of her American-born counterparts.

"For me the most important thing is to study," she said. "For them it's boyfriends, going places, and buying clothes. That doesn't matter to me. A person's worth isn't what they wear, but what they are and how they feel."

Her friends at home, she insists, were different. "We were more united over there," she said. "I think sometimes that those who grew up here are more superficial. There may be more opportunities here, but over there people looked out for you."

Even the people she meets at El Puente, a youth center two blocks from her home, don't always understand what she is going through. Some don't even understand her language, although they are children of Hispanic parents. Her closest

FACT

More than 6 million legal immigrants came into the country during the 1980s, nearly double the number who arrived during the 1960s. The number of new arrivals has grown from 1.5 million between 1960 and 1964 to 5.6 million between 1985 and 1990.

(Source: Census Bureau.)

friends are Lilin Fong and Danilda Torres, both of whom came from the Dominican Republic several years ago.

The three are active in a natural healing class at El Puente, and they often sit together, chatting in Spanish. Lilin thinks Asenhat is adapting as well as she can.

"I used to count the days I had been here," she said. "I knew the hour I arrived."

Asenhat nodded. "I count the months, too," she said. "I wanted to return home." She lowered her voice. "Sometimes I still feel like going."

Doña Mercedes: Dispensing Advice to "Daughters"

Good thing Mercedes Mendez didn't hear that. The last time Asenhat revealed her homesickness, Doña Mercedes — as she is known to all — looked at her as if she were insane. "Don't even think of going back!" she scolded. "You have to be with your mother."

Each day, Asenhat passes by Doña Mercedes's apartment for lunch and a brief visit with her mother, who works as a home attendant caring for the 71-year-old Puerto Rican woman. Doña Mercedes, who walks stiffly because of knee replacement surgery a dozen years ago, busily looks after Asenhat, calling her "one of my adopted daughters."

Doña Mercedes is one of several women who have rallied around Asenhat, intent on making sure that nothing keeps her from her goals. Doña Mercedes, who came to the mainland in 1946 and worked for years packing tomatoes and cooking for the field hands on a New Jersey farm, often regales her with tales of how hard her life was when she arrived. She cautions her against talking to strangers or following the crowds.

"Most of all, take care of your virginity," Doña Mercedes admonished. "Don't wander off with boys; you can get easily lost out there."

Esperanza nodded in agreement. But far from worrying that her daughter will be led astray by friends, she frets that she spends too much time alone.

She also wishes Asenhat would be a little more accepting of her new husband, who, she says, has had a hard enough time

---

FACT

In 1990, about 1 in 12 Americans (21 million, over 8 percent of the population) was foreign-born. The foreign-born total was a record high, nearly five times the number counted in 1970.

(Source: Census Bureau.)

FACT

One recent immigrant in four has a college degree, and one in three has a high-school diploma.

(Source: Census Bureau, 1990.)

coping with his extended unemployment and his mother's illness.

Asenhat would like to get a job, to help the family out. She has looked a few times, to no avail.

"She talks about work, anything she can do," said Cecilia Figueroa, a health coordinator at El Puente. "But there's not much she can do with no language and no experience. She doesn't have anything."

Esperanza says she only wants her daughter to keep striving toward her goal of becoming a doctor. To help her learn English, she is buying her a $950 set of language cassettes, on the installment plan.

"There are few mothers who would do what Esperanza did," said Doña Mercedes. "She's only had God's help."

And the help of Esperanza's sister, Mirope Ortiz-Lisardo, who took in the three children when she came to the United States. Asenhat is so close to her aunt that she calls her "Mami," and after almost a year apart, she could barely contain her glee during Mirope's recent visit.

When it came time to leave, on a bitter cold Saturday, the house grew quiet. Mrs. Ortiz-Lisardo walked up to Asenhat and reached out to her. They hugged, gazing into each other's eyes. A kiss, another hug, and then her aunt stepped into the hallway and began her journey back to the friends and places in the homeland her niece had left behind.

Quietly, Asenhat flopped onto the couch and sank into a corner, clutching her sister's talking teddy bear. Her mother sat next to her and stroked her arm. The girl shook her head when asked if she was sad.

Asenhat hugged the toy, and its voice broke the silence.

"Dream with me," the bear sang in tinny, electronic tones. She hugged it tighter.

"Dream with me."

FROM: A ten-part series of articles, *Children of the Shadows: Ten Lives of the Cities*, published in 1993 in *The New York Times*.

YVCA

Youth Volunteer Corps of America

![Youth Volunteer Corps of America logo]

Bringing together teens from diverse backgrounds to learn the values of cooperation, cultural understanding, and community service is what drives this national organization of volunteers.

The brainchild of David Battey, Youth Volunteer Corps of America (YVCA) started out as a college paper creation. Several years later, the United Way of Kansas funded start-up costs for Battey's plan to coordinate a national corps of youth volunteers. The not-for-profit organization now totals 15 corporate and private foundations plus individual funders.

In Vero Beach, Florida, 16-year-old Marie "Red" Watson sings at the player piano to residents of a nursing home. One of the 15,000 young people, ages 11 to 18, who have contributed more than 500,000 volunteer hours through YVCA-sponsored projects, Red enjoys her contribution. "They taught me that they are people just like me, and I relate to them," said Red, who has been volunteering at the home for three years.

In the community of Vero Beach, an unexpected benefit of the 96 local youth volunteers is that their dozens of outreach efforts have revitalized their local sponsor, the YMCA.

YVCA likes to work with local agencies such as the YMCA or the United Way to coordinate the kinds of community services most necessary and appropriate. Teens are recruited from all areas to encourage a diverse cross section. YVCA provides extensive training and leadership programs for volunteer leaders and assists with fund-raising, publicity, and information-sharing tasks.

Seventeen states and one Canadian province are affiliated with YVCA.

For more information, contact Youth Volunteer Corps of America, 6310 Lamar Avenue, Suite 125, Overland Park, KS 66202-4247; (913) 432-9822.

Photo: Michael Regnier

City Year

Urban-based public service for 17- to 23-year-olds

City Year is a Boston-based "urban Peace Corps" that channels the natural idealism of young people into community service. Founded in 1988, the program puts teams of youths from all backgrounds to work full time on public-service projects throughout the city. Participants receive $125 a week and, at the end of their nine months of service, either a $4,725 stipend toward college tuition or a smaller cash award.

City Year members — young men and women ages 17 to 23 — spend their time on such projects as tutoring kids, rebuilding urban playgrounds and gardens, and running food pantries. For those members who are school dropouts, City Year offers high school equivalency classes.

Created exclusively with private funding from corporations, foundations, and individuals, the program has since attracted federal and municipal support as well.

City Year aims to inculcate responsible citizenship and, with its emphasis on racial and socioeconomic diversity, to break down barriers to integration. As one former member put it, "City Year allows everyone to be on the same page, despite color, sex, or education. I've been exposed to so many different types of people. Everyone is valued here."

During his presidential campaign, Bill Clinton visited City Year and later cited it as a national model for youth community service programs. In 1994, his administration launched AmeriCorps (see page 219), an initiative bearing many similarities to

City Year. Boston's City Year corps now numbers 300 people annually, and the program has been replicated in five other metropolitan areas, with plans to expand to 25 cities and 3,000 to 5,000 young recruits by 1996.

For more information, contact City Year, 11 Stillings Street, Boston, MA 02210; (617) 451-0699.

LVA

Literacy Volunteers of America

As many as 35 million adult Americans today are functionally illiterate, lacking the necessary skills to fill out a job application, read a newspaper, or decipher the instructions on a bottle of medicine. For more than three decades, Literacy Volunteers of America (LVA) has mobilized volunteers nationwide to help people acquire basic reading and writing skills that can open many doors.

LVA is a national, nonprofit network of community programs that train volunteers to teach adults and teens to read and write through one-on-one or small-group instruction. Reaching some 61,000 learners annually with nearly 55,000 volunteer instructors, the organization is most effective with nonreaders whose skills are below the fifth-grade level — and who therefore may not be ready for traditional classroom learning.

LVA reports that after just 35 to 40 hours of tutoring, students in the program improve their reading skills significantly. Such skills can be particularly empowering for the poor, among whom illiteracy is rampant. The report of the U.S. Department of Education's 1993 National Adult Literacy Survey put it this way: "Literacy can be thought of as a currency in this society. Just as adults with little money have difficulty meeting their basic needs, those with limited literacy skills are likely to find it more challenging to pursue their goals —

whether these involve job advancement, consumer decision-making, [or] citizenship."

LVA has its roots in Syracuse, New York, where it was founded as a local organization in 1962 by Ruth Colvin. The organization grew quickly throughout New York and in neighboring states, with LVA affiliates today numbering 455 in 44 states. In addition to basic literacy training, LVA offers instruction in English as a Second Language and GED classes and also conducts tutoring in special settings such as prisons and workplace programs.

For more information, contact Literacy Volunteers of America, Inc., 5795 Widewaters Parkway, Syracuse, NY 13214; (315) 445-8000.

In the Fields of King Coal

FENTON JOHNSON

Why do some people stay in communities that are losing economic viability? For some, the fact that they are the third, fourth, or fifth generation in their family to live in a community is reason enough. For those who refuse to surrender to the economic forces beyond their community, the challenge to renew economic health, as described in this article by Fenton Johnson, is a significant and sometimes rewarding task.

Driving into the Appalachians from my childhood hometown in lowland Kentucky, I wait for the superhighway to end but it keeps rolling itself out. Wider than the towns it passes, bound from nowhere to nowhere on the premise that someday somewhere might arise along the way, this vast road offers the most tangible remnant of the War on Poverty's aspirations and failures.

These are not the Appalachians of upstate New York or of Pennsylvania or Virginia, with their long, parallel valleys conducive to commerce and transportation. Eastern Kentucky is serrated as a corncob, a plateau raised millions of years ago and eroded ever since by countless creeks forming countless hollers. Trees cling to slopes so steep that climbing them is an exercise more of arms than legs, a process not of walking but of hoisting oneself from one tree limb or outcrop to the next. A two-lane road, broken and potholed from coal trucks, takes all the flat land on one side of a creek; houses, equally broken, occupy the other side, with maybe a rickety bridge in between. Coal tipples rise from hillsides flecked with white and pink dogwood. Creeks flow red with runoff from abandoned mine shafts. In more accessible towns, Wal-Marts and brick tract houses sprout on reclaimed strip-mine lands, islands of prosperity sustained by what remains of the coal industry and by a burgeoning ser-

Fenton Johnson is the author of *Scissors, Paper, Rock* and the award-winning *Crossing the River*. He is also a frequent contributor to *The New York Times Magazine*. His stories and essays have appeared in anthologies, including *Best of the West* and *How We Live Now*.

Summary

It is projected that by the year 2000, the only categories that will significantly increase their share of the job growth will be high-skilled ones, while the most significant loss will affect low-skilled laborers.

Low-Skilled Jobs Are Declining

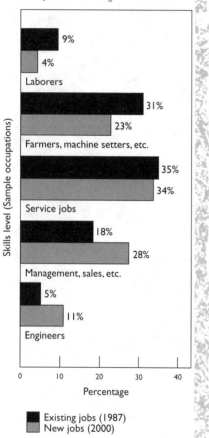

9%
4%
Laborers

31%
23%
Farmers, machine setters, etc.

35%
34%
Service jobs

18%
28%
Management, sales, etc.

5%
11%
Engineers

Skills level (Sample occupations)

0   10   20   30   40
Percentage

■ Existing jobs (1987)
■ New jobs (2000)

Source: *Workforce 2000*, Hudson Institute (1987).

vice sector based on transfer payments — black lung, or Social Security, or welfare benefits.

For a century America's prime rural battlefield for industrial magnates, labor unions, and social reformers, the coal fields of eastern Kentucky are in a period of transition no less portentous than that heralded by the arrival of the coal and steel barons. America continues to depend on coal — 58 percent of the nation's electricity is coal-generated — and coal production is at record highs. But mechanization in eastern Kentucky has dramatically reduced total mine employment from 1960 levels, with more layoffs to come. Here, union locals have all but disappeared, victims of internal bickering and corruption, the mountaineers' resistance to organization, and a growing number of people desperate for jobs and willing to work without union protection. And the coal itself is starting to run out —assuming current technology and levels of production, state geologists predict that in 20 to 30 years, it may no longer be profitable to continue mining.

With the decline in mine employment has come challenges to King Coal's once-absolute dominance of eastern Kentucky's politics and economy. Capitalizing on the Great Society's legacy of political action, grass-roots activists are asserting the right of communities to shape their futures. In politics, in business, in education, in the nonprofit sector, they are searching for local solutions to local problems — maybe too late, and certainly out of desperation, but searching all the same.

Their ambitions and efforts illuminate critical choices of the coming years. With the region's large population losses of the last decade, public and private leaders are questioning if the nation can afford the attendant price tag — in transfer payments to those who remain, and in social upheaval and its consequences among those who leave. The answer is relevant not just to eastern Kentucky but also to any of the nation's capital-poor rural regions that are losing population, and to the over-taxed cities to which those people move.

What follows is a collage of snapshots from a journey through the coal fields, one of the distant backyards on which urban and suburban America depends. Like the third world countries to which it's often compared, eastern Kentucky confronts any visitor with big questions. In a world dominated by urban values and priorities, can those who wish to stay in rural areas create a place where they can survive? What is at stake for urban societies in the survival, or death, of rural cultures?

Founded with Great Society money, dedicated to the fostering and preservation of southern Appalachian culture, Appalshop is among the nation's most successful rural cultural centers. Once regarded by locals as a hotbed of radical agitators, today "the Shop" has earned respect for its programs training young people in fields as diverse as radio, television, theater, and recording.

Each year Appalshop sponsors a group of local high-school seniors in writing and performing a play about an issue of pressing importance to the mountains. Last year's play, "Home Place," examined a scattered nuclear family, each of whose members are searching to find, or keep, a place they may call home.

Achingly young, shouting each other down in their eagerness to tell their stories, the "Home Place" actors form a cast within the cast: the olive-complected girl from the wrong side of the mountain; her sultry boyfriend, arms crossed, biceps bulging — a passable James Dean; the pudgy blonde who alternates between yakking and passing notes; the quiet, bespectacled guy who gets my silent vote for most likely to get going and stay gone.

A sample of their conversation:

"Anybody with any get-up-and-go has got up and went."

"My dad, who's a miner, asked me what I wanted to do when I graduated. I said something that made him prouder than anything else I could have said — I said I wanted to get a job where I could wear a coat and tie."

"You have to ask the question: 'What's happiness?' I've been to Chicago and seen people sleeping in the streets. I'll never recover from that."

For a heated hour and a half they argue whether they wanted to stay (most did), whether they would be able to stay (most thought not), what would be required to enable them to stay. Toward evening's end, the teacher, Jeff Hawkins, who moved

FACT

Between 1985 and 1990, 37 percent of Americans moved within their own state and 9 percent moved to another state.

(Source: Census Bureau, 1990.)

FACT

The average American moves 11 times in his or her lifetime.

(Source: Larry Long, *International Regional Science Review*.)

away from Appalachia to attend college, later to return, poses this question: "Do you want to be like Lexington?" — which is to say, an imitation of the suburbs of California and New York. "Or can you create and sustain something that's unique to here?"

That high-school students are confronting these questions is an extraordinary change from my own high-school days in rural Kentucky, when the unchallenged assumption was that opportunity lay in distant and golden cities, and anybody of any count flew the coop.

"You have to ask the question: 'What's happiness?'" The issues implied in the high-school student's query are relevant to all depressed areas where community and cultural ties remain strong. The question eastern Kentucky faces is how to achieve the economic diversity that might allow for political and social stability, which might in turn sustain the social values that substitute for the material wealth of a consumer society.

"Maybe we won't have the income standards of the rest of America," said Ron Eller, director of the Appalachian Center at the University of Kentucky in Lexington and himself a native of Appalachia. "But maybe we'll have other things. The bottom line here is value systems. Do you value wanting to be like Lexington or do you value other things — family ties, for example, and community ties — that a lot of folks in Lexington would like to have?"

But it's one thing to talk "less is more" community values and another to practice them, in a society whose advertising, news and entertainment media and popular mythology glorify the rugged individualist who in the end owns it all. The same education that enables students to understand what's at stake gives them the tools they need to leave and the dissatisfaction with home ties to fuel their departure.

Is it possible to empower people through education while preserving and enhancing community ties and values? "Television is bringing us these questions anyway," said Bill Weinberg, a prominent mountain lawyer and former state representative. "Our hope is that we can learn from the experience of industrial America. We don't see ourselves as playing catch-up — we're trying to make a leap, adapting a society with agrarian values to a postindustrial society."

THESE ARE THE REGION'S OPTIONS, as outlined by Dr. Grady Stumbo, chairman of the Kentucky Democratic Party and co-founder, with State Senator Benny Ray Bailey, of the East Kentucky Health Services Center. "We can rear people here and export them elsewhere. We can stay here and accept transfer payments from the rest of the country. Or we can try to change the economy, encouraging lots of little enterprises to create a new kind of environment." He foresees a combination of all three, but he and other activists are working for the last.

Together with Bill Weinberg and Senator Bailey, Dr. Stumbo forms the nucleus of a group working for change in eastern Kentucky, familiarly called the "Knott County mafia." Along with community activists statewide, they have engineered changes no one once thought possible. In 1988 they won a 20-year battle over the broad-form deed, a 1903 statute that allowed companies in possession of subsurface mineral rights to do anything they considered necessary to extract coal, with little or no compensation for current landowners. In an emphatic rejection of the coal companies' statewide media campaign, more than 80 percent of the electorate voted to pass a constitutional amendment enlarging owners' ability to protect their property.

That coal interests lost so overwhelmingly is an indication of the loosening grip on the region and the state. "Political leadership in the mountains has been handed to a new generation," Dr. Stumbo says with undisguised glee. "You can like it or not but you got to deal with it."

DEEP IN HARLAN COUNTY, Lynch was one of the segregated company towns founded by U.S. Steel to house labor imported to work the mines. Donna Cockrel grew up in its black neighborhood, then left to get a B.A. degree in 1988 from the University of Kentucky in Lexington. She returned to Lynch to be near her parents and to teach elementary school.

It's late in the evening when I arrive, but Cockrel's mother lays out a spread. Our conversation is underscored by the rasp

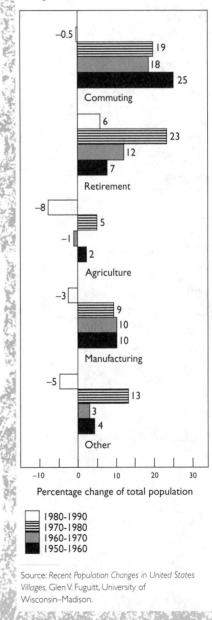

Summary

Across the United States, small towns are dying. During the 1980s, almost three quarters of towns with populations under 2,500 lost residents, mainly due to the farm crisis and the elimination of manufacturing jobs.

Leaving Main Street

Percentage change of total population

☐ 1980-1990
▤ 1970-1980
▦ 1960-1970
■ 1950-1960

Source: *Recent Population Changes in United States Villages*, Glen V. Fuguitt, University of Wisconsin–Madison.

Summary

As of 1990, the United States was spending much more on defense and much less on social expenditures than countries like Germany, France, Sweden, and the United Kingdom.

Defense or Social Spending?

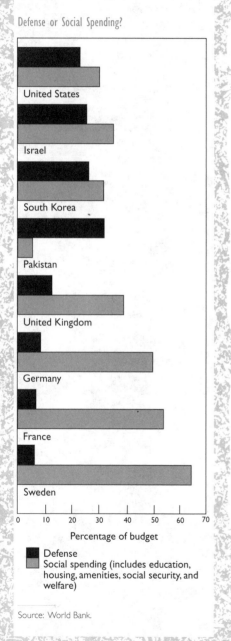

Percentage of budget

■ Defense
▨ Social spending (includes education, housing, amenities, social security, and welfare)

Source: World Bank.

and heave of Cockrel's father, disabled by black lung and hooked to his twice-daily infusion of oxygen.

Cockrel is a dynamo, a heavyset woman of bright colors and boundless energy who's "geared towards change." She incorporates multicultural elements into her teaching, and laughs at the thought that locals view her as an *activist* — *"They call me a troublemaker!"* she crows. She paraphrases Martin Luther King, Jr. — "Everybody can serve," she says, adding, "It's empowerment from the bottom."

After supper she takes me on a drive through Lynch, built as a model of company paternalism. Once home to the world's largest coal loading facility, now it hangs on as a handsome, built-to-last ghost town. Every second or third house is empty. About a quarter of the town has been demolished.

As we drive past boarded-up brick and limestone buildings, she articulates a vision of change at the most local, personal level.

"I have a dream that some day I'll be a business executive and I'll invite kids in to learn business skills," she says. She drops me at my car with a last bit of philosophy. "Stop complaining about what you don't have and use what you've got," she says, executing a little jig.

Cockrel's life since our conversations illustrates the troubles of those trying to remain in the mountains. At the school year's end she was laid off in part because there are too few children to justify keeping her school open. Now she lives and teaches a four-hour drive from Lynch and returns each weekend to see her family, to continue her work with her church, and to broadcast a Sunday morning gospel program.

The day after speaking to the Cockrels, I seek out John F. Tate, the property supervisor of Cyprus Mountain Coals Corporation in Perry County. Cyprus, which has the reputation of being among eastern Kentucky's most environmentally conscious companies, has won community awards for hiring from the local work force and for environmental awareness.

In place of rugged mountains, Tate describes his vision of industrial parks and subdivisions with split-level ranch houses built on flattened land reclaimed from the strip mines. I think of the Cockrel family's town, built as the ideal city of an earlier generation of outsiders, now a place of boarded-up storefronts and polluted creeks and empty houses. Has Tate visited Lynch? He's puzzled at my question. "Why would anyone go there?" he asks.

Who will buy and occupy the ranch houses he envisions, I ask, in a county with 30 percent real unemployment, that lost 10 percent of it's population in the last decade? Who will build industrial parks in a region long unsuccessful at attracting outside investment? How will he supply water to his newly created mesa, when streams are already clogged with silt and polluted with acid from mine runoff? Where should the people who wish to stay in eastern Kentucky put their faith — in promises for what might be, or in what experience has shown them to be true? He answers the question as he shows me the door. "I have faith in technology," he says. "I believe in Horatio Alger. I believe in Pollyanna."

STEVE MENG BEGAN AS A YOUNG, venture capitalist at Kentucky Highlands Investment Corporation, a public-private venture capital company specializing in encouraging the area's economic development. Meng left Kentucky Highlands to become president of one of its successes, a nonprofit organization with two small manufacturing plants that make store fixtures and desk accessories for retail chains and that are some distance into the mountains. "My guess is that these communities would prefer to attract a branch plant from an established company," he says. "But the fact is it doesn't happen very much."

"My vision for the area is to look for internally generated opportunities instead of branch plants," Meng says. He has high praise for his workers, while decrying their lack of training. "If these people were trained and educated to consider more sophisticated approaches to business they could start their own 10-percent businesses," he says. "The problem is that they think only in terms of the familiar — laundromats, or auto repair shops."

THE TWO APPROACHES — industrial park developments and small, homegrown operations — are not necessarily exclu-

> Action is typical of the American style, thought and planning are not; it is considered heresy to state that some problems are not immediately or easily solvable.
>
> DANIEL BELL
> Sociologist, Educator

213

Summary

In 1990, almost 50 percent of the poor in the United States were white, compared to less than 30 percent black and 17 percent Hispanic.

White Poverty versus Black Poverty

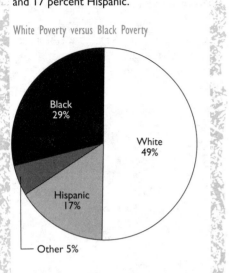

- Black 29%
- White 49%
- Hispanic 17%
- Other 5%

Source: Bureau of the Census, *Poverty in the United States*, 1992.

sive, but development patterns in eastern Kentucky illustrate their applications in isolated, rural regions. In counties with easy access to interstate highways and urban economies, industrial park development has scored some significant coups. But outside interest wanes in those counties — like Harlan and Letcher —that are remote from the prosperous lowlands and inaccessible to them.

Tom Miller, program officer at the Ford Foundation and former president of Kentucky Highlands, underscored the problem with initiating home-grown development in underdeveloped economies. "In my years at Kentucky Highlands we always had more money than we needed," he said. "Our constraint was the number of opportunities we could uncover."

As eastern Kentucky loses population, that problem worsens. "In more isolated counties the people leaving are those with the most resources and ambition," Miller said. "And when those people leave they often carry their troubles to the place they move to. That cost to society provides a fiscal as well as human compassion reason to develop the region."

LOOKED AT IN LIGHT OF THE HARSH economic realities of the late 20th century, what does it finally matter, the disappearance of Appalachian culture, the emptying of the mountains? The late Governor Bert T. Combs, among the original architects of the Great Society's Appalachian projects, was not alone in conceding that perhaps there are too many people in these hills, and that the most productive and humane approach is in fact encouraging a good number of them to move to cities, provided they are offered relocation assistance and job training.

In an era of shrinking government funds, that sounds good, but relocation programs themselves cost money and (in another echo of the third world) have the potential of shifting the undereducated and chronically underemployed from the countryside, where they have at least their family network and cultural identity and big garden to help them get by, to city streets, where their economic, social, and emotional future is considerably more uncertain.

More to the point, such a policy implies giving up not just on eastern Kentucky but on whole regions of the world — in America, parts of the Great Plains and the rural South come to mind. These are places where cultures once flourished, that are now being depopulated to the verge of extinction. At a time when capitalism and democracy are seen as triumphant worldwide, for a whole region of America to slide into a depopulated environmental wasteland represents an unnerving failure at least of capitalism, perhaps — in its betrayal of its citizens — of democracy itself.

NONE OF THE ACTIVISTS argue that coal mining will or should disappear tomorrow. The most strident among them acknowledge that, so far as the outside world is concerned, eastern Kentucky is immediately important only for its underground resources. The question is how those resources will be taken, and what will be left for the land and its people. Implicit is consideration for the area's future once the coal is gone.

"Nobody's going to help us out of this — it's got to start from within." This refrain I heard from community activists and concerned business leaders throughout the region. That's a vast change from the company town-government subsidy mentality that dominated the region in the past.

In 1966, Joe Begley, who owns a general store in Letcher County, organized the region's first protests against strip mining; in 1977 he stood at Jimmy Carter's side for the signing of the national strip-mine regulation bill. Speaking now of the difficulties of convincing people that they may take charge of their futures, he describes how "people here have been taught to say yes instead of no. They don't know how to say no, and that's been their ruination." But listen to Donna Cockrel: "I want to teach my kids that they can learn to be assertive about saying no and learn when to say yes. Anything that can be learned can be unlearned. They got to have a vision. If they lack vision they perish."

Everywhere I went people were scratching their heads and pondering when to say yes, when to say no. It is this babble of voices that I heard throughout eastern Kentucky, that is energizing, inspiring, different from the decades when the coal com-

FACT

Farm output is still rising but farms, home to 40 percent of Americans a century ago, now house less than 2 percent of the population.

(Source: U.S. Department of Agriculture; U.S. Census Bureau.)

panies called the tune. Whether this growing pluralism can make a difference, whether the coal industry can be engaged constructively, whether the region can sustain a place that people are willing and able to call home — the answers to these questions have short-term implications for the amount of tax money required to keep eastern Kentucky from starving. In the long term, their answers will say a great deal about what the nation is able and willing to do in the face of the depopulation of rural America. For the moment, there's some small pleasure to be taken just in hearing the questions asked, in the noise of those competing voices.

FROM: *The New York Times Magazine*, November 22, 1992.

Working with the volunteers

AN INTERVIEW WITH SUE ELLA KOBAK

Sue Ella Kobak was born, raised, and still lives and works in eastern Kentucky. In the sixties she worked with the Appalachia Volunteers (AV) — a program within VISTA. This excerpt is compiled from film and phone interviews conducted by the producers of Blackside, Inc.'s documentary series, America's War on Poverty.

When I was growing up, my sense about power — about how it manifested itself — was very real. We talked about it. We pointed at it. We realized that there were certain people in the county who controlled everything and I mean everything, even down to whether you got commodities or not. We didn't have welfare when I was growing up, like free lunches or AFDC or anything like that. The one thing some poor people could get was commodities. But you had  to be the right political party. They [political operatives] controlled everything...and the only way you could deal with them was to either leave the county or be under their control.

They [the VISTA volunteers in Appalachia] were amazed at how local politicians would be little demagogues and would put up stumbling blocks, because the things the volunteers were trying to get made good sense to them...any good middle class community would move toward improving the roads or improving the school system or help children get free lunches. That doesn't sound like such a radical idea. It was always amazing to the volunteers that there were obstacles to us having access to the power to make those changes. They grew up feeling the power and the right to have a decent way of living. In the community that they came from, it was part of who they were.

The major problem with the AVs coming into the area was that they operated as if *they* had the answers to ending poverty. They never believed we had an agenda. Through the funding for the War on Poverty, they had resources, which meant power outside our local power structure. We worked to get access to some of that power. They saw us as needing help and they were going to manipulate us to help us. They didn't mean to be paternalistic, in fact, many tried not to be, but they couldn't see us as equals or partners in this process. This struggle against poverty didn't involve them personally the way it involved us. That's why they were able to switch priorities. For many of them the fight against the war in Vietnam became a more important issue than their fight against poverty in Appalachia. Of course, that wasn't an option for us. We couldn't abandon the fight against poverty.

The AVs really kind of got into "going native" a lot of times. Most of the time it was, we felt, humorous. We'd laugh about it. But it was offensive at times, too, because that wasn't what we wanted to move toward. I mean, we didn't want to stay where we were. We wanted to move toward being the "haves." And it seemed like they were kind of romanticizing our poverty and that was offensive. The same thing is true about various paternalistic things they would do. We would try in nice ways to let them know that this wasn't coming across too well. Most of the time they didn't hear it [chuckles]. They were young, you know, these people were 22, 24 years old. They were very idealistic and just full of themselves and didn't hear as much as you do when you get a little bit older.

A lot of those people became my friends, are still my friends. I think that their world was a bigger world and they shared that with me. Getting experiences with going to New York City for the first time, or flying planes for the first time, or even having dinner with a steak and a glass of wine, I mean that was very sophisticated as far as I was concerned. I never experienced anything like that when I was growing up. We didn't have wine. We come from a dry county in east Kentucky. Getting to know the names of the colleges they went to like Smith or Harvard or Yale and so forth, I knew about those schools, but by talking about [the schools] I got a sense of what [the AVs] knew and how they had been

educated and I would copy and emulate that. I started feeling like I was getting a college education from that point of view.

I came from a family that did not have access to anything other than Poorbottom and Hellier [High School] and getting out. If I thought I had a right to college, that would mean that I thought I was in some way part of the privileged class and only certain families had access to go to college or do things like that.

I went to Hellier High School. The principal's name was Louie Owens. Mr. Owens was not a real nice person. I always knew I was going to go to college and I went to him in my senior year. I remember it so clearly. I went into his office, I was standing up and he was sitting down. I said "Mr. Owens, you know I'm a senior now and I really want to go to college and so I wanted to find out if you had any information about scholarships or any kind of financing I can get for college." He just kind of squeaked the chair back and he got up, he was a big man, he looked down on me and he said, "You stupid little hillbilly, don't you know that you can't do anything like that?"

I wasn't on the slate to make it out. I remember my first-grade teacher saying, when I met him about five years ago, "I never thought you'd be a lawyer."

AmeriCorps

A community-based national service program

AmeriCorps is the Clinton Administration's national service program whereby young Americans contribute a year of community service in exchange for financial aid for college tuition or repayment of school loans.

The program was launched in September 1994, with the goal of enlisting some 20,000 volunteers in the first year to serve community-based agencies working in four areas: education, health and human needs, crime abatement, and the environment.

Heralded in its program literature as "the new domestic Peace Corps," AmeriCorps is made up of youths aged 17 and up who "look like America" by representing a wide range of racial and ethnic groups, economic backgrounds, and regions. Recruits work on such jobs as helping to rebuild hurricane-ravished homes; mentoring teenage parents to help them complete school; developing crime prevention workshops; or counseling young mothers on prenatal care. The work is carried out in concert with grassroots organizations selected by the government through a competitive process.

In return for their work, AmeriCorps members receive a minimum-wage salary and free health care, plus an education credit of $4,725 per year of service, for up to two years.

AmeriCorps also includes the 30-year-old Volunteers in Service to America (VISTA) and the new Civilian Community Corps, which focuses on environmental issues and which houses and trains its members on military bases. The AmeriCorps program is administered by the Corporation for National Service, which was created by congressional legislation in 1993.

For more information, contact the Corporation for National Service, P.O. Box 438, Beltsville, MD 20704; (800) 94-ACORPS.

Ideas, Strategies, and Resources

"THEM" OR "US"?

MICHAEL KATZ

We can think about poor people as "them" or "us." For the most part, Americans have talked about "them." Even in the language of social science, as well as in ordinary conversation and political rhetoric, poor people usually remain outsiders, strangers to be pitied or despised, helped or punished, ignored or studied, but rarely full citizens, members of a larger community on the same terms as the rest of us. They are, as Vice President Dan Quayle said in his debate with Senator Lloyd Bentsen, "those people," objects of curiosity, analysis, prurience, or compassion, not subjects who construct their own lives and history. Poor people seem cardboard cutouts, figures in single dimensions, members of inferior categories, rarely complex, multifaceted, even contradictory in the manner of other persons. Their poverty therefore results from some attribute, a defect in personality, behavior, or human capital. Whether their deficiencies stem from family, genes, or deprivation doesn't really matter very much. The consequences are the same. Poverty in America is profoundly indi-

vidual; like popular economics, it is supply-side.

By individualizing poverty, many American social scientists have aided the mystification of its origins and obscured its politics. In much American social science, poverty remains profoundly apolitical. Discussions on how to influence the level of social benefits along a fairly narrow band of possibilities pass for political discussion. About the real politics of poverty, American social science remains largely silent. For finally, the politics of poverty are about the process of inclusion and exclusion in American life: Who, to put the question crudely, gets what? How are goods distributed? As such, it is a question of race, class, gender, and the bases of power. Poverty is not an unfortunate accident, a residue, an indication that the great American mobility machine missed a minority of the people. On the contrary, always it has been a necessary result of America's distinctive political economy. Although poverty hardly has been unique to America, here, as everywhere, it assumes its particular configuration as a consequence of its temporal and national context.

Relatively few writers have tried to show American poverty whole, and they have had less influence than they merit. Among the more recent, the most notable are the National Conference of Catholic Bishops in their pastoral letter on the economy, and Michael Harrington in *The New American Poverty*. The "structures of misery today," writes Harrington, "are the results of massive economic and social transformations and they cannot be understood apart from an analysis of them." The result of global economic trends, especially the international division of labor, was a new poverty, "much more systematic and structured" and hence "more difficult to defeat than the indignities of twenty years ago."

Like Harrington, Europeans today write about the "new poverty," which they understand in a similar way. They do not write very much about the "underclass," which highlights the peculiarly American tendency to transform poverty from a product of politics and economics into a matter of individual behavior. In his summary of a twelve-country survey of poverty, Graham Room of the University of Bath points to the recent consensus that poverty has assumed new forms within the European Community. He finds their sources in economic restructuring and recent demographic trends that have exposed "new weaknesses in the postwar systems of welfare provision and social security; new lines of social division and new patterns of dependency." With this orientation, European discussions of the "new poverty" focus on unemployment and structural dislocation far more than on the behavior and deficits of the poor.

Indeed, European scholars often find American approaches to poverty, including those of the most respected social scientists, bizarre. In American controversies about social policy, notes Swedish social scientist Walter Korpi, "the European observer finds lively debates on issues that he or she has previously met only in the more or less dusty pages of historical accounts of the development of social policy at home." In his comparison of national American and European poverty research, Korpi points out how American social science and public policy obscure inequality by stressing only absolute measures of poverty, in contrast to the Europeans' reliance on relative ones. Unlike Europeans, American poverty researchers, he adds, neglect both unemployment and politics. American poverty research lacks theories that accord economic resources and political power a central role or that explain inequality as the outcome of "conflicts over distribution." To Korpi, this silence about politics remains "striking," given the "high degree of conflict in American society." Equally striking is the neglect by American poverty research of the consequences for the poor of extremely high levels of unemployment throughout the postwar period. Despite living in a "sea of unemployment," American poverty researchers have focused their efforts on the work motivation of the poor.

BOTH RESEARCH AND policy require the reconstruction of discourse about poverty and welfare. Europeans offer important points of departure; so do aspects of the fragmented American liberalism of the last two decades. These include:

Moral outrage at the persistence of hunger, homelessness, inadequate medical care, and other forms of deprivation.

The substitution of human dignity, community, and the realization of democracy in place of classification, work incentives, and the obligation of the poor as the foundation of public policy.

Finding ways to talk about poor people as "us" that expand ideas of citizenship and transcend the stale historic preoccupations that have constricted ideas, research, and policy during the last two centuries.

Restricting market models of human behavior and distributive justice within appropriate boundaries by defining, and defending, in Michael Walzer's phrase, "spheres of justice."

Enhancing the political acceptability of progressive social policy by connecting it with widely shared American values: for instance, by reviving Charles Reich's concept of the "new property," which defends redistributive policies through an appeal to private property and liberty and by

showing how the persistence of poverty undermines both family life and economic growth.

The main theme is very simple: By attacking poverty, America will become a better nation. As Michael Harrington predicted, "When we join, in solidarity and not in noblesse oblige, with the poor, we will rediscover our own best selves…we will regain the vision of America."

Reconstructing the way we think about poverty is partly an intellectual challenge. As such, it draws on creative resources, in which America is rich. Acting on those ideas is another matter. It requires material resources, which America also has, and political will, which it has lacked. The fundamental questions are not about the details of policy or the sources of revenue; they are, rather, about the basis of community, the conditions of citizenship, and the achievement of human dignity. They are, that is, about our definition of America and just how much we are willing to do to realize it.

FROM: *The Undeserving Poor*, 1989.

RESPONSIBILITY FOR REDUCING POVERTY

PETER B. EDELMAN

Government at all levels, the business community and trade unions, foundations and churches, civic leaders and ordinary citizens, and poor people themselves all have a role and a responsibility in reducing poverty.

1. The Federal Government

The federal role in the twelve years preceding the 1992 election was tragically and cynically inadequate in terms of all three dimensions — leadership, funding, and standard-setting. The president, however, can provide leadership to set a positive tone, and the federal government can alter priorities to provide increased funding, basic guidelines, and adequate standards.

A key point to remember is that insofar as government is the institution to carry out and implement some of the policies, local and state governments are primarily the ones to do this, and it will often be the case that private, generally nonprofit entities should be the ones that actually deliver services financed in part with public funds. (The private sector in all of its manifestations must also play a greatly enhanced role.) Other than through the Social Security Administration, the Veterans Administration, and some aspects of agriculture policy, the federal government has never delivered services directly to the general public. Conservatives continue to attack proposals for partial federal financing of activities as efforts to create a massive new federal bureaucracy — when no one is suggesting anything of the kind.

2. State Government

One major change that has occurred since the 1960s is the revitalization of state government. The states in Lyndon Johnson's time were still suffering the effects of decades of legislative malapportionment. They were still in the thrall of the rural interests that had controlled the legislatures for so long, and they were managed like the mom and pop stores of small rural towns.

While nirvana has surely not arrived, the states today are far more competently staffed and managed, and are in general relatively more responsive to their urban citizens. This is not so evident at the moment, with the recession having forced state after state to cut budgets that have long since been cut past fat. The budget cuts have resulted in the decimation of work forces to the point that the states are severely crippled in their ability to deliver some basic services. States today do, however, have the capacity to play a very different role in poverty-related initiatives than they did in the 1960s, when they were bypassed by many programs, especially those administered by the Office of Economic Opportunity and the Departments of Housing and Urban Development and Labor.

3. Public Funds and the Role of Private Nonprofit Organizations

Another significant change is the public sector's role, which is still evolving; the change concerns the extent to which publicly funded services are delivered by private, generally nonprofit organizations. To some extent, there is less here than meets the eye, because America has always had an active and extensive nonprofit sector that delivers services of various kinds, especially health and welfare services. But increasingly, questions are being asked about the efficacy of public service delivery by public employees. Critics are troubled by the moribundity and unresponsiveness that seem to attend delivery of services by people with civil service job protection, especially delivery of services to constituencies with very little political power. Public employee unions are understandably quite concerned about this line of questioning, which implies that replacement of unionized civil service workers by nonunion, nontenured private workers would be appropriate. The trend toward additional privatization will most likely continue unless public sector managers and union leaders can find ways to demonstrate that they can improve productivity and responsiveness.

At the same time, privatization contains significant pitfalls, even when confined largely to nonprofit entities. While private organizations do not face the barriers created by civil service laws in discharging unsatisfactory workers, quality control of the performance of service deliverers who work for private groups is difficult to achieve. Hard as it is for a central office, or even a regional or district office, to know what is going on in a series of decentralized offices or sites among employees who are all directly on the public payroll, it is even more difficult to monitor the performance of groups that are separately incorporated and organized.

Running a holistic system in which people are successfully referred for different kinds of required assistance is another challenge that is made more difficult by utilizing private agencies to deliver services that need to be part of a larger system. Difficult as it is to get people who all work for the same government to coordinate and cooperate with one another, it is vastly more difficult to get agencies that are chartered for only one or even a number of limited purposes to work actively as part of a genuine system of service delivery.

4. The Business Community

The business community has increasingly come to see that it has a role to play in reducing poverty in America. Concerned about the labor force of the future, the corporate community in the 1980s began to speak out nationally on the need for policies and programs to develop and educate children to the fullness of their potential. Locally, in city after city, businesses began to get involved in school improvement efforts, and often participated in blue-ribbon commissions to diagnose school systems' problems and propose remedies. In some states and communities, businesses have stayed with the process to help press for implementation of proposed reforms, including adequate funding to make change occur.

These efforts have been largely confined to the corporate sector of the business community, and they have been, as implied, mainly limited to "prevention" policies such as child development, prenatal care, and education. A major challenge for the 1990s is to interest a larger portion of the business community in the poverty problem, and to broaden topics of interest, particularly to add a focus on employment and immediate preparation for employment. Given the sick economy of the past few years, it is understandable that the business sector's antipoverty efforts have not focused on employment. Self-sufficiency, however, will not be forthcoming for any significant number of the poor without the availability of jobs; and, even when jobs are available, proactive steps need to be taken to ensure that low-income people are ready to perform in those jobs and are given a chance to apply. The business community needs to play a role in publicizing available jobs and in helping people, especially young people with no experience in the labor market, to understand what is involved in pursuing employment.

A particular agenda item for the business community (as well as for law enforcement) concerns employment discrimination, which is still widespread and operates to intensify poverty for people of color. Both nationally and in particular locales, business leaders can work with civil rights advocates and with public agencies charged with enforcing antidiscrimination laws to foster public understanding about the degree to which widespread employment discrimination continues to exist.

5. Foundations

Foundations have undertaken major new initiatives against poverty over the past decade, particularly in designing new services for families and children in low-income neighborhoods, and also in funding studies to sort out which policies work and which do not. There is an unprecedented level of sophistication about poverty issues in the foundation world at this time. With the advent in Washington of a more responsive administration, there is a possibility of translating the foundation initiatives of recent years into public policy, and of new foundation-government partnerships leveraging greater resources into various demonstrations and initiatives.

6. Religious Institutions

Religious institutions must become more deeply involved in reducing poverty. Some individual churches have played a critical role for a long time, delivering services to families, running Head Start programs, sponsoring mentoring programs, and building low-income and elderly housing. Many denominations have been outstanding in their national commitment to public action.

These efforts, both local and national, need to be expanded, but a new dimension of activity is needed as well. There is a moral breakdown in the inner city. As suggested earlier, there are competing stories about why that has occurred, but there is no question that it has. Violence, drugs, and unduly early pregnancy involve issues of economics, law enforcement, and public health, but they are also moral questions. The long-term answers to these questions may lie in greater economic opportunity and in social, economic, and racial justice. The short-term answers may include incarceration and community policing, drug treatment, and prenatal care and family preservation services. But additionally, a message needs to be sent about values and personal responsibility, the importance of marriage and family, the avoidance of out-of-wedlock pregnancy, abstinence from drug use (and drug dealing), and the value of work at a legal job. These messages can do little good without accompanying public policy, but they are crucial messages all the same, and we need religious and spiritual leaders to make an extra effort to join in sending them. We have had a politics of values about the poor for some time (for centuries, in fact), but in recent years this has involved using values as weapons to divide rather than as tools to teach and build.

7. Individuals

This leads to the last point on the issue of who must take responsibility — individuals must take responsibility for themselves and their families. Children need to hear that the counterpart of opportunity is responsibility and that, with all the barriers that confront them if they are poor, and even more so if they are poor and of color, there exists no substitute for their own effort. The message needs especially to be repeated through the years of adolescence and young adulthood.

That individuals must take responsibility is a message that must be understood carefully by those who send it and those who make policy based on it — it is hard for a person to take responsibility who cannot find a job and it is hard for a person to take responsibility who has no way to pay rent or buy food. There are millions of the poor who are not disabled within the legal definition of that term, but who are nonetheless so damaged by the ravages of life that they are simply not in a position to take responsibility. Asking people to take responsibility for themselves who are unable to do so is not wise public policy. Nonetheless, if the responsibility of all is a basic tenet of antipoverty strategy in the 1990s, it must be extended to the poor themselves.

FROM: "Toward a Comprehensive Antipoverty Strategy: Getting Beyond the Silver Bullet," *The Georgetown Law Journal*, 1993.

COMMUNITARIAN VS. INDIVIDUALISTIC CAPITALISM

LESTER THUROW

In March 1990 the two biggest business groups in the world, Japan's Mitsubishi and Germany's Daimler Benz-Deutsche Bank, held a secret meeting in Singapore to talk about a global alliance. Among other things, both were interested in discussing how to expand their market share in civilian aircraft production.

From an American perspective, everything about that Singapore meeting was highly illegal, violating both antitrust and banking laws. In the United States, banks cannot own industrial firms and businesses cannot sit down behind closed doors to plan joint strategies. Those doing so get thrown in jail for extended periods of time. Yet today Americans cannot force the rest of the world to play the economic game as they think it should be played. The game will be played under international, not American, rules.

With economic competition between communism and capitalism over, this other competition...between two different forms of capitalism...has quickly taken over the economic playing field. Using a distinction first made by Harvard's George C. Lodge, the individualistic, Anglo-Saxon, British-American form of capitalism is going to face off against the communitarian German and Japanese variants of capitalism: The "I" of America or the United Kingdom versus "Das Volk" and "Japan Inc." The essential difference between the two is the relative stress placed on communitarian and individualistic values as the best route to economic success.

Shareholders and Stakeholders

America and Britain champion individualistic values: the brilliant entrepreneur, Nobel Prize winners, large wage differentials, individual responsibility for skills, easy-to-fire-easy-to-quit, profit maximization, hostile mergers, and takeovers. Their hero is the Lone Ranger.

In contrast, Germany and Japan trumpet communitarian values: business groups, social responsibility for skills, team work, firm loyalty, growth-promoting industry, and government strategies. Anglo-Saxon firms are profit maximizers; Japanese and German business firms play a game best termed "strategic conquest." Americans believe in "consumer economics"; Japanese believe in "producer economics."

In the Anglo-Saxon variant of capitalism, the individual is supposed to have a personal economic strategy for success, while the business firm is to have an economic strategy reflecting the wishes of its individual shareholders. Since shareholders want income to maximize their lifetime consumption, their firms must be profit maximizers. For the profit-maximizing firm, customer and employee relations are merely a means of achieving higher profits for the shareholders. Using this formula, lower wages equals higher profits…and wages are to be beaten down where possible. When not needed, employees are to be laid off. For their part, workers in the Anglo-Saxon system are expected to change employers whenever opportunities exist to earn higher wages elsewhere.

Whereas in Anglo-Saxon firms the shareholder is the only stakeholder, in Japanese business firms employees are seen as the No. 1 stakeholder, customers No. 2, and the shareholders a distant No. 3, whose dividend payouts are low. Because employees are the prime stakeholders, higher employee wages are a central goal of the firm in Japan. The firm can be seen as a "value-added maximizer" rather than a "profit maximizer." Profits will be sacrificed to maintain either wages or employment.

Workers in the communitarian system join a company team and are then considered successful as part of that team. The key decision in an individual's personal strategy is to join the "right" team.

In the United States or Great Britain, employee turnover rates are viewed positively. Firms are getting rid of unneeded labor when they fire workers, and individuals are moving to higher wage opportunities when they quit. Job switching, voluntary or involuntary, is almost a synonym for efficiency. In both Germany and Japan job switching is far less preva-

lent. In fact, many Japanese firms still refer to voluntary quits as "treason."

Coalesce for Success

Beyond personal and firm strategies, communitarian capitalists believe in having strategies at two additional levels. Business groups such as Japan's Mitsui Group or Germany's Deutsche Bank Group are expected to have a collective strategy in which companies are financially interlocked and work together to strengthen each other's activities. At the top of the pyramid of Japanese business groups are the major *zaibatsu* (Mitsui group, 23 member firms; Mitsubishi group, 28 member firms; Sumatomo group, 21 member firms; Fuji group, 29 member firms; Sanwa group, 39 member firms; Dai-Ichi Kangyo group, 45 member firms). The members of each group will own a controlling block of shares in each of the firms in the group. In addition, each member firm will in turn have a group of smaller customers and suppliers, the *keiretsu*, grouped around it. Hitachi has 688 firms in its family; Toyota has 175 primary members and 4,000 secondary members.

Similar patterns exist in Germany. The Deutsche Bank directly owns 10 percent or more of the shares in 70 companies: It owns 28 percent of Germany's largest company Daimler-Benz; 10 percent of Europe's largest reinsurance company Munich Rai; 25 percent of Europe's largest department store chain,

Karstady; 30 percent of Germany's largest construction company, Philipp Holzmann; and 21 percent of Europe's largest sugar producer, Sudzucker. Through its trust department, Deutsche Bank indirectly controls many more shares that don't have to be publicly disclosed.

When the Arabs threatened to buy a controlling interest in Mercedes Benz a few years ago, the Deutsche Bank intervened on behalf of the German economy to buy a controlling interest. Now the bank protects the managers of Mercedes Benz from the raids of the financial Vikings: It frees the managers from the tyranny of the stock market, with its emphasis on quarterly profits, and it helps plan corporate strategies and raise the money to carry out these strategies. But it also fires the managers if Mercedes Benz slips in the auto market and prevents the managers from engaging in self-serving activities such as poison pills or golden parachutes, which do not enhance the company's long-term prospects.

Government's Role in Economic Growth

Both Europe and Japan believe that government has a role to play in economic growth. An example of this philosophy put into practice is the pan-European project called Airbus Industries, a civilian aircraft manufacturer owned by the British, French, German, and Spanish governments, designed to break the American monopoly and get Europe back into civilian aircraft manufacturing. Today it is a success, with 20 percent of the aircraft market and announced plans to double production and capture one-third of the worldwide market by the mid-1990s.

Airbus' penetration into the aircraft manufacturing industry has severely affected U.S. manufacturers. In 1990 Boeing's market share of new orders dropped to 45 percent...the first time in decades it had been below 50 percent. McDonnell Douglas' market share has been reduced from 30 percent to 15 percent. In this particular industry, a greater European share can only mean a smaller market share for Boeing and the demise of McDonnell Douglas.

The Europeans now have a number of pan-European strategic efforts underway to catch up with America and Japan. Each is designed to help European firms compete in a major industry. European governments spend from 5½ percent (Italy) to 1¾ percent (Britain) of the GNP [gross national product] aiding industry. If the United States had spent what Germany spends (2½ percent of GNP), $140 billion would have gone to help U.S. industries in 1991. In Spain, where the economy grew more rapidly than any other in Europe in the 1980s, government-owned firms produce at least half of the GDP [gross domestic product]. In France and Italy, the state sector accounts for one-third of the GNP.

"Social Market" vs. "Market" Economy

Germany, the dominant European economic power, sees itself as having a "social market" economy and not just a "market" economy. State and federal governments in Germany own more shares in more industries...airlines, autos, steel, chemicals, electric power, transportation...than any noncommunist country on the face of the globe. Public investments such as Airbus Industries are not controversial political issues. Privatization is not sweeping Germany as it did Great Britain.

In Germany, government is believed to have an important role to play in insuring that everyone has the skills necessary to participate in the market. Its socially financed apprenticeship system is the envy of the world. Social welfare policies are seen as a necessary part of a market economy. Unfettered capitalism is believed to generate levels of income inequality that are unacceptable.

The United States, by contrast, sees social welfare programs as a regrettable necessity brought about by people who will not provide for their own old age, unemployment, or ill health. Continual public discussions remind everyone that the higher taxes required to pay for social welfare systems reduce work incentives for those paying taxes and that social welfare benefits undercut work incentives for those who get them. In the ideal Anglo-Saxon market economy social welfare policies would not be necessary.

Administrative Guidance

In Japan, industry representatives working with the Ministry of International Trade and Industry present "visions" as to where the economy should be going. In the past these visions served as guides to the allocation of scarce foreign exchange or capital flows. Today what the Japanese know as "administrative guidance" is a way of life, and it is used to aim R&D funding at key industries.

An example of this can be found in the Japanese strategy toward semiconductor chips, which was similar to Europe's Airbus plan in that it was lengthy, expensive, and eventually successful in breaking the dominance of American firms. The government-financed "very-large-integrated-circuit-chip" research project was just part of a much larger effort, where a combination of patience, large investments, and American mistakes (a reluctance to expand capacity during cyclical downturns) paid off in the end.

The idea of administrative guidance could not be more foreign to the minds of American officials. According to the politically correct language of the Bush administration, the U.S. government has no role in investment funding and a "legitimate" R&D role only in "pre-competitive, generic, enabling technologies." These rules are sometimes violated in practice, but the principle is clear: Governments should protect private property rights, then get out of the way and let individuals do their thing. Capitalism will spontaneously combust.

History as Destiny

These different conceptions of capitalism flow from very different histories. In the formative years of British capitalism during the 19th century, Great Britain did not have to play "catch up" with anyone. As the initiator of the industrial revolution, Great Britain was the most powerful country in the world.

The United States similarly had a head start in its industrial revolution. Protected by two great oceans, the United States did not feel militarily threatened by Britain's early economic lead. In the last half of the 19th century, when it was moving faster than Great Britain, Americans could see that they were going to have to catch up without deliberate government efforts to throw more coal into the American economic steam engines.

On the other hand, 19th-century Germany had to catch up with Great Britain if it was not to be overrun in the wars of Europe. The rulers of German states were expected by their subjects to take an active part in fostering the economic growth of their territories. To have its rightful place at the European table, Prussia had to have a modern industrial economy. German capitalism needed help to catch up.

The Japanese system similarly did not occur by accident. Admiral Perry arrived in the mid 1800s and with a few cannon balls forced Japan to begin trading with the rest of the world. But the mid-19th century was the height of colonialism. If Japan did not quickly develop, it would become a colony of the British, French, Dutch, Germans, or Americans. Economic development was part of national defense...perhaps a more important part than the army itself, for a modern army could not be built without a modern economy.

In both Germany and Japan, economic strategies were important elements of military strategies for remaining independent and becoming powerful. Governments pushed actively to insure that the economic combustion took place. They had to up the intensity of that combustion so that the economic gaps, and hence military gaps, between themselves and their potential enemies could be cut in the shortest possible time. Under these circumstances, it was not surprising that firms were organized along military lines or that the line between public and private disappeared. Government and industry had to work together to design the national economic strategies necessary for national independence. In a very real sense, business firms became the front line of national defense.

American history is very different. Government's first significant economic act...the Interstate Commerce Commission...was enacted to prevent the railroads from using their monopoly power to set freight rates that would rip off everyone else. A few decades later, its second significant act...the antitrust laws...was to prevent Mr. Rockefeller from using his control over the supply of lighting oil to extract everyone else's income. The third major source of government economic activity flowed from the collapse of capitalism in the 1930s, when the government had to pick up the resultant mess.

As a result adversarial relations and deep suspicions of each other's motives are deeply embedded in American history. While very different histories have led to very different systems, today those very different systems face off in the same world economy.

Let me suggest that the military metaphors now so widely used should be replaced with the language of football. Despite the desire to win, football has a cooperative as well as a competitive element. Everyone has to agree on the rules of the game, the referees, and how to split the proceeds. One can want to win yet remain friends both during and after the game. But what the rest of the world knows as football is known as soccer in America. What Americans like about American football…frequent time-outs, lots of huddles, and unlimited substitutions…are not present in world football. It has no time-outs, no huddles, and very limited substitutions. It is a faster game.

FROM: *New Perspectives Quarterly*, 1992.

GIVING SERVICE:
Resources for Action as Citizen, Neighbor, Community Member, and Employee

Who is responsible for helping people out of poverty...for keeping people from becoming trapped in poverty? If we've learned one thing about fighting poverty since Lyndon Johnson declared war on it in 1964, it is that we each must share in the responsibility of ensuring justice, compassion, and access to opportunity and resources for ourselves, those around us, and those we may never meet. There is a real danger in abdicating responsibility for action to a church group, or a government body, or a private program. If we don't each strive to take action ourselves, by voting, advocating, volunteering, and setting an example in our everyday encounters, our society will have a hard time mustering the general goodwill necessary to build a civil society and to launch a new war on poverty — a broadbased war on poverty that uses the government effectively, but only as one tool among many.

In each of the programs profiled in this book we've included information on how you can find out more about their work or get involved yourself. In addition to these programs, which were selected either because of the innovative nature of their work or because they offer an example of combatting specific problems detailed in the articles, there are numerous other agencies and programs. Below is a brief bibliography citing sources of information to help you get involved.

American Homelessness: A Reference Handbook, Mary Ellen Hombs, ed. National Coalition for the Homeless, 1990.

A Common Cause Guide to Citizen Action: How, When and Where to Write to Your Elected Officials, Common Cause, Washington, DC, 1990.

Directory of Services for Refugees and Immigrants, Alan E. Schorr, ed. Denali Press (P.O. Box 021535, Alaska, USA 99802-1535), 1990.

The Elements of a Successful Public Interest Advocacy Campaign, Advocacy Institute, Washington, DC, 1990.

Encyclopedia of Senior Citizen Information Resources, 1st. ed. Wasserman, Koehler, and Lev, ed. Gale Research Co., Michigan, 1987.

Enough Is Enough: The Hellraiser's Guide to Community Activism, by Diane MacEachern. Avon Books, New York, 1994.

50 Ways to Help Your Community, by Steve Fiffer and Sharon Sloan Fiffer. Doubleday, New York, 1994.

Fighting Hunger in Your Community: A Guide for the Development of Community Action Projects, League of Women Voters Education Fund, Washington, DC, 1990.

How to Win a Local Election, by Lawrence M. Grey. Evans & Company, New York, 1994.

Impact on Congress: A Grassroots Lobbying Handbook for Local League Activists, League of Women Voters, Washington, DC, 1987.

It's Our World, Too!: Stories of Young People Who Are Making a Difference, by Phillip Hoose. Joy Street Books, Little, Brown & Company, Boston, 1993.

Organizing for Social Change: A Manual for Activists in the 1990s, by Kim Bobo, Jackie

Kendall, and Steve Max. Seven Locks Press, Cabin John, Maryland, 1991.

PRRAC Network Directory. Poverty & Race Research Action Council. Washington, DC, 1994.

Public Welfare Directory, Amy J. Weinstein, ed. APWA. Washington, DC, 1994.

Revolution X: A Survival Guide for Our Generation, by J. Cowan and R. Nelson. Penguin Books, New York, 1994.

Wasting America's Future: The Children's Defense Fund Report on the Costs of Child Poverty, by Arloc Sherman. Beacon Press, Boston, Massachusetts, 1994.

You Can Change America: How to Make a Difference Right Now in Your Community, in Congress and in the Country. EarthWorks Group, Berkeley, California, 1991.

POLICY, HISTORY, AND POVERTY:
An Annotated Bibliography

JAMES JENNINGS

The literature on poverty in the United States is vast and continually growing. In these few pages, therefore, it is impossible to cite all of the numerous books, government and foundation reports, articles, and newspaper accounts related to poverty in this country. The purpose of this short and introductory bibliographic review, based on but a few selected writings is, simply, to provide the reader with a map by which to obtain basic information about the problem of poverty and how it affects poor and nonpoor people. Hopefully, the selections included here will also serve to challenge how the American public thinks about this growing problem in our society.

There are numerous sources of data describing the characteristics, location, and duration of poverty for the millions of Americans who are poor. The U.S. Bureau of the Census publishes various reports focusing on poverty. One report, *Poverty in the United States: 1990* (Washington, D.C.: August 1991), is particularly useful because it provides a comprehensive overview of poverty and some of the latest official indicators and characteristics about poverty organized by individuals, families, age groupings, race and ethnic groups, and other categories. The *Statistical Abstract of the United States*, also published by the U.S. Bureau of the Census, and updated yearly, provides a wealth of data on many aspects

of the social, economic, and educational characteristics of the entire nation.

Another source of data and information regarding poverty characteristics in the United States is William P. O'Hare's *Poverty in America: Trends and New Patterns* (Washington, D.C.: Population Reference Bureau, 1987). In addition to reporting various kinds of poverty data, O'Hare discusses some of the major explanations for changes in American poverty over the last several decades. He also examines selected social welfare programs that have been instituted to fight poverty in the United States. Sar A. Levitan's *Programs in Aid of the Poor* (Baltimore, Md.: The Johns Hopkins University Press, 1990) is also an excellent source that describes poverty characteristics as well as programs instituted to reduce poverty or its effects. This work, published in several editions, continues to be a useful introduction to the characteristics of poor Americans, as well as a thorough description of national programs designed to assist poor people.

Nathan Glazer's *The Limits of Social Welfare Policy* (Cambridge, Mass.: Harvard University Press, 1988) explains how the civic values presumably held by Americans temper and limits the kinds of political strategies adopted for reducing poverty. Glazer discusses how racial perceptions about poverty tend to limit the supportive responses of white Americans to attempts to reduce or eliminate poverty for some Americans. It seems that whites have been resistant to supporting antipoverty programs that they perceive as beneficial to blacks, and, today, also Latinos. An article by Charles V. Hamilton and Dona C. Hamilton, "Social Policies, Civil Rights, and Poverty," shows that even under the universal framework of President Roosevelt's New

Deal, when a broad range of programs was instituted presumably to benefit all Americans, blacks were systematically excluded initially from some of the key antipoverty and work programs of this period. This essay is found in a reader by Sheldon H. Danziger and Daniel H. Weinberg, *Fighting Poverty: What Works and What Doesn't* (Cambridge, Mass.: Harvard University Press, 1986). This collection of articles covers several important topics related to poverty, including characteristics of the poor; the relationship among education, employment, and poverty; legal issues related to poverty; and governmental responses to the problem of poverty.

There are several books that the reader can use to obtain an understanding of the history of poverty. Michael B. Katz's *In the Shadow of the Poorhouse: A Social History of Welfare in America* (New York: Basic Books, 1986) describes how poverty existed and was dealt with by government and private groups throughout American history, from the colonial period to the present. The critical work by Michael Harrington in 1962, *The Other America* (New York: Macmillan, 1969), should still be read by those interested in the face of poverty in the United States in the 1950s and early 1960s, and, importantly, in how poverty was ignored and invisibilized during that period by the government and the general public.

Another significant and reader-friendly book detailing important historical information about poverty and focusing on the last three decades is also written by Katz: *The Underserving Poor: From the War on Poverty to the War on Welfare* (New York: Pantheon, 1986). This book is useful in explaining how various categories of poor people have been,

and continue to be, treated differentially by the government and by the general public; i.e., the "deserving" and "undeserving" poor. This work also documents how poor people themselves have attempted to overcome their poverty status in local and national political arenas.

Many writings on this topic are devoted to examination of the causes of poverty in the United States. One of the most popular books, which maintains that poor people are kept in poverty status and politically weak by societal institutions, is *Regulating the Poor* (New York: Pantheon, 1971) by Frances Fox Piven and Richard A. Cloward. One thesis in this study is that the economic and political system should be the target of reform as a response to poverty; thus, poor people should mobilize themselves to change a system that basically maintains and exploits the existence of poverty. From a different ideological perspective, Charles A. Murray in *Losing Ground: American Social Policy, 1950-1980* (New York: Basic Books, 1984) as well as Lawrence M. Mead in *Beyond Entitlement: The Social Obligations of Citizenship* (New York: Free Press, 1986) argue that it is the social behavior of poor people that should be the target of reform because poverty is caused not by inadequacies or inequities in the economic and political system, according to these authors, but rather by moral, cultural, and intellectual flaws in those afflicted with poverty.

Much of the current political and policy discussion about poverty revolves around issues related to welfare reform and dependency. David T. Ellwood's book, *Poor Support* (New York: Basic Books, 1988), offers a wealth of information and data about the characteristics of poor people, as well as the development of Aid to Families with Dependent Children (AFDC). This book, as does Harrell R. Rodgers, Jr.'s, *Poor Women, Poor Families: The Economic Plight of America's Female-Headed Households* (Armonk, N.Y.: M.E. Sharpe, 1990), debunks many of the popular misconceptions that have been associated with poverty and the notion of welfare dependency.

In terms of introducing the reader to some of the current policy and political debates regarding poor people and antipoverty policies, William J. Wilson's *The Truly Disadvantaged: The Inner City, Poverty, and Public Policy* (Chicago: The University of Chicago Press, 1987) examines how broad social and economic transformation has impacted negatively on poor and working-class communities in urban America. Wilson's thesis, focusing on loss of jobs, lower education and training skills, suburbanization, and other systemic factors, suggests that the causes of poverty and, therefore, its resolution, are far more complex than is suggested by such writers as Murray, Mead, and others. A recent anthology by Katz, *The Underclass Debate: Views from History* (Princeton, N.J.: Princeton University Press, 1993), also offers several critiques of writers who blame the condition of poverty on the attitudes, behavior, or culture of poor people, rather than on the kinds of systemic forces identified by Wilson.

Perhaps there is much that Americans can learn about the causes and resolution of poverty by reading about the experiences of other postindustrialized nations. Peter Townsend's *Poverty in the United Kingdom: A Survey of Household Resources and Standards of Living* (Berkeley, Calif.: University of California Press, 1979) is a comprehensive and encyclopedic study of poverty in England, both in the current period as well as in that nation's history. Fiona Williams's *Social Policy: A Critical Introduction* (New York: Blackwell Publishers, 1989) can also be referred to in order to obtain a comparison of how poverty is approached in the United States and in the United Kingdom. Peter Alcock provides a thorough analysis of how poverty is defined and debated in England in his work *Understanding Poverty* (London: Macmillan Co., 1993).

My own work, *Understanding the Nature of Poverty in Urban America* (Westport, Conn.: Praeger Publishers, 1994), may be useful as an introduction to various facets of poverty. This book is based on a review of hundreds of books, reports, and articles about poverty in the United States. Each chapter is devoted to a major question geared to providing the reader with preliminary understanding of some facet of poverty: What is poverty? How is poverty measured by the federal government? What kinds of national policies have been utilized to manage poverty from the New Deal to the Clinton administration? What are the major explanations for persistent poverty in the United States? What are the major characteristics and themes reflected in the U.S. welfare system and anti-poverty policies? How is the underclass defined and explained? How have the poor utilized political mobilization to fight poverty in the United States? How does social welfare policy directed at poverty in the United States compare to that of other countries?

When one asks what government might do, or what one can do, in response to the problem of poverty, many answers have been proposed. Some proposals are found in the literature reviewed for this bibliographic essay. But a very useful article in helping the reader organize antipoverty strategies by various kinds of institutional sectors is Peter B. Edelman, "Toward a Comprehensive Antipoverty Strategy: Getting beyond the Silver Bullet" (*Georgetown Law Journal*, Vol. 81, No. 5, June 1993). In this essay, Edelman provides a synopsis of what strategies can be pursued by the federal government, state and local governments, foundations and civic organizations, religious institutions, the business community, and finally individuals. Edelman's essay illustrates that poverty is a multi-faceted problem that affects negatively all Americans, and exists at all levels of American life.

There are many other books and sources that would serve the same purpose as the materials cited above. I have attempted to identify only a handful of those that a broad range of readers may find not only interesting and useful in following and participating in the nation's public discourse on poverty but also challenging to the ways we all think about this national problem.

STORIES AND VOICES:
Thirty-Five Novels to Continue the Dialogue

ARTHUR I. BLAUSTEIN

Socially conscious novels speak out against social, economic, and political injustice; and they extend our capacity for compassion. When we read these novels, we learn about who we are as individuals and as a nation. They inform us, as no other medium does, about the state of our national soul and character—of the difference between what we say we are and how we actually behave.

Robert Penn Warren, our first poet laureate, warned us, "History is dying.... If this country loses its sense of history, it has lost its sense to complicate men's feelings and emotions. If I could, I would re-evaluate the education system in this country, to emphasize history and literature." Warren gets to the heart of the issue: The identity of society is determined by its connection to history and the moral values passed on through its literature. The valuing process is the lifeblood of civilized and humane society, necessary for a shared sense of national purpose.

Novels offer genuine hope for learning how to handle our daily personal problems—in a moral and human way. They can help us to understand the relationship between our inner lives and the outer world and the balance between thinking, acting, and feeling. They can give us awareness of place, time, and condition, about ourselves and others. As William Faulkner, our great Nobel Prize winner, said, the best literature is far more true than any journalism.

Novels that focus on themes of social consciousness force us to confront our society's inability to distinguish between authentic moral behavior and abstract moralizing. By doing so, they remind us of our commitment to the democratic covenant—that what unites people to form a national character is not color or gender or religion, but moral conscience.

Literature, and the novel in particular in modern times, has functioned historically as our most dependable source of human awareness and self-consciousness. Good literature can function as a conscience, a moral brake; it unmasks what ideology conceals. It serves as an indispensable corrective for false consciousness. Through the pleasure and power of stories, reinforced by identification with characters, we learn values.

Serious novelists remind us that we have cultural choices other than conformity, greed, terminal consumerism, and escapism. Socially conscious novels can be crucial in the struggle to activate people.

The 35 novels I recommend here can help us confront the difficult problems we face in the 1990s and beyond. They can help us deal with the real-world conflicts of ordinary people who must struggle to achieve genuine freedom and justice, equality and opportunity, individuality and community, sanity and human connection. It is essential that we examine the complexities and ambiguities of the contemporary human predicament if we are to survive as a sane and civilized nation.

Several of these novels are political; most could be referred to as "social realism" and some, "social protest." The realism and the protest are offered as a patriotic vision. What the writers of protest and realism are doing is no less than reminding us of our traditional American values—freedom, justice, equality, and opportunity. They know that to point a finger at the pain of poverty or the hypocrisy of inequality and injustice, or to expose the deceit of false myths and symbols, is an act of allegiance to our nation and our values as a people. It is the task of a novelist to remind us of who we thought we were and to give us a glimpse of what we might become—the most important of all human endeavors.

Dorothy Allison, *Bastard Out of Carolina* (Dutton). An unsparing, passionate, and gritty work about a young girl growing up in poverty. It resonates with integrity, empathy, and realism.

Lisa Alther, *Original Sins* (Bantam). An intelligent and absorbing novel—set in the south—that bridges the differences between races.

Harriet Arnow, *The Dollmaker* (Avon). A family moves from the hills of Kentucky to industrial Detroit. An epic novel that tests the strength of the human heart against the bitterest odds.

James Baldwin, *Another Country* (Dell). A magnificent, tumultuous, and disturbing work about racism that rings with authenticity. A master work of American fiction.

Russell Banks, *Continental Drift* (Ballantine). A totally absorbing story about a frost-belt family who move to Florida to find the good life. Instead, they find a nightmare.

Wendell Berry, *The Memory of Old Jack* (Harvest). Remarkable and graceful, set in Appalachia, offering keen insights into the life of an aging farmer and America's changing values.

Dorothy Bryant, *Confessions of Madame Psyche* (Ata). The 20th century as experienced by a Chinese-American woman. A moving account of Mei-li Murrow's saga—a metaphor for California's and our nation's multicultural experience.

Sandra Cisneros, *The House on Mango Street* (Knopf). A coming-of-age novel in the Latino section of Chicago. Poignant and moving with unforgettable characters.

Ralph Ellison, *The Invisible Man* (Vintage). The powerful and classic novel about race, individuality, and the quest for identity. A southern black man moves to New York and learns the many ways whites are unable to see him.

Gretel Ehrlich, *Heart Mountain* (Penguin). Explores the experience of Japanese Americans exiled into a relocation camp in Wyoming and their relationship to local ranchers.

Louise Erdrich, *Love Medicine* (Harper Perennial). Stunning and haunting insight into life for today's Native Americans, on and off the reservation.

Denise Giardina, *The Unquiet Earth* (Ivy). From the devastation of the Depression to the hope of the War on Poverty, this is a moving and passionate story of a West Virginia community's struggle for survival.

Davis Grubb, *Shadow of My Brother* (Zebra). Perfectly paced, a dramatic tale of a Tennessee town in the 1950s caught in the midst of a moral crisis over racial violence.

Ernest Hebert, *The Dogs of March* (New England Press). Brilliant, sensitive, and funny. A tour de force that captures what it's like to be unemployed or underemployed in the 1980s. Set in New England, it's the American dream going belly-up.

Linda Hogan, *Mean Spirit* (Ivy). A magical and compelling story about whites robbing the Osage Indian tribe of their oil wealth in Oklahoma.

John Irving, *The Cider House Rules* (Bantam). A fine writer brings his instructive story-telling gifts to fruition with this excellent novel about choice, class, and Yankee common sense.

Arthur Islas, *Migrant Souls* (Avon). A beautiful tale of the conflicts of a Chicano family in south Texas; and a keen insight into the workings of the human heart.

William Kennedy, *Ironweed* (Penguin). Pulitzer Prize winner's shrewd study of the diceyness of fate. This modern Dante's Inferno about life on "skid row" is especially poignant during a time when homelessness casts a shadow across our land.

Barbara Kingsolver, *Animal Dreams* (Harper Perennial). A wonderful tale of multiculturalism, set in Arizona, about authenticity, community, integrity, truth, and all those other virtues that have become unfashionable and unhip.

Maxine Hong Kingston, *The Woman Warrior: Memories of a Girlhood among Ghosts* (Vintage). Brilliant and haunting account of the Chinese-American experience. Kingston's account of growing up Asian and poor adds a cultural richness to the landscape that is an absolute must.

Ella Leffland, *Rumors of Peace* (Harper Perennial). A young, fierce California girl comes of age during World War II, making her own sense of racism, the rise of Nazism, the bombings of Pearl Harbor and Hiroshima, and the coming of peace.

Carson McCullers, *The Heart Is a Lonely Hunter* (Bantam). This enduring masterpiece, set in small-town Georgia, is a compassionate study of how people confront the problems of poverty, race, class, gender, and, most important, the conflicts of the human condition.

Toni Morrison, *Beloved* (Plume). Winner of the Nobel Prize, this is a powerful story of the legacy of slavery. The underlying theme, that of the relationship between slave and master, examines the tragic complications underlying our historical experience.

Bharati Mukherjee, *The Middleman* (Fawcett). Winner of the National Book Critics Circle Award, this is a profound, intelligent, and often funny book about recent immigrants to America and their struggle to survive.

Faye Ng, *Bone* (Harper Perennial). In a clear and emotionally powerful novel, Ng takes us into the heart and inner secrets of a family in San Francisco's Chinatown.

John Nichols, *The Milagro Beanfield War* (Ballantine). Provides no-nonsense insights into how the economic and political "shell game" is being run on ordinary Americans. Part of the author's New Mexico trilogy, it is a contemporary *Grapes of Wrath*, with Mark Twain's down-home humor.

Joyce Carol Oates, *Them* (Vanguard). A poignant account of the hopes, strategies, and chaos of urban community organizing during the time of the 1960s riots.

Tillie Olsen, *Yonnondio* (Laurel). A remarkable, poetic, and timeless book about a young family's struggle to overcome poverty during the Great Depression.

Chaim Potok, *Davita's Harp* (Fawcett). A compassionate coming-of-age novel about a young New York girl developing a social, moral, and political consciousness.

Marge Piercy, *Gone to Soldiers* (Fawcett). A sweeping epic of women's lives during World War II that seamlessly blends a canvas of political, social, and economic issues on the home front.

E. Annie Proulx, *Postcards* (Collier). Winner of the Pulitzer Prize, Proulx has written a remarkable story of the struggle of New England farmers to confront the loss of home and place because of economic hard times.

Mary Lee Settle, *The Scapegoat* (Ballantine). Stirring account of a historic strike in the coal fields. The real-life struggle between immigrants (Italian, Greek, Polish, Slavic, et al.) and the robber barons. You won't find this in history texts.

John Steinbeck, *The Grapes of Wrath* (Penguin). This classic novel of farmers forced to move west during the Great Depression electrified the nation and reminded us of our historical commitment to compassion, opportunity, and social justice.

Kurt Vonnegut, *Jailbird* (Dell). An unflinching mix of wit, politics, and class. Vonnegut's hilarious tale about Nixon's social policies of "benign neglect" and the Watergate era should be required reading.

Alice Walker, *Meridian* (Fawcett). A powerful novel about civil rights activism in the South in the 1960s. Warm, generous, and complex, this book challenges each of us to examine what it is to become a decent, responsible, and honorable person.

ABOUT THE CONTRIBUTORS

Biographies of authors for each story, essay, or report appear at the beginning of each article. Biographical information on authors of the frontmatter, prologue, conclusion, and appendices follows:

ARTHUR I. BLAUSTEIN

Mr. Blaustein was the chairman of the President's National Advisory Council on Economic Opportunity (under Jimmy Carter) and former director of the National Economic Development and Law Center. He teaches Urban Policy at the University of California, Berkeley. Two of his books are *The American Promise: Equal Justice and Economic Opportunity* and *Man Against Poverty: World War III.*

PETER EDELMAN

Mr. Edelman is Counselor at the Department of Health and Human Services. He is on leave from his position as Professor of Law at Georgetown University Law Center, where he teaches constitutional law and directs a family poverty clinic. He served as Legislative Assistant to Senator Robert F. Kennedy from 1965 to 1968. He is the author of numerous articles on poverty, constitutional law, and issues relating to children and youth.

HENRY HAMPTON

Mr. Hampton is the founder and president of Blackside, Inc. He is the executive producer of the documentary series, *America's War on Poverty*, to which this book serves as a companion. He was also the executive producer of the multiple award-winning television documentary histories *Eyes on the Prize* and *America's Great Depression.*

JAMES JENNINGS

Dr. Jennings is Professor of Political Science and Director of William M. Trotter Institute at University of Massachusetts in Boston. He is the author of *Understanding the Nature of Poverty in Urban America* and the editor of *Blacks, Latinos, and Asians in Urban America.*

MICHAEL KATZ

Mr. Katz is Chair of the History Department and the co-director of the Urban Studies Department at the Uni-

versity of Pennsylvania. He is the author of seven books, including *The Undeserving Poor* and *The "Underclass" Debate: Views from History.*

ROBERT REICH

Mr. Reich is Secretary of Labor under President Bill Clinton. Prior to that appointment, he was on the faculty of the Kennedy School of Government at Harvard University. He has published seven books, including *The Work of Nations: Preparing Ourselves for 21st-Century Capitalism*, published in 1991.

CAROLYN SHAW BELL

Ms. Bell holds the Katherine Coman Chair of Economics as an emeritus professor at Wellesley College in Massachusetts, where she taught from 1950 to 1989. She has published articles in *The Public Interest*, *Social Research*, *The Los Angeles Times*, *The New York Times*, *The Wall Street Journal*, *The Washington Post*, and *The Boston Globe*, for which she writes a monthly column.

LESTER THUROW

Mr. Thurow is professor of Management and Economics at The Sloan School of Massachusetts Institute of Technology. He has authored several books on economics, including *Head to Head: The Coming Economic Battle Among Japan, Europe and America*, *The Zero-Sum Society*, *The Zero-Sum Solution*, and *Poverty and Discrimination*, which received the David A. Wells Prize in 1968.

ROBERT LAVELLE is the editor of this collection. He is an award-winning editor and producer of books and new media for Blackside, Inc., with whom he's worked for nine years. He is also a co-founder of the New Learning Project, a multimedia production company (now called Illumina Productions). Earlier he was a senior editor at Addison-Wesley Publishing Company. He works with numerous organizations and educational institutions on book and new media projects.

NOTES

Sources are listed with the graphs and facts that appear in the margins of this book. Sources for the introductory notes to each section and selection follow:

PAGE

3 "When Lyndon Johnson announced…": *America's Struggle Against Poverty: 1900-1980*, James T. Patterson, Harvard University Press, 1986.

4 "In 1991, 16 percent…": *The Condition of Education: 1993*, U.S. Department of Education, National Center for Education Statistics, 1993.

18 "Roughly one third…": *New York Times*, June 19, 1994. "The ratio of white…": *Findings of the 1973 AFDC Study*, National Center for Social Statistics, January 1975; *Aid to Families with Dependent Children: 1983 Recipient Characteristics and Financial Circumstances of AFDC Recipients*, Family Support Administration, 1986.

31 "In fact, out of every dollar…": *Wasting America's Future: The Children's Defense Fund Report on the Costs of Child Poverty*, Arloc Sherman, Beacon Press, 1994.

41 "At least 5.5 million…": *Current Health*, December 1992. "As of 1993, 10 percent…": U.S. Department of Agriculture, Food and Nutrition Service, 1994.

45 "According to a 1989 report…" and "The high school dropout…": *Boston Globe*, August 20, 1989.

53 "As the Children's Defense Fund…": *Wasting America's Future*, ibid.

65 "In 1959, the top 4 percent…":, Kevin Phillips, *The Politics of Rich and Poor*, Random House, 1990.

79 "In fact, this family model…": *The Way We Never Were: American Families and the Nostalgia Trap*, Stephanie Coontz, Basic Books, 1992.

"Fewer than 27 percent…": *Who We Are: A Portrait of America Based on the Latest U.S. Census*, Sam Roberts, Times Books, 1993.

"The federal government's aid…?": *Programs in Aid of the Poor*, Sar A. Levitan, Johns Hopkins University Press, 1990.

"Today, only half of America's…": *Who We Are*, ibid.

80 "The federal minimum wage…": *The State of Working America: 1992-1993*, Lawrence Mishel and Jared Bernstein, Economic Policy Institute Series, M.E. Sharpe, 1993.

"In 1979, a minimum wage…": *Working but Poor: America's Contradiction*, Sar A. Levitan, Frank Gallo, and Isaac Shapiro, Johns Hopkins University Press, 1993.

88 "Since 1980, over 300,000…": *America: What Went Wrong?*, Donald J. Barlett and James B. Steele, Andrews and McMeel, 1992.

101 "Currently, nearly 50 percent…" and "The highest rate in the world…": *Just the Facts: A Summary of Recent Information on America's Children and Their Families*, National Commission on Children, Washington, D.C., 1993, cited in *The Index of Leading Cultural Indicators: Facts and Figures on the State of American Society*, William J. Bennett, Touchstone, 1994.

"It is worth noting…": *Criminal Victimization in the United States*, 1990, U.S. Department of Justice, 1991, cited in *The Index of Leading Cultural Indicators*, ibid.

"The number of people serving…": *Washington Post*, June 2, 1994.

"The United States has the highest…": *Forbes, What's Wrong with America?*, September 1992, cited in *The Index of Leading Cultural Indicators*, ibid.

118 "According to the 1990 census…": *Statistical Abstract of the United States: 1993*, U.S. Bureau of the Census, 1993.

"In five of six large cities…": *Boston Globe*, February 6, 1994.

127 "There are over 1.9 million…": FDCH Congressional Testimony, May 17, 1994.

142 "Furthermore, with more than...": *New York Times*, July 11, 1993.

151 "In his book...": *Broken Heartland: The Rise of America's Rural Ghetto*, Osha Gray Davidson, The Free Press, 1990.

151 "After participating...": *Boston Review*, June–September 1994.

163 "Ernesto Cortes learned...": *Let Them Call Me Rebel: Saul Alinsky — His Life and Legacy*, Sanford D. Horwitt, Alfred A. Knopf, 1989.

176 "Over the last 30 years...": *Who Will Tell the People: The Betrayal of American Democracy*, William Greider, Touchstone, 1992.

196 "The Immigration Act of 1965...": *The American People: Creating a Nation and a Society, Volume 2*, Gary B. Nash, Julie Roy Jeffrey, et al. editors, Harper & Row, 1990.

Prologue: Everything Has Changed, Except the Way We Think

1. "The Secession of the Successful." An adaptation of *The Work of Nations: Preparing Ourselves for 21st-Century Capitalism*, by Robert B. Reich. (New York: Knopf, 1991). First published in *The New York Times Magazine*, January 20, 1991. Used by permission of Robert B. Reich. Copyright 1991 by Robert B. Reich.

2. "Beating Poverty with Power," by James Jennings. First published in the *Boston Review* (June–September 1994). Copyright © 1994 by James Jennings. Reprinted by permission of the Robert B. Reich.

3. "Are We a Humane Nation?" by Arthur I. Blaustein. First published in the *San Jose Mercury News*, December 24, 1989. Copyright © 1990 by Arthur I. Blaustein. Reprinted by permission of the author.

Part I. When Children Are Poor

4. "Sawdust." From *Kentucky Straight* by Chris Offutt (New York: Random House, 1990). Copyright © 1990 by Chris Offutt. Reprinted by permission of Random House, Inc.

5. "What Is Poverty?" by Carolyn Bell Shaw, Katherine Coman Professor of Economics, Emerita, Wellesley College. First published in *The Boston Globe* on July 12, 1994. Copyright © 1994 by Carolyn Bell Shaw. Reprinted by permission of the author.

6. "So How Did I Get Here?" by Rosemary Bray. First published in *The New York Times Magazine*, November 8, 1992. Copyright © 1992 by Rosemary Bray. Reprinted by permission of the author.

7. "Sharers," excerpt from *All-Bright Court* by Connie Porter (New York: Houghton Mifflin, 1991). Copyright © 1991 by Connie Porter. Reprinted by permission of Houghton Mifflin Co. All rights reserved.

8. Excerpt from *Bastard Out of Carolina* by Dorothy Allison (New York: Plume Fiction, 1992). Copyright © 1992 by Dorothy Allison. Reprinted by permission of the author.

9. "The Circuit" by Francisco Jiménez. First published in *The Arizona Quarterly*, Autumn 1972. Copyright © 1973 by Francisco Jiménez. Reprinted by permission of the author.

10. "First Born, Fast Grown: The Manful Life of Nicholas," by Isabel Wilkerson. First published in *The New York Times*, April 4, 1993. Copyright © 1993 by The New York Times Company. Reprinted by permission.

11. "The Lesson." From *Gorillas, My Love* by Toni Cade Bambara (New York: Random House, 1972). Copyright © 1972 by Toni Cade Bambara. Reprinted by permission of Random House, Inc.

Part 2. Poverty, Families and Friends

12. "Getting Nowhere" by Tony Horwitz. First published in *The Wall Street Journal*, June 14, 1994. Reprinted by permission of *The Wall Street Journal*, © 1994, Dow Jones & Company, Inc. All Rights Reserved Worldwide.

13. "Getting the Facts of Life," by Paulette Childress White. Copyright © 1991 by Paulette Childress White. Reprinted by permission of the author.

14. "Douglas Wyoming: An Oral History by Connie Arthur." From *Below the Line* by Eugene Richards (New York: Consumers Union, 1987). Copyright by Consumers Union of U.S., Inc., Yonkers, NY 10703-1057. Reprinted by permission from *Consumer Reports*.

15. "Editorial Notebook/Confronting Slaughter in the Streets," by Brent Staples. First published in *The New York Times*, November 5, 1993. Copyright © 1993 by the New York Times Company. Reprinted by permission.

16. "On the Meaning of Plumbing and Poverty," by Melanie Scheller. First published in *The North Carolina Independent Weekly* (January 4, 1990). Copyright © 1990 by Melanie Scheller. Reprinted by permission of the author.

17. "The Death of a Farm," by Amy Jo Keifer. First published in *The New York Times* (op ed pages), June 30, 1991. Copyright © 1991 by The New York Times Company. Reprinted by permission.

18. "Circling Raven." Excerpt from *Bloodlines: Odyssey of a Native Daughter,* by Janet Campbell Hale (New York: Random House, 1993). Copyright © 1993 by Janet Campbell Hale. Reprinted by permission of Random House, Inc., New York.

19. "Daniel." From *Travels with Lizbeth* by Lars Eighner (New York: St. Martin's Press, 1993). First published in *The Threepenny Review,* Winter 1993. Copyright © 1993 by Lars Eighner. Reprinted by permission of St. Martin's Press, Inc., New York, NY.

20. Excerpt from *Rachel and Her Children* by Jonathan Kozol (New York: Crown Publishers, 1988). Copyright © 1988 by Jonathan Kozol. Reprinted by permission of Crown Publishers, a subsidiary of Random House, Inc.

Part 3. Communities in Poverty

21. Excerpt from *Milagro Beanfield War* by John Treadwell Nichols (New York: Henry Holt, 1974). Copyright © 1974, 1994 by John Treadwell Nichols. Reprinted by permission of Henry Holt & Co., Inc.

22. "Interview with Ernesto J. Cortes." From *Bill Moyers: A World of Ideas II* by Bill Moyers. Copyright © 1990 by Public Affairs Television, Inc. Used by permission of Doubleday, a division of Bantam Doubleday Dell Publishing Group, Inc.

23. "Travels." From *Meridian* by Alice Walker (Orlando, FL: Harcourt Brace, 1976). Copyright © by Alice Walker. Reprinted by permission of Harcourt Brace & Company.

24. Excerpts from "Inside Trey-Nine" by Peter Goldman. From *Newsweek,* March 23, 1987, Newsweek, Inc. All rights reserved. Reprinted by permission.

25. "Like a Prison" by David Gonzalez. From *The New York Times,* April 20, 1993. Copyright © 1993 by The New York Times Company. Reprinted by permission.

26. "In The Fields of King Coal," by Fenton Johnson. Copyright © 1992 by Fenton Johnson. Reprinted by permission of the author.

Conclusion: Ideas, Strategies and Resources

27. "'Them' or Us'." From *The Undeserving Poor* by Michael Katz (New York: Pantheon Books, 1989). Copyright © 1989 by Michael Katz. Reprinted by permission of Pantheon Books, a division of Random House, Inc.

28. "Responsibility for Reducing Poverty." An excerpt from *Toward a Comprehensive Anti-Poverty Strategy: Getting Beyond the Silver Bullet* by Peter Edelman. *The Georgetown Law Journal,* Vol. 81, No. 5, June 1993. Reprinted with permission of the publisher, copyright © 1993 by *Georgetown Law Journal* and Georgetown University.

29. "Communitarian vs. Individualistic Capitalism," by Lester Thurow. Copyright © 1992 by Lester Thurow. Reprinted with permission from *New Perspectives Quarterly,* Winter 1992 issue.

ACKNOWLEDGMENTS

This book is a companion volume to the five-part historical documentary series, *America's War on Poverty*, produced by Blackside, Inc., of Boston, Massachusetts. In compiling this book, we drew extensively on the research conducted for that series as well as the expertise developed by the Blackside staff and the guidance of the film project's numerous advisors. A list of film staff, advisors, and funders is included below, but two people deserve special thanks for the trust they showed in us: Terry Rockefeller, the knowledgeable and energetic series producer who kept the entire project moving forward; and Henry Hampton, the series executive producer who made this ambitious undertaking possible and whose vision kept it moving in the right direction.

This book was developed on a grant from the Ford Foundation and published with the financial and professional assistance of KQED Books. At Ford we offer heartfelt thanks to Andrea Taylor, Robert Curvin, and Lynn Huntley. At KQED Books we thank the publisher, Pamela Byers. We are grateful as well to Ms. Byers for her help in working through editorial and design issues.

Working directly on this book were: Ann Bennett, research coordinator and general assistant, whose calm was matched by her capacity to work long hours with good cheer; Lalitha Rajan, researcher, who skillfully unearthed program information, articles, and artwork; Patricia Garcia-Rios, researcher, who quickly became renowned for her ability to locate facts, figures, and background data. Additionally, Hannah Benoit wrote many of the program profiles in this book and provided expert line-by-line editorial help. Roger House and Susan Pittman each wrote program profiles with professional aplomb. Marc Mandel, intern, helped with general support and research (particularly with the selection of quotations).

We thank our literary agent, Doe Coover, for working with us and helping us find a publisher who understood the unusual nature of this project.

Janis Owens is a talented and gracious designer who undertook this project with a degree of equanimity that is remarkable.

The principal advisors to this book project discussed with us the approach, the selections, and the overall scope of our work. Their guidance has been invaluable. This book has many components and became more complex than we had anticipated. If any errors slipped through, it is certainly not due to a lack of diligence, intelligence, or sensitivity on the part of our advisors:

Arthur Blaustein, of the University of California at Berkeley, shared firsthand experience — based on his work at the Office of Economic Opportunity during the War on Poverty — of the history that undergirds this project. He also lent the unique insights of one who has used literature to teach issues of poverty and social justice. We're grateful as well for the bibliography he prepared for this book (Appendix C).

Pablo Eisenberg, President of the Center for Community Change (Washington, D.C.), offered us the benefit of his years of experience dealing with complex issues concerning poverty and social change as well as guidance on anti-poverty programs.

Chester Hartman gave generously of his time despite the many demands confronting him as President of the Poverty and Race Research Action Council (Washington, D.C.). His thoughtful and critical assessment of the manuscript was greatly appreciated.

Rob Hollister, Director of the Lincoln Filene Center at Tufts University, helped both in subtle ways — gauging what we should emphasize — and in direct ways — with names, numbers, and solutions to specific problems. He originally brought many of the book's advisors together and was instrumental in directing the community outreach initiative of this project.

James Jennings, Director of the William Monroe Trotter Institute at the University of Massachusetts, who recently completed a review of selected topics and the research literature on poverty (published now as *Understanding the Nature of Poverty in Urban America*, Praeger, 1994), gave generously of his wealth of information. We thank him also for the bibliography he prepared as Appendix B in this book. His guidance was always on target and extremely helpful, and his enthusiastic encouragement was heartening.

Others to whom we owe thanks for their help and encouragement include: Dorothy Stoneman, Martha Fowlkes, Ceasar McDowell, Nancy Benjamin, Karen

Johnson, Michael Greene, Lorraine Kiley, Jessica Slattery, Jacqui Santiago, Kathy McGuinness, Andrea Boxill, Sue Ella Kobak, Daniel Schorr, Marianne Neuman, Kathy Lykes, Donna Dunlop, Alison Bassett, Rafe Sagalyn, Henry Horenstein, Judy Richardson, Judy Samelson, and Ann Beaudry.

On behalf of the book team, I offer our sincerest thanks.

Robert Lavelle, Editor

America's War On Poverty
FILM PRODUCTION CREDITS

Executive Producer	Henry Hampton
Series Producer	Terry Kay Rockefeller
Supervising Producer	Alison Bassett
Narrator	Lynne Thigpen
Series Researcher	Tracy Heather Strain
Series Archivist	Katy Mostoller
Production Coordinator	Andrea Kathleen Boxill
Music Supervisor	Rena C. Kosersky
Music Composers	Nik Bariluk
	Brian Keane
Series Consultants	Lillian Benson
	Jon Else
	Steve Fayer

EPISODE ONE   **In This Affluent Society**

Producer/Director	Susan Bellows
Associate Producer	Noland Walker
Editor	Sharon Sachs
Production Assistant	Patricia Garcia-Rios

EPISODE TWO   **Given a Chance**

Producer/Director	Dante James
Associate Producer	Elizabeth J. Carver
Editor	Jon Neuburger
Writer	Sheila Curran Bernard
Production Assistant	Ann Bennett

EPISODE THREE   **City of Promise**

Producer/Director	Werner Bundschuh
Associate Producer	Christie L. Taylor
Editor	James Rutenbeck
Production Assistant	Wendell Hanes

EPISODE FOUR   **In Service to America**

Producers/Directors	Paige Martinez & Sam Sills
Production Associate	Lauren Cooper
Editor	Joanna Kiernan

EPISODE FIVE   **My Brother's Keeper**

Producer/Director	Leslie D. Farrell
Associate Producer	Lulie Haddad
Editor	Betty Ciccarelli
Production Assistant	Ed Burley

SERIES ADVISORS
Mary Coleman, Jackson State University; Robert Curvin, The Ford Foundation; Peter Edelman, U.S. Department of Health and Human Services; Pablo Eisenberg, Center for Community Change; Gerald Gill, Tufts University; Linda Gordon, University of Wisconsin; Vincent G. Harding, Iliff School of Theology; Wil C. Haygood, *The Boston Globe*; Thomas Jackson, Smith College; James Jennings, University of Massachusetts at Boston; Jacqueline Jones, Brandeis University; Michael B. Katz, University of Pennsylvania; Robin D.G. Kelley, New York University; Nicholas Lemann, *The Atlantic Monthly*; Helen Lewis, Berea College; Lawrence M. Mead, Princeton University; James Patterson, Brown University; Dianne Pinderhughes, University of Illinois; Barbara Sabol, University Research Corporation and Center for Human Services; Lisbeth Schorr, Harvard University Project on Effective Services for Children and Family; Komozi Woodard, Sarah Lawrence College.

BLACKSIDE, INC., STAFF

President	Henry Hampton
Executive Assistant to President	Carole Weiss Flink
Vice President, Development	Martha Fowlkes
Vice President, Marketing and Licensing	W. Michael Greene
Editor and Producer, Books and New Media	Robert Lavelle
Education Director/Producer	Judy Richardson
Promotion Director	Richelle Tarlin
Business Manager	Lorraine Flynn Kiley
Production Accountant	Jessica Slattery
Rights Coordinator	Cindy Kuhn
Promotion Coordinator	Jass Stewart
Production Assistants	Terlonzo Amos EuReco Blair
Office Administrator	Jacqueline Santiago

"America's War on Poverty" — the television series and related educational materials — was produced by Blackside, Inc. The project's nonprofit partner is the Civil Rights Project, Inc. President: Ceasar McDowell. Administrative Assistant: Betty Hugh. Education Director: Judy Richardson. Program Associate: Marianne Castano. Director of Development: Martha Fowlkes. Director, Community Outreach Initiative: Lisa Gregory.

FUNDING CREDITS

Funding for the television documentary series was provided by:

The Ford Foundation, the Charles Stewart Mott Foundation, the John D. and Catherine T. MacArthur Foundation, the Corporation for Public Broadcasting, and public television viewers. Additional funding was provided by: the William Penn Foundation, the Surdna Foundation, the Joyce Foundation, the Cummins Engine Foundation, the Victoria Foundation, the Arca Foundation, the Boston Foundation, the Maurice Falk Medical Fund, and the Ruth Mott Fund.

Funding and/or services for community outreach, educational materials, and the public opinion poll was provided by: The Charles Stewart Mott Foundation, the Ford Foundation, the Hyams Foundation, the Ruth Mott Fund, the Friedman Family Foundation, the Surdna Foundation, the Friedman/Cohen Fund, the Joyce Foundation, the Americans Talk Issues Foundation, and the Circle Foundation.